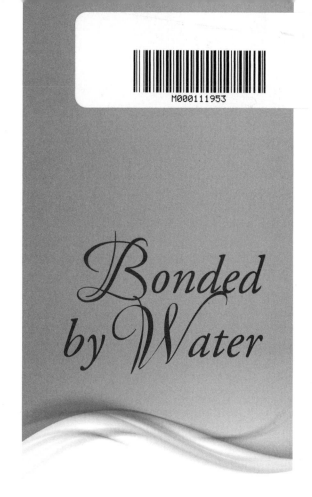

Bonded by Water

Memoirs and a chronicle of many lives,
Primarily of a father, a brother, a daughter, and a few friends,
Lived mostly in the Pacific Northwest and Southeast Alaska.

Praise for
Bonded by Water

"A unique original historical chronicle of success, failure, surprise, comedy, and tragedy, three generations of diverse family and friends of the author, to move you from laughter to tears with creatively linked true stories lived mostly in the Pacific Northwest and Southeast Alaska.

"*[Bonded by Water]* captures the flavor of living in the 'good old days' with hard working fishermen and families who made their lives count in the last frontier."

— Frank H. Murkowski,
former Alaska governor and U. S. Senator

"Olson provides a glimpse of his past with poignant stories of family and faith that inspire us to reflect on our own stories that bond us together."

— Kevin P. Haggerty, Ph.D.

"A richly textured account of exceptional people and their adventures at sea and on shore making waves in Alaska, and much more."

— Joe Upton, author of *Alaska Blues*

"... inspiring stories of nonconformists showing up for adventures in life and faith."

— Vaughn Sherman, author of *Sea Travels*

To John,

Bonded by Water

Memoirs of Family and Friends

Best Wishes

David R. Olson

Dave Olson

Edmonds, Washington

Published by Patos Island Press
705 Spruce Street
Edmonds, Washington 98020
www.patosislandpress.com

Hardcover ISBN: 978-0-9847225-6-3
Trade Paperback ISBN: 978-0-9847225-5-6

Printed in the United States of America

Cover painting, "The Christian"
by Brenda Schwartz, Wrangell, Alaska
Maps by Joe Upton
Book and cover design
Jeanie James, www.Shorebird-Creative.com

Dedication

Dedicated to my mother, Ida—for watering my curiosity and freeing my brothers and me at an early age to go outside, wander, explore, and try anything that turned us on.

And to my wife, Betty, because I couldn't have lived my life the way I've lived it without her tolerance, participation, courage, support, enthusiasm, eternal optimism, and steadfast love.

And to our daughter Jenifer (Jef) and my brother Ken, who both died too young in the outdoors they loved—a day never passes when I don't think of each of you and miss you.

Acknowledgments

Writing this book was a family and friends project.

So my first expressions of gratitude begin with my wife Betty for graciously leaving off from whatever she was doing hundreds of times to read drafts from paragraphs to pages and offer candid opinions. Next would be to our son Alan for assisting his computer illiterate Dad through writing a book in the computer age and our daughter Susan for designing and creating my web site.

This work would be just another memoir were it not for the contributions of poems, letters, and other written contributions from relatives and friends. You added a unique dimension to make it a different book. Thanks are also due the many people who responded to my quests for information adding authenticity to the stories.

From the beginning I was fortunate to have a circle of well wishers who early on kindly read drafts of the introduction and various chapters—and encouraged me to "keep writing." Friends Gene Dyer, Mary Norton, Mary Brown, Diane Murphy, and Heather Griffiths were important supporters in this group. Special thanks are due Barbara Kerlin and Kevin Haggerty for reviewing the manuscript draft and gently pointing out weaknesses asking for rewriting, reorganization, or deletion.

Eventually, reflecting more good fortune for me, the writing was far enough along for me to attract the interest of author/publisher, and close friend for over six decades, Vaughn Sherman. Without him, the odds are good this work would never have made it to print – certainly not as a professionally produced product. He introduced me and my book to Stephen Lay, managing director of Epicenter Press/Aftershocks Media. Stephen placed my manuscript with Joanne Haines for editing, and Vaughn secured designer Jeanie James to put the finishing touches on the book.

I'm grateful to all of these people for making it possible for me to share this book of my dreams.

Table of Contents

Over the years, after hearing some of my stories, a few friends have said, "Dave, you should write a book." This number has not included my daughter Susan who, in response to a suggestion from friend Grace Raube, said, "Don't bother, Dad, no one will believe you!" Nor did it include my wife, Betty, who, I surmise, foresaw what a pain in the butt I'd be during the pregnancy and birthing of the book. I decided to write it, though, because I have many tales to tell of living bravely that aren't about me.

Since Garrison Keillor made his mark on the national scene, I've seen myself as a representative son of his mythical Lake Wobegon. This view has its roots in my Minnesota upbringing, especially junior high years, when I was awakened to my inability to make the first string on the church basketball team or compete with John Beers for the affection of my first love, Marion Odberg. So mine has been a life spent in relative obscurity beyond the circles of my various communities. Success eventually found me, but often it has been wildly mixed and elusive enough to give me second thoughts about trying anything new—like writing a book.

That said, I am the principal living witness to the lives of my father, Roy, and brother Ken—lives worthy of being recorded in a book. My daughter Jef's inspiring life also calls for a valedictory story, singing out to be shared. All three lived creative lives, never hesitating to take roads less traveled. (People will say the same is true of me.) I'm also a living library of other worthy tales compiled over eight-plus decades of family and friends leading a kind of Huckleberry Finn existence afloat on the river of life. Beyond the shelves of my retention are old books and fascinating files of tattered newsprint, letters, photos, and almost-forgotten poems. If I don't record all this, who will? I also sense a debt to Pacific Lutheran College professor Anne Knudson who instilled in me a serious love of literature and the belief I was a good writer. Equally important, she taught me to write skillfully—a craft that has contributed to modest success in so many aspects of my life. Obviously, the challenge of those realizations—and papering my reminiscences for family, friends, and the hell of it—got the best of me.

You'll find water in all its manifestations—including ice, snow, and clouds—a magnet and personal link in these pages, connecting me in myriad ways to family and friends, including the dogs. Also, water is the bridge to the flora and fauna living in and on the rivers, lakes, and oceans that have had a conscious and abiding fascination in my life. My brothers Ken and Tim shared this attraction with me, as poetically expressed by each of us in these pages. As sons born into a Christian family, we were, from the beginning, bonded by water and the Word through baptism to the community of faith.

Ancestral Bokn Island Home of Grandfather Rasmus Olson
in Southwestern Coastal Norway
Taken on visit in 1978
Photo by Dave Olson

Dad's maritime Norway ancestry must have genetically driven him to never accept living far from bodies of water. He didn't and I haven't. I found out why on a visit Betty and I made to Norway in 1978 to explore my roots. We took the coastal ferry north from Stavanger and got off at the very rural and sparsely populated Bokn Island. Obviously farming and fishing were the historical occupations. A general store and fuel outlet appeared to be the extent of commercial development. The storekeeper spoke almost no English. Fortunately, he found the bilingual Liv Lund, a second cousin of mine, at home. She came down to meet us. Dumbfounded by our mission, she made a couple of calls and then left us at the store. Thirty minutes later, she was back to report all had been arranged. We were on our way to a magical day with Liv as our tour guide and interpreter. She told us her husband was a ferryboat captain. We passed a lake, leading me to conclude that no one living on the island lived far from water. Then we arrived at the farm, including the home where my grandfather was born. We explored the property, still owned by family members, with the house available as a rental. The next stop was at the home of Great Aunt Anna Haaland, who spoke no English. She had already prepared a traditional lunch complete with lefse. She also had old photos of the family, including Grandfather Rasmus. All of us were amazed at reestablishing these connections after the passage of nearly a century.

* * *

Ken and I grew up sharing a room from preschool through my graduation from college. Swimming, fishing, boating, skating, and skiing were compulsions we pursued together and with friends. Commercial fishing in Alaska was part of our lives in our late teens and into our early twenties. We took advantage of opportunities to work together. We did it all unconscious of the binding threads weaving into the tapestry of our lives.

It all began growing up in a very literate Lutheran minister's family. My father accumulated scrapbooks and boxes of his writings, plus assorted articles by and about him from newspapers and magazines. Dad's expertise on matters of crime and punishment, gleaned from his experience as a representative of his denomination in prison missions and participation in Minneapolis, Minnesota, reform politics, made a splash big enough to be listed in *Who's Who In America* in the late 1930s and early 1940s. He authored two books. *The Plumbline of Education* was a circa 1960 guidance book for college-bound high school seniors that was unanimously adopted for distribution by the Association of American Lutheran Colleges. *Christians and Trouble*, published in 1982, was a treatise on evil and our trust in God to accept and surmount bad things happening to good people. I think his best writing was a weekly column for newspapers in Ketchikan, Alaska, and Concrete, Washington. "Picked Up Along The Way" was a weekly religious column carried by the *Ketchikan Chronicle* for over a year and later, for a few years, by the *Concrete Herald*. The *Herald* column twice won top honors in the Washington State Sigma Delta Chi Professional Journalism Competition.

Dad saved these writings and recollections because he thought his life, especially the first fifty years, made enough significant history to deserve preservation through his autobiography. I agree, but regretfully he never wrote more than a rough-draft digest of his life. This he typed in shaky "hunt and peck" style in his eighty-eighth year. He died a year later—a vocal maverick to the end.

In retrospect, my father made a difference in the lives of many people. His lasting gifts to me were lessons in where and how to show up for life, including my later propensity for political activism supporting controversial movements like civil rights (I was there for the March On Washington and Martin Luther King's "I Have a Dream" speech in 1963) and opposing optional wars in Vietnam and Iraq. Though failing often, I continue to strive to do my best and hope it's good enough.

Ida, my mother, who retired from teaching high school English and literature to marry my father, never actually stopped teaching. Mom read books of fairy tales and adventure to my brothers and me in early childhood. Later she introduced us to the power of poetry. This fostered a love for verse that led Ken, Tim, and me to eventually write our own. An eternal optimist, I recall hearing Mom's version of the old G. K. Chesterton quote, "When it rains on your parade, look up rather than down. Without the rain, there would be no rainbow," which is advice I've thought about more than once over the passing decades. She was also a talker who remembered everything. She could deliver verbatim "So-and-so said this" and "I said that" accounts of past conversations, driving my father crazy and amazing the rest of us. Near the end of her life she could still remind us of forgotten events from our family history. As for correspondence after we left home, you could count on two or three letters from Mom for every one from Dad. She was the chronicler of our family life. I wish more of her letters had been saved as some brought more than just family updates. I'm glad I had the opportunities to fly up from California for long visits during the months before she died—a day short of her eighty-eighth birthday. It's all only memories now.

Ken was a waterman cut from different cloth to become a clergyman. The modest, risk-taking, entrepreneurial daredevil I grew up with evolved into a mystic visionary and missionary. All of his talents, traits, and characteristics led him to successfully pursue a dream of unique ministry aboard a boat. Articles appeared in various newspapers and periodicals over the years covering various aspects of Ken's inspiring journey with the M/V *Christian*. Through it all he appeared oblivious to the abiding influence he was having on various youth aboard the *Christian* that became central to their recollections in these pages. As the creative and enduring spirit of this ministry, from conception through its present service, he left a unique legacy. This includes most of a decade with his wife, Nancy, aboard the *Christian* bringing ministry to isolated communities in Southeast Alaska. This period was preceded by a storybook romance leading to their partnership. They established a precedent followed by successors.

Throughout his life, Ken wrote poetry and essays as the spirit moved him. In 1976, he self-published a collection of some of his work titled *Just A Few Poems For My Friends From The Summer I Knew I Was A Poet*. Over the course of 1986 and 1987 he wrote and compiled an anthology of his theological, philosophical, and poetic works, *Salmon Are Christian*, subsequently printed for limited distribution among friends and relatives. He also left behind an incomplete personal journal begun in midsummer of 1986, covering the period of his escape to a new life sailing a small boat to Alaska, romance with Nancy, and reconnection with the *Christian* in the spring of 1988. Unfortunately, for some reason, numerous pages are missing. Nancy, in loaning me the journal for this book, says she thinks these were the "dark pages." Certainly, there were many dark days for Ken up to his meeting Nancy. We can only speculate as to what Ken might have written about during those low times in his life, or what he would have written had he had the chance to pen the narrative history of the *Christian* itself—now in its fifth decade of evolving mission. Ken's tragic end came too soon; he would have been the ideal author for the biography of the *Christian*. Instead, its life has become his legacy.

All of us who knew Ken also know his life would not have been the same without his personal theology. Thus, this work would have been incomplete without recognizing the convergent place his theology had in his life and providing insight into the meaning of those writings. I found this insight in a, dare I say, brilliant letter by our brother Tim written shortly after Ken died. Through Tim, you'll find that he left us with a lot to think about on the enigma of "the real" Ken Olson.

We had no surviving sisters, but you will find one women's lib story. I wish I had known more of the courageous women who, in my day, were already refusing to be denied participation in the kinds of ventures that are at the heart of this book.

* * *

Digressions herein are researched accounts of rather extraordinary people I knew and incidents in a world where shit happened and the outcomes ranged from humorous to lucky. Two tales are of uncommon boat captains, Harky Tew and John Knaplund, whom I decked for in my youth. They reflect fascinating family histories generously shared with me by relatives. Stories about Tew include a summary biography of Selma Swanson Tew MacKenzie, an independent and feisty woman I met but never knew. What she pulled off as a businesswoman in a macho frontier town deserves at least honorable mention in the history of Ketchikan, Alaska, and the women's movement within that state. Another side story is the implausible tale told to me, that I've been telling for over six decades, of the double collision of the M/V *Kiska* and the M/V *Mayflower*. You'll find it fleshed out with legal documentation of the basic facts. Believe it or not!

Some of the others are my stories and adventures. You'll find a few skiing stories get some play because this is where Ken and I spent many winters. Part three, "Forrest Gump Live," is mostly an account of my twenties to forties—CIA, flying, and sailing adventures. A year of living on isolated Tachen Island off the coast of China during the Korean War era foreordained me to witness escapades that make up a sliver of history. I justify the flying adventures because they are good yarns. You may think a couple cross the border between fact and fiction, but my partners on those flights are still alive and tell the same stories. It's now or never to put them in a book. Besides, water is so much a part of air and flying is so much like sailing, I think the attractions to the brotherhoods of pilots and sailors are the same.

From the beginnings of this writing I also sensed the necessity to tell my daughter Jef's story. Her life carries a family thread of fourth generations of Olsons. Fortunately, I have been able to fall back on the writings of those who loved her to fill out the mosaic of her life and the many lives she touched along the way. All who thoughtfully shared their memories following Jef's death were contributors to what you'll find in "The Inspired Life of Jenifer Ann Olson."

Finally, "River Life Retrospective" reflects fifteen years of vibrant life on a wild river with living waters.

None of this could have been shared without the contributions of family and friends. They not only filled a multitude of gaps in my recalled narratives, but also triggered my interest in their related stories.

I hope those still alive and discovering themselves on these pages will find pleasure in the reading. If you find a bone to pick, that's OK. I've done my best to research and relentlessly track down sources to verify story details with mixed success. Investigation to minimize errors in names, times, and places dependent solely on my recollection has been less than diligent because it really doesn't matter anymore, does it? Dad's Alaskan friend Ed Sande often closed his tall tales by saying, "If you don't believe this, write [name] in [place] and he will confirm every word of it." One memorable evening Nellie, his wife, responded, "C'mon, Ed, he died twenty years ago." Ed, unfazed, moved on to his next yarn. It's just water over the dam now, isn't it?

Or maybe it isn't. I ask myself, "What if my father had not pursued an opportunity to go to Alaska for a year when he was a twenty-six-year-old seminarian, or go back when he was a forty-four-year-old Lutheran minister with a family and make a little history in the politics of the Territory? Or my brother Ken, what if he had not plunged into buying his own salmon troller in Seattle to fish in Alaska when he was barely twenty years old? Or, when he was a thirty-nine-year-old minister with a parish and a family, to pursue the building of a floating youth Bible camp that weighed one hundred tons and measured sixty-five feet in length? What if Jef had not followed her spiritual calling from her early teens to be an unforgettable blessing and inspiration in so many lives in so few years? Finally, what if I had not jumped at a unique opportunity to learn to fly in far away Taiwan in 1954? In this regard, I revel in stories of people of all ages from all walks of life who say yes to taking roads less traveled in their lives. Perhaps this small work will help awaken some reader of any age to do the same—to courageously seek out, welcome, and embrace opportunities and adventure as they come along. Having that impact on just one person would make me think this book had been worth writing.

PART ONE

Family Roots—Minnesota To Alaska

Every memory passed on is a strand in the family rope linking past to future.
Together, they braid to a strong cable spanning time,
Connecting generations past with those yet to come.
My family's history is the foundation for all that follows.

Roy and Ida wedding portrait
Married July 2, 1927, in Mansfield, Minnesota

UPWARDLY MOBILE FAMILY

ROY AND IDA

For Mom and Dad, it all began on a Greyhound bus.

My father, Roy; my brothers Ken, Jerry, and Tim; and I are all Olsons, but our surname should be Bokneberg. Dad's father Rasmus, no doubt taken from his mother's maiden name Rasmusson, was born to this family name on Bokn Island at the mouth of Boknafjord about twenty miles north of Stavanger, Norway. Rasmus was born on May 31, 1861, among the youngest in a large family. His father, Ole, was a successful farmer with probably some reliance on nearby fishing for additional food and possibly income. The island's sons grew up learning those trades. With no inheritance and no land to divide for younger siblings, the most attractive choice was migrating to America.

Young Rasmus made his move at age twenty. Perhaps Rasmus thought Bokneberg too long or complex a name. When he arrived at Ellis Island, he denied his surname by listing his name as Olson. Maybe he decided to become another Olson as an adaptation of his father's first name. Maybe he did it in response to unhappiness with his parents, siblings, or himself that was nourished before sailing for America. This is more likely because the family he left behind on Bokn Island never heard from or of him again.

Roy's mother, Engel, was a Severeid from a farming area by that name located along the south shore at the upper end of Akrafjord about seventy miles north of Boknafjord. The Severeids were a large extended family of farmers. Apparently unsuccessful at attracting a qualified suitor by age twenty, Engel joined other Severeids already settled across the ocean in Story City, Iowa. Soon after her arrival in 1881 she met Rasmus, and they married in 1885. He listed his occupation as "laborer" on the marriage certificate. Success stories of other local Norwegian immigrants led the couple to stay in the upper Midwest. Nine children followed, of which eight survived to grow up and experience the hardscrabble life of immigrant tenant farming in northern Iowa, despite all their ancestral roots that were in the shorelands and islands of the fjords along the west coast of Norway. So perhaps love of the sea was a quiet voice passed to my father, and on to me and my brothers, in latent genes by this hardy couple who had to take what they could get.

Roy was the seventh child, born December 20, 1900. His memories of his boyhood are bittersweet. This is how he described early schooling in his memoir:

> *It all took place in a little one room school, eight grades. We all drank well water from the same dipper. Snot noses never stopped running. Someone was always bringing head lice to school. I can still feel the torture of that fine-tooth comb dipped in kerosene when mother went to work on us. Somebody always had one of the childhood ailments—the "Grippe," chicken pox, measles, mumps, pink eye, and occasionally epidemic diphtheria or scarlet fever that meant weeks of quarantine. But we were tough. I can't remember one death from disease.*

* * *

In his teens, Roy found his way to nearby rivers and lakes to discover the magic of water and fishing. Maybe his father or an older brother took him fishing to catch his share for family dinner. He told me that a cane pole, some line, a bottle cork bobber, a machine nut for weight, a hook, and worms for bait were his first outfit. Sunfish, crappies and blue gills were his catch. Panfish were his fry. He was a fisherman his whole life.

High school was followed by work and two years at Ellsworth College in Northern Iowa qualifying him to teach grammar school. Summer evenings were for fishing. When the fish weren't biting, I'm sure Dad was instead falling into hypnotic raptures on the wonders and marvels of God's outdoor creation. He said he felt chosen by Jesus to be a fisher of souls through Christian ministry from his early teens. Perhaps he had already also discovered God had given him a gift of gab and enough charisma, strong convictions, and sense of humor to sell an icebox to an Eskimo. At age twenty-four, though he didn't meet the bachelor's degree requirement, he talked or impressed his way into acceptance at Luther Theological Seminary in St. Paul, Minnesota.

Fishing was one of the few approved pastimes for Norwegian Lutheran seminarians in those days. Perhaps Roy found it a complementary outdoor activity he could surely pursue for a lifetime along with ministry. With his line in the water, he could mull over ideas for future sermons. In his junior year, Roy made his luckiest catch, a fisherman's dream, even if he thought it a call from God. The call was a notice to the seminary from the bishop whose synod included the U.S. Territory of Alaska. He was looking for a seminarian interested in serving his intern year, customarily a school year under tutelage of the minister at a church, in remote Ketchikan, reached only by sea. The interning seminarian would be chaplain of the Lutheran Seaman's Mission, lead Lutherans in Sunday worship services, and continue a predecessor's groundwork establishing a congregation. Fluency in Norwegian and an adventurous spirit were prerequisites. Duly qualified and raring to go, Roy got the job.

He took the steamship from Seattle, arriving in Ketchikan in July 1926. Sited on an island in Southeast Alaska, six hundred miles north of Seattle, Ketchikan was primarily a fishing village of about two thousand people. Roy's first flock were all Norwegian immigrants engaged in commercial fishing or related pursuits, including marriage and raising families. The people and Roy took to each other like ducks to water.

There was no church but, lucky for Roy, the Lutheran Home Missions department owned a twenty-eight-foot wood pilothouse cabin boat, M/V *North Star*, powered by a one-lung[1] gas engine. The department had wanted its own boat for clerical visits to serve Norwegian Lutherans settled on outlying islands. Roy soon discovered there were no such folks to call on. But in exchange for maintenance, he could use the *North Star* for fishing and exploring local waters.

Young Roy on Mission Boat M/V *North Star* in Ketchikan in 1926
Photo by Roy Olson

All this makes you think God knew how to put Roy Olson in heaven for his intern year in Ketchikan. Wild salmon and trout, among the sacred fishes of

---

1   "One-lung" was the vernacular term for a single-cylinder engine. Large, heavy single-cylinder gas engines turning at low RPMs were common during that era.

myth, mystery, legend, and faith, were there in bountiful abundance testifying to God's eternal presence and handiwork. They were there to make an exciting catch with no license required and no limit on numbers. They were there for taking to the table as a staple of Ketchikan cuisine. I remember him reminiscing about his introduction to fishing with a fly rod for trout in Ketchikan Creek just a short hike from where he lived at the Seaman's Mission. There was talk, too, about overnights in secure anchorages, surrounded by mountains, and going to sleep to the music of waterfalls. Friends were no doubt often invited along for company on these pocket cruises.

Ketchikan, Alaska Water Front in 1926
Courtesy Gene and Joyce Dyer, Holdal Family Archive

Equally important were his accomplishments as Lutheran apostle to the Norwegian immigrant community in Ketchikan. Going door to door, sharing the vision of building a church over many cups of coffee, $1,800 was raised for the project. By the time he left, start-up membership for a congregation was organized and ground had been purchased on which to build a future church.

An important secular legacy, never forgotten and forever appreciated by old timers, was Roy's language class taught to Norwegian immigrants who had come to Ketchikan knowing hardly a word of English. Thora Vig née Holdal was one of them. A personal friend in the years before she died, Thora told me, in her inimitable, soft, musical Norse accent, about attending Roy's class. She said, "Some of the single ladies hoped to catch the eye of Reverend Olson, but it never happened."

Already thinking ahead to the first-person tales he could tell to church groups back home in the Midwest, he carried a camera everywhere, taking photos of everything. It was a "never pass up an opportunity" eager seminarian's field year.

Due to return to Minnesota, Roy had some bright ideas on how to get there. Steamship passage to Seattle was a no-brainer, but once there, he figured an alternative more exciting than taking a train the rest of the way might be buying a clunker Model T and driving instead. Besides, his brother Jesse, back in Iowa, had written to him in Ketchikan saying he had some savings and an urge to see the West. He proposed meeting Roy in Seattle. It all worked. How far they got in the clunker is hazy, though. They made it, but Roy told tales later indicating they weren't driving a Model T on the home stretch.[2]

Roy returned to flatland Minnesota flat broke with a box full of photos and lantern slide negatives he could project on a screen, in addition to a well-honed spiel about the marvels of life and starting a church on the last frontier.

He also returned to the love of his life, Ida, a graduate of the University of Minnesota who was teaching high school English and literature in Fessenden, North Dakota, while he was in Alaska. They had met two years before on a southbound bus from Minneapolis. Roy left the story in his memoir:

> *The bus was crowded. There was only one vacant seat, just behind a seat shared by an elderly gentleman and a young lady. In the course of their conversation, which I couldn't help overhearing, she said she was on her way home to attend her grandparents' golden wedding [anniversary] and mentioned a university student friend who had been a high school classmate of mine. That was all it took to bring me into the conversation. It developed we had other acquaintances. At the next stop the gentleman suggested exchanging seats.*

On the rest of the ride, Ida probably also told him she was a farmer's daughter and a senior at the University of Minnesota. Perhaps she let him guess her age (she was born December 28, 1901), but I'm certain she never told him her nickname was "Pee-Wee" because she was not quite five feet tall. Who knows what Roy told her. What we do know is by the time she got off the bus one hundred miles down the road in Albert Lea, Roy had convinced her to tell him that her name was Ida Louise Brewer and what her family farm address was

---

2   After hearing Roy's tales of Alaska, Jesse went on to Lutheran missionary service in far north Teller, Alaska, south of Nome.

in Alden, Minnesota. That's all Roy needed. Ida came from a laid-back German, English, Dutch, and Yankee farm family. They had successfully farmed a quarter section (160 acres) of rich black dirt for almost a quarter century by the time Ida met Roy on the bus. It was a home built on hard work, faith, and imagination.

James (Jim) Brewer, Ida's father, was a third-generation American. His grandparents had farmed in Ohio. His father, looking for more room, eventually settled in Iowa. Jim initially learned the butter maker's trade, but left it to return to farming—for which all of us who have followed are thankful.

Martha, née Wichmann, Ida's mother, was born in Germany. Her family migrated to America in 1882 when she was seven years old. They homesteaded in southern Minnesota to build a successful farm just a few miles from Ida's home farm.

The Brewers were a generous, gregarious, and full-of-fun family who never missed church, a free show, or the county fair. They belonged to a much more liberal American Lutheran church with German roots and were much more attuned to the good things of life like dancing, movies, playing cards, and Grain Belt beer. How could young Roy not be attracted to this family and their way of life?

Ida was bright-eyed and quietly determined from early girlhood. Similar to Roy, she discovered and fell in love with books early on in the one-room, one-teacher, grades one to eight country school not far from home. A fortunate supporting presence at home was her father, Jim, who believed in education and served on the school board for decades, even after his three children had graduated.

Ida was the first from her extended family to push on to high school and, from there, to the university. We know she was an excellent teacher loved by her students. She was so good, a former student, Margaret Erdahl Shank, later wrote of her in the memoir *The Coffee Train*:

> She (Miss Brewer) left us with an abiding sense of beauty in our memories. For with this small, gentle teacher we had stormed the citadels of power with Sir Walter Scott; we heard the clash of arms and rumble of chariots on the plains of Troy. She taught us to honor words as the sound of the human race in its slow ascent up the ladder of knowledge.

Pursuit of Ida hadn't been easy. As Roy put it in his memoir:

> The time came (within a year of first meeting) and I proposed during Christmas vacation. She had visions of a master's degree at Columbia. She wasn't ready to promise to spend her life with a man still teaching country school. But she didn't say no.

They missed each other when Roy went to Alaska. So much so they reached agreement, apparently by love letter, to marry as soon as the penniless suitor returned home. How broke was he? Here's what Roy had to say in his memoir:

Well now, get this straight, when she paid for the marriage license and the ring, I knew I had a wife who knew what "for better or for worse" could mean. If I was crazy, she ran me a close second. She should have turned and fled.

They were married July 2, 1927. Was there a honeymoon? No mention, but Roy tells us what they did on their return:

I doubt that many newly married have had more fun than we did that summer. We hit the road with me "lecturing" on Alaska, and Ida dipping into her purse for gasoline money if the last night's collection hadn't been sufficient.

As the magic summer ended they found a tiny house near the seminary. Roy went back to class. Ida was already pregnant. She gave birth to a daughter whom they named Elaine. She died a week later. Roy wrote in his memoir, "To this day, Ida's composure and resignation remain a source of mystery to me."

Roy resumed life on the lecture circuit that summer. His final year at the seminary was uneventful. He graduated and was ordained in the Lutheran ministry. Ida, though she probably never aspired to be one, became a minister's wife.

* * *

CORNUCOPIA OF OPPORTUNITIES

My father's first parish was Bethlehem Lutheran in St. Cloud, Minnesota. This small city was home to lots of Norwegian Lutherans and close to nearby fishing lakes. Maybe Garrison Keillor saw the same two regional attributes decades later when he located Lake Wobegon near St. Cloud. It was also the location of the Minnesota State Reformatory. My guess is if Reverend Olson had a choice of churches, he also chose St. Cloud for the opportunity to serve as Protestant chaplain at the prison. While learning about prison life, he might lead inmates away from evil and to redemption and salvation in Christ. He could combine all this with starting a family.

I was born on June 24, 1929, and named David in honor of the Bible psalmist. Kenneth was born March 11, 1931, with no significance attached to his name according to Mom. Both of us were born in a Catholic hospital.

Mother said she always trusted we would turn out to be good boys because the nuns prayed for us. To her dying day, she thought those prayers were answered. I'm thankful for that.

By the time I was four and Ken was two, Dad was taking us to the reformatory for our haircuts in the prison barbershop. The barbers were also inmates. On the way out we would stop by the warden's office to pick up a cake or cookies. These "goodies" had been received from inmates' families, but were undeliverable to the cellblocks. Perhaps these experiences influenced my views of incarceration to this day. Around that same time, Mother was reading to us *Just So Stories* by Rudyard Kipling and, our favorites, the *Billy Whiskers* series by Frances Trego Montgomery. Looking ahead to future school days, she was instilling a love of reading and learning in us.

By 1933, Reverend Olson was looking for new challenges. He was intrigued by the possibilities for accomplishments doing the Lord's work in the prison environment, so he sought the opportunity to be appointed the Norwegian Lutheran Church's first (and perhaps only) national director of prison missions.

Our family moved to Minneapolis and into a home that was small by today's standards but big enough back then to have space for Dad's national prison missions office. This included space for bachelor Hans, missions assistant and secretary, to work and live with us. Lucky for me, we were just a few blocks from Lake Nokomis's swimming beach.

Our first visits to the beach were with Mother or Hans. A summer later, trusting and fearless for our safety, mother gave Ken and me each a nickel for popcorn and let us take off for the beach to teach ourselves to swim. We loved the water. The next summer I was swimming out to the diving dock to practice off the low boards, preparatory to working my way up to the tower high dives. Ken was not far behind. Dad introduced us to fishing on Lake Nokomis as well. A *Minneapolis Daily Times* news photographer captured Ken and me doing our best to figure out how to rig the leaders and lures in Dad's tackle box.

One project of the prison missions director's was a tour of federal and state prisons to investigate conditions and other chaplaincy programs. In those days there were few airlines or car rental services. Travel by personal auto was the practical way to go, and Dad thought taking his family along would make it more enjoyable. So he bought an ugly home-built four-wheel pop-up house trailer, which was painted dark green so it could be hidden in the forest. There were beds for all of us. Backing it up was next to impossible and Dad never got the hang of it.

That summer we drove south to Galveston, Texas, through the Gulf states and back up the Atlantic coast to Washington, D.C., New York, and home again.

One of the trip's highlights for Dad was catfish fishing not far from a Bible camp near Waco, Texas, where he was guest preacher for a week. The highlight for me was eating the catfish pan fried by the camp cook, a big, jolly, black guy who loved kids. He was the first black person I had ever actually experienced as a real person. Maybe he sparked the dawning of my eventual activist participation to achieve desegregation.

Another highlight was camping on the ocean beach at Galveston. Dad took Ken and me wading into the surf. Feeling the undertow and awed by the height of the waves, I was glad to have my hand firmly in Dad's hand.

Another memory is approaching New York, cruising through the Holland Tunnel and into the eye-popping madness of Manhattan. We went to the top of the Empire State Building and the Statue of Liberty, and dined at a Japanese restaurant on dishes stir-fried at our table. From New York we accompanied Dad to Sing Sing Prison. He investigated inmate conditions and the rest of us got a brief tour. I knew I didn't want to spend any more time there.

Thanksgiving 1934 was at the farm of one of Dad's brothers. We met our cousins and had a farm tour, after which we little boys were sent to an upstairs bedroom to play until dinner was ready. The room was over the kitchen. In the floor, directly over the old-fashioned cob-and-wood-fired oven, was a one-foot-square iron grate set into the floor. This was to allow heat from the range to heat the bedroom. Peering through the grate at the cooking going on below, a mischievous cousin decided to tinkle through the opening and watch the drops sizzle on the range top—not to mention a few falling into Grandma's gravy. That's when all hell broke loose. Grandma and mothers whooped it up from the kitchen and fathers quickly arrived upstairs. The unfortunate perpetrator's father did not spare the rod.

* * *

Back home, after Hans moved out and left a vacant bedroom, Dad brought home Billy Markinen, a teenager down on his luck at Redwing Juvenile Reformatory. Dad thought he deserved a better chance in life. Mother graciously took him in, but after a year she had seen enough of Billy. Beggarly Billy kept us informed of his whereabouts by calling Dad when he was short of money. Dad thought we had seen the last of him when he joined the army. Final contact was a call one morning from a base in Texas. Billy had lost some money in a poker game. He was about to take a beating if he didn't pay up. Dad hung up.

In 1935 Dad was lured away from the prison missions by an offer to become executive secretary of the Lutheran Brotherhood, the denomination's national organization for men. He loved the job—visiting churches and successfully organizing men's clubs to contribute to their congregational programs. One of the approaches he used to give the men, almost all fathers, something worthwhile for their club to do was to interest them in sponsoring scout troops. Scout officials appreciated his work. When he visited a church where the minister was a fisherman, he could also occasionally fit in a day off on the water.

The downside to Dad's job as the executive secretary was the continuous travel. He wasn't home much except for vacations, holidays, and some weekends. Mother tried to learn how to drive, but quit after ending up in a snow bank during the winter of 1936. It didn't matter. We only had one car (owned by the Lutheran Brotherhood), we couldn't afford another, and women drivers were only beginning to be accepted. Since we lived too far away to walk to Lake Nokomis Lutheran Church for Sunday school, worship services, and other activities when Dad wasn't home, later that year we moved to a home closer to the church.

Ken and I soon discovered we lived one block from a valley with short, open, snow-covered slopes in the winter. Kids were sledding and skiing down those short hills and we couldn't wait to join them. Skis appeared to offer more challenge and fun than sleds, and when I was eight years old, I got my first pair. They were made of pine with leather toe straps. We used rubber bands cut from an old car tire inner tube for harnesses to keep our boot toes from coming out of the straps. Some older boys built a small jump at the bottom of one of the hills with firewood as a support base. It was about two feet high and you could fly airborne for about six feet. I was unable to get enough of it, forgetting to go home, continuing to jump after dark and getting into some trouble when Dad came looking for me to come home for supper. But he understood: snow, frost, and ice were God's winter works of art with water. Dad reveled in their beauty and appreciated my attraction to skiing. How could his sons be more Norwegian? Ken got his first skis a year later.

* * *

From 1935 through 1937, Ken and I spent two or three weeks each summer down on the family farm where Mom had grown up. Grandma and Grandpa Brewer, along with our mother's brother, Ted, and his wife, Leona, somehow found room for us and our cousins Curt and Russ, sons of Mom's sister, Marie. We had grand times learning and doing all the things farm kids do. Grandma and Leona put us to work picking produce from the garden, gathering eggs from the hen house, plucking (defeathering) roosters dipped in boiling water after Grandma laid them one at a time on the chopping block to cut their heads off with an ax, and shelling corncobs from the previous year's crop for fuel to fire the kitchen range. Grandpa and Uncle Ted taught us to help milk cows and turn the crank on the manual separator, producing a small stream of cream to sell to the butter maker plus a large stream of skim milk to feed the calves and slop the hogs. Grandpa gave words like "hell" and "damn" new meanings not taught at church. He also communicated in conversation and body language the subtleties in the usage of words like "shit" and "horseshit" that remain a part of my vocabulary today.

Grandma Martha Brewer, me, and Grandpa Jim Brewer
On the farm in 1943
Photo by Leona Brewer

Uncle Ted had no problem letting us risk life and limb, like discovering for ourselves the limits of climbing the vertical ladder up the barn wall to the small wooden platform at the ceiling's peak to jump off into the loose hay piled ten to twelve feet below. Another attraction was climbing the one-and-a-half-inch-diameter manila line running about thirty-five vertical feet from the barn floor up to a block pulley attached to a rafter. This "hay rope" was part of a system for raising slings of fresh alfalfa from the horse-drawn hayrack up to the second story hayloft for storage. It was perfect for climbing to the pulley or swinging over to a crossbeam halfway up from where you could launch yourself and pretend to be a trapeze artist at the fair. Ted's young son, Roland, watched us and by the time he was five, he had surpassed all of us. City kids just didn't know what they were missing.

While fooling around on the hay rope, I discovered the ecstasy of sex. Working the rope bound between my legs was the turn-on. What did I know? Innocence was bliss! Sometime after returning home I learned a new word, "masturbation," a sinful act that might stunt my growth. I was old enough to understand its association with fun on the hay rope, and it scared the hell out of me for a year or two.

How fearless was Uncle Ted? Grandma and Grandpa liked to tell how their Holstein bull broke through the fence onto the neighbor's farm. Ted was sent over to retrieve the bull, and he returned home riding it. Challenged to do likewise, we cousins broke a young cow named Betsey to tolerate us riding her down the lane from pasture to barnyard for evening milking. This lasted until our family reunion. Another city relative saw us do this and wanted a ride. So we held her while he got on. Betsey immediately lit out across the barnyard to dump him, in his Sunday best, in four inches of barnyard mud and cow shit. Grandma was not pleased.

Uncle Ted was my first hero, but he was more than that. He was gentle in caring for the stock on the farm, especially the draft horses. They knew him and he knew them. He also gave me my first introduction on how to be respectful of wildlife. There was a slew in the back forty that was home every summer to a few pairs of wild mallard ducks. When one of the hens made her nest one spring up in a grain field and Ted noticed it, he went out of his way to till and plant around the nest, giving the hen room to incubate and hatch her brood of ducklings.

* * *

Back home, we lived only two miles from the Minneapolis airport. The Army Air Corps operated a flight training program there so the local air space was pretty busy. I was fascinated watching the air traffic, especially the Stearman biplanes, flying training and formation patterns. By age nine I was building twenty-five-cent balsa wood models. I wanted to fly. For my tenth birthday I got a couple of one-dollar bills. Mac McGinnis Air Service charged two dollars for a ten-minute plane ride. Dad was easy to talk into for a ride to the airport. McGinnis himself was flying that day. I was the only customer buying a ride. He wanted to take me up in a Piper Cub, but I had my heart set on a ride in his open cockpit biplane that was a much bigger three-seater. When I persisted, Dad, though not eager, paid and joined me for the ride.

After landing, with no other customers waiting, Dad and Mac got into a casual conversation with Dad entertaining us both with a joke to explain his earlier hesitation about going up for the flight. It was about a guy who couldn't be sold on taking a ride. To change his mind the barnstormer pilot bragged of his flying hours and said he was a fatalist—when your time is up, it's up! To which the prospect responded, "What if we get up there and your time is up?" This brief conversation led to a meaningful second meet-up for Dad and Mac a year later.

Also in the late 1930s, our family continued to grow. We welcomed the births of Jerry on February 15, 1937, and Tim on December 15, 1938, who came home just in time for Christmas. Mother and child customarily spent ten days in the hospital in those days. I thought giving birth was major surgery requiring lengthy convalescence. I think that's what Dad led us boys to believe. We were told to be helpful and behave ourselves.

* * *

In early 1939 the elderly minister at Lake Nokomis Lutheran Church retired. The Pastoral Call Committee decided they couldn't do better than calling their fellow member, Reverend Olson. Dad responded to the committee, informing them that, after considerable prayer, God had told him to accept their call. I speculate Mother's gentle persuasion was the deciding factor. With four sons to raise, she was ready for Father to spend more time closer to home. He was installed as pastor on October 1, 1939.

Apparently settled into a long ministry, tired of renting, and wanting a home of their own, Mom and Dad soon found a fine house on Woodlawn Boulevard, a block from Lake Nokomis. We moved again.

Ken and I quickly found friends among the boys in the new neighborhood. Dick Edwards and his older brother Egbert (Egg), Denny Buck and his older brother Don, and Dale Lindquist made up our loose-knit group of bright, hyperactive youngsters left to our own devices with a talent for finding fun and excitement. The older boys in high school were the organizers and leaders. The rest of us were learners, followers, and occasional opportunistic mischief-makers.

All of us were members of a scout troop meeting at my father's church. It was a very successful troop, so large it had a separate Explorer Patrol for older scouts. They met at a nearby private home on the same night as the troop met, and it was on the way home for my friends and me. One winter evening with snowbanks piled up to two feet high along the roads, as two of those friends and I were walking home from a scout meeting, we were accosted by two Explorer Scouts proposing participation in some seemingly innocent rascality.

One of their pals had just acquired a Model A Ford. It was parked in front of the home where the Explorers were still meeting. Their proposal was for the three of us to help them push their friend's Model A down the street a couple of blocks so he'd have to look for it after the meeting. Whoopee! What fun! We pushed it to a "T" in the road where we could go left or right. Straight ahead was a short hill that emptied out onto the Keewaydin Bowl outdoor ice skating rink. There was no hesitation—we pushed hard to get momentum up and over the curb and shoved it down the hill. It cut through the snow and finished its trip with a graceful 360-degree spin on the ice. Instantly we knew we had gone too far. My buddies and I took off for home and so did the two Explorers.

The owner reported his car stolen when he couldn't find it after the meeting. A tow truck was needed the next day to get the car back on the street. The cops didn't take long determining that the culprits included me and my two scout friends. A police officer was sent to pick us up at the junior high school. He met with us in the assistant principal's office where he told us we were being charged with car theft—they thought the five of us took a joy ride around South Minneapolis in a pilfered Model A. Our troop scoutmaster and other scouting officials got involved and asked the policeman to leave us boy scouts at school. The Explorers paid the towing bill, and all of the culprits received orders to attend a meeting at the scoutmaster's home the next Sunday afternoon. From a holding room, each of us was called to appear separately before the troop committee. One spokesman told me the trouble they had experienced getting the charges dismissed. Another emphasized damage done to my reputation, not to mention the embarrassment caused to the Boy Scouts of America, my church, and my father. Dismissed in tears, I cried on the way home. Mother cheered me up, and Dad must have decided there was nothing to add to the scout committee's inquisition, so the incident was never discussed until it was good for a laugh many years later.

* * *

On a clear, cold, windy midwinter afternoon, when Ken was eleven and I was thirteen, we looked out at a snowless ice-bound Lake Nokomis and wished we had an iceboat. We put our heads together, mounted a mast with a square sail on a Flexible Flyer sled long enough for both of us to sit on, and headed for the upwind end of the lake to see how fast we could go. I still remember the initial acceleration—the thing just took off!

Totally out of control and unable to see where we were going as we sat in tandem behind the sail, we hung on. Unfortunately, at the same time, two men on a large sloop-rigged iceboat were on a fast track across the lake, putting them on a collision course with us. We couldn't see them and they had no reason to look our way to avoid hitting us. About a mile or more from our start, perhaps halfway across the lake, the inevitable happened. In its photo story of the accident, the *Minneapolis Daily Times* reported, "David Olson, 13, and his brother Kenneth, 11, today were abed in Fairview Hospital with painful injuries because they learned to make their sled skim over the ice with a gunnysack sail, but forgot until too late that they hadn't mastered the technique of steering their comic-strip craft."

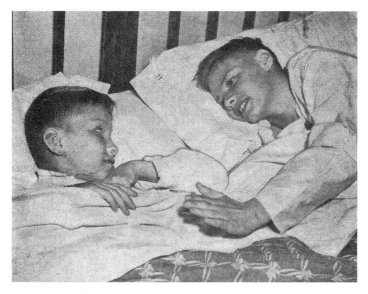

Ken and me in the hospital after our sailing sled collision with a large ice boat on Lake Nokomis in Minneapolis in 1942
Ken was 11 and I was 13 years old. Our "ice boat" was a sled
with a make-shift mast and powered by a gunny-sack sail.
Photo by *Minneapolis Daily Times*

Though the adults piloting the large iceboat would have been found at fault in any court for not seeing Ken and me, Dad and Mom never mentioned it or, to my knowledge, considered making an issue of it. It was just an accident to forgive and forget. I turned out to be more seriously hurt with several broken bones in my right foot. The bones guy did a great job of casting it, and I was sent home after a week in the hospital.

Most memorable about the hospital stay was Miss Hermansen, a young, very blond, very blue-eyed minister's daughter from northern Minnesota, who was a student nurse on my floor. She was the nicest, prettiest thing I'd ever seen. I remember her getting me ready to go home; I thought I'd never see her again. Then a week later, my broken big toe, with a wire through it for traction, became infected. I was sent back to the hospital for another week. They put me in a room on a different floor from my first stay—so no Miss Hermansen. She heard I was back in the hospital, though, and came in one day to visit me. Unfortunately, she wanted a look at my foot, which was in a bed tent. Raising the sheet, she looked in far enough to see not only my foot, but also an unmistakable twitterpated teenager's erection, standing tall. I remember her blushing, dropping the sheet, and wishing me well on the way to a hasty retreat. My sword fell. I was crestfallen the rest of the day. Eventually I read Hemingway's *Farewell To Arms* and realized I wasn't the first to fall in love with his nurse.

By the next winter, the two older neighborhood teenagers, Egg and Don, had completed a neat two-seat sloop-rigged iceboat. They not only took their younger brothers, Dick and Denny, who were my friends, and me for rides, but they also taught us to sail it ourselves. They let me take it alone. So I invited Ken for at least one breezy Saturday morning of numerous round-trip crossings of the lake. Careening across a frozen lake in an open-cockpit iceboat at dizzying speeds with no brakes remains an unforgettable thrill.

* * *

The move to Woodlawn Boulevard, along with Dad working in a nearby congregation, also coalesced into a family life that was never dull. Dad often brought guests home for dinner. Some were friends picked up from various walks of life. Most were ministerial buddies who happened to be in town. Guest preachers, especially foreign missionaries on home leave, would almost always stay over for Sunday dinner. The missionaries were occasionally accompanied by their wives; together they told the best stories. And finally, contributing to our family experience was Dad's continuing inability to resist bringing home deserving teenagers to live with us.

Shortly after moving to the bigger house, probably the midsummer of 1940, Dad drove down to Nebraska to guest preach at a dust bowl country church. I went with him for the ride. The minister, Reverend Turmo, had some number of children, including a daughter, Eldred, who had just graduated from high school and felt beckoned by the big city. So that afternoon she packed her belongings in our car and returned to Minneapolis to live with us while she found a job. She was a wonderful addition to our family. We had a grand piano and Eldred knew how to play it. This led to sing-alongs accompanied by Eldred as standard entertainment. After two months, she left us to become a nurse, but we remained her home away from home.

A year or two later she caught the eye of Ensign Perry Roberts, a handsome young naval aviator. They married and eventually raised five or six children. During the summer of 1956, working in Washington, D.C., I had the pleasure of being invited down to their home on Chesapeake Bay for weekends of water skiing and other fun. Never would have happened if Dad hadn't done what he did long ago on that dusty Sunday afternoon.

The bed vacated by Eldred didn't stay empty for long either. Walt Gravrock, a shirttail seminarian relative of Dad's, prevailed on my parents to rent the room to his fiancée, Lorraine Trehus. She was a nice young Christian lady with a weakness for occasionally shoplifting clothes she liked and couldn't afford. Mom caught on and reported to Dad. He apparently successfully exercised his considerable powers of pastoral persuasion, casting out her casual addiction. She eventually moved on to a long and successful life as Reverend Walt's wife, raising a fine family.

* * *

On a late summer evening in 1940, Dad was invited down the street for a neighborly chat with Mr. Von Levern, the principal of nearby Roosevelt High School. He introduced Dad to the bright and talented Jim Smith who was president-elect of the student body, but facing homelessness due to family dissolution. Jim was feeling forced to forego his senior year to find a job and support himself. Von Levern wanted Dad's help finding a home for Jim.

My belief is Dad took an instant liking to Jim. He went straight home to talk Mom into inviting him to live with us for the year. The idea was that Jim would help around the house to help pay his way. He also talked to Ken and me, who shared a bedroom with twin beds, about Ken moving over to another bedroom to share with Jerry while I would stay in the bedroom to be shared with Jim, who needed his own bed to accommodate an almost 6'4" frame. Finally, Mom and Dad returned Tim to his crib in a corner of their master bedroom. The next day Jim moved in. I had no idea I had just gained the best big brother a mixed-up young teen could ever imagine.

There was never a boring moment while Jim and Lorraine lived with us. The house was open to a constant flow of their friends, plus Eldred, plus friends and relatives of Mom and Dad, not to mention us four brothers. Jim had a particularly keen sense of humor. I remember him teasing Lorraine by calling her "Shrub-hut" as a spin-off from her last name, Trehus. He also had a girlfriend, Marion Scudder. I don't know what he did with that last name, but I will never forget him chasing Ken and me back upstairs when he caught us spying on him smooching with her. We retreated to the upstairs bathroom, the sole secure place of privacy in the house, to get the door locked just in time. The next night I found my bed short-sheeted.

All eight of us plus guests shared this upstairs bathroom with a toilet, small sink, standing bathtub, and no shower. Family towels were shared, along with a bar of soap, and it's hazy as to when brushing our teeth became a habit. People, especially men, used a lot of toothpicks in those days. A small cabinet over the sink contained bandages, iodine for more serious cuts, aspirin for headaches, Alka-Seltzer for stomachaches, Ex-Lax for constipation, Sloan's Liniment for aching muscles, and Vicks VapoRub to treat colds. We got along just fine.

The kitchen was modern by the standards of the era with a gas range and an electric refrigerator with a small freezer box. Mother did the cooking, assisted by a day maid from time to time and the rest of us. On Sundays, before she went to church, Mom would put a roast in the oven and timed it to be done when she got home. At the end of Sunday dinner, Dad would often give one of us boys a quarter to run down to the drugstore a block away and bring back a quart of ice cream for immediate consumption or sometimes as topping for pie. All dirty dishes were piled up to be hand washed by everyone able and available except Dad. In 1940 we got a magical electric Bendix clothes washer, but clothes were still hung outside to dry, including through the cold winters. Fresh cotton sheets dried on the clothesline still feel better to me than machine dried, but Mother had no regrets about eventually giving up the old ways.

A grand piano was the major player in the living room. Near it was a standalone AM radio (there was no FM) shared by all of us. Ken and I reserved the hour before supper to listen to fifteen-minute serials like *Navarre of the North* and *Renfrew of the Royal Mounted*, which got us caught up in the enchantment of adventures in Alaska and Canada. On Sunday evenings we all listened to *Amos 'n' Andy*, Fred Allen, Jack Benny, Gracie Allen and George Burns, and Edgar Bergen with Charlie McCarthy.

Toward the end of the high school year, Jim busied himself applying for every available college scholarship he might qualify for. An interesting two days transpired when he received notice of winning a four-year all-expense-paid scholarship to Williams College in Williamstown, Massachusetts. They required acceptance within twenty-four hours. Jim wanted to go to Harvard, but he believed that a bird in the hand was worth two in the bush, so he accepted the Williams offer. A day later he received a similar scholarship from Harvard. This led to a spirited discussion with Dad over the ethics of reneging on the Williams acceptance. In the end, he didn't. Years later he told me he never regretted it either, as the decision left him with his integrity intact and was worth more than the year he might have spent at Harvard before going off to war.

Williams was a small, select, elite, and expensive private men's college. It offered a liberal arts education to the sons of the wealthy plus a paltry contingent of bright, deserving, white Protestant young men like Jim. Every student, including Jim, was a resident in one of the fraternities. One of the brothers in

Jim's house was the scion of a wealthy family, the Delaware DuPonts, and a skier. When he bought a different pair of skis he discarded the other. These, like new and including bindings, were of the right length for me, a short twelve-year-old, to use on local jumping hills in Minnesota. Jim packed and shipped them to me as a Christmas gift. Fortuitously, my neighborhood friend Dale Lindquist also got a pair of jumping skis for Christmas. We were soon on our way to Minnehaha Park where a local ski club had a hill for jumps from sixty to eighty-plus feet. After our first jumps we were hooked on the thrill of the sport.

Meanwhile, Lake Nokomis Lutheran Church was on a roll. The congregation thrived and grew to about fifteen hundred members under the Reverend Olson's leadership. He was a sought-after speaker and savored forever the accolades he received on one occasion from a group of pastors at a Methodist conference. As humorously recalled by Dad: "Bishop Cushman said, 'Brethren, it's interesting to find a Lutheran who can give a good speech.' I replied, 'It's equally interesting to find a Methodist who knows a good speech when he hears one.'"

* * *

KABEKONA SUMMERS

The informal brotherhood of fishing buddies Dad had run with during seminary years were now pastors of churches scattered over the Midwest, including Al Rogness, later president of Luther Seminary; Loyal Tallakson, later a bishop; and Jerry Moilien, whose parish wasn't that far away from Dad's. When they would meet, much of their talk was of fishing and outdoor life. One of them noticed a tract of shorefront acreage for sale on Lake Kabekona in an obscure undeveloped forest area a few miles from Walker, Minnesota. Walker is at the center of the Minnesota Lakes Country. The lake was a clear spring-fed body of water seven miles long and perhaps two miles wide teaming with walleyed and northern pike. Pairs of nesting loons with their haunting evening call were annual summer residents. Wildlife and blueberries were abundant. The only access to the property was a single-lane rutted dirt road skirting along the shore about fifty yards inland from the lake. No effort was made in the early years to improve the road beyond hand shovel work to level potholes and make passing possible.

No doubt these enterprising ministers felt God's guiding hand as they banded together to buy the property and subdivide it into lots for sale to themselves and other like-minded Lutheran pastors. As a member of the original group, Dad got one of the better lots. He drew level ground for a cabin and front yard, from which a short and rather steep slope with wooden steps descended to a natural crystal-clear spring at the shore for water. Though the shore was rocky, Dad was able to excavate a site to keep a boat. Kids like Ken and me never had any trouble wading out into the clear waters for swimming.

In early March 1938, Dad took Ken and me with him for a brief trip to Kabekona to ribbon the trees outlining the cabin site on the lot. We were blessed with a beautiful day and one or two feet of snow still on the ground. The closest we could get to our lot by car was the cabin resort well over a mile of shoreline away. Undaunted, Dad led Ken and me on the hike. On the way we stopped at the isolated one-room log cabin of a bearded bachelor trapper who wintered there. All the talk was at the door, but Dad wanted to make a new friend; and he did. Dad told us later the man was not very happy about the prospect of a bunch of preachers building summer cabins in his woods on his lake.

We helped Dad with the measuring tape. Using standing birch trees for posts, he ribboned the site carefully, placing the cabin far enough away to save a handsome Norway pine still standing today. He talked about the beautiful white birch to be fallen for burning in our cabin fireplace. All in all, it was a magical day none of us ever forgot. Before returning home, Dad stopped at a boatyard in Walker and bought a sixteen-foot traditional round-bottom fishing boat. Dithering over decisions or price was not his way.

By July the cabin was finished, complete with a natural stone fireplace and full-length screened porch overlooking the lake. Mom and Dad put a table for eating on one side of the porch and the other side was allocated for cots and kids' sleeping quarters. Cooking was on camp stoves on the porch and over coals in the fireplace.

Our Minneapolis neighbors must have been pleased to see us packing for the cabin because Dad turned the run-down house trailer from the prison mission trip into a cargo trailer to haul our furnishings. When he finally got it up the rutted driveway near the cabin, it collapsed, never to move again. Thereafter, it served as storage space and spare bunks when Dad and Mom had guests at the cabin. Dad took his month's vacation in July and the rest of us stayed through most of August with Dad coming up to join us during mid-week breaks when he could get away.

Big walleyed pike were biting. No one knew better than Dad where, when, and how to catch them. Shiner minnows were the bait, trolling or still-fishing over hot spots was the way, and early evening was the time. Dad would usually take a friend. Ken and I were invited along mostly for the experience and to mind the flashlight when landing fish after dark; we weren't quite ready to handle those big ones ourselves. After boating each fish he would quickly and carefully put it on a stringer and back in the water to keep it alive all the way back to the cabin. Dad was so successful at catching walleyes that he added a screened in-the-water fish-holding box to the small boat dock he had built. He would keep extra fish alive in the box for up to a week sometimes. This provided us with a source of fresh fish while he was back in Minneapolis tending to his ministerial duties. It was fascinating.

**Roy with his catch of trophy size Northern Pike caught
in Minnesota Lake circa 1930's**
Photo by Roy Olson

Fishing rods with Pflueger or Shakespeare casting reels were our next birthday presents. Shortly after receiving mine, I was out practicing casting off the boat some yards offshore from the cabin. On one cast, I let go of the rod by accident and watched the whole outfit sink to the bottom of the lake. We dragged a grappler for it, but no luck. A week later, trolling through the same waters, Ken got an unusual bite on a plug. He had hooked a fish line. On the end of it was my rod and reel.

When Dad was away, Ken and I were free to take the boat out fishing on our own. We found our favorite fishing to be casting red and white striped daredevil spoons for northern pike. These could be as big as walleyes with twice the fight. They lurked in shallow water along shorelines of cattails and bulrushes. The trick was to skillfully cast your spoon to hit the water within a foot or two of the line of cattails, but not in them where the spoon hook would snag. Although often a featured entrée in today's restaurants, northerns were thought of as inferior to walleyes according to Dad. Fortunately, Mom wasn't so fussy when Dad was away and the fish box was empty.

In August 1939 the Jensen family—Mom's sister Marie, Marie's husband Curtis, and their four children—came to spend a week with our family at the cabin. The morning after their arrival, Ken and I took our cousins Curtis Jr. and Russell for a hike on the rough trail crossing the lots to the boundary of the Kabekona ministers' property. We returned by hiking the lakeshore. Russ, only six, had a hard time scrambling along the rough and rocky beach. So halfway back he left us to hike up the short slope to the trail we had been on a few minutes before. When we got back to the cabin, though, Russ wasn't there. Ken and I immediately ran back up the trail shouting and looking for him. No Russ! Dad and Uncle Curt were out on the lake fishing. Mom sent Ken and me off to spread word of the disappearance and seek help. I can still hear Mother saying, "Ken, you go out the driveway and down the road; Dave, you and Curt go down the path again toward Rogness and out his driveway to meet Ken on the road." There was no telephone.

The next three days were a blur. By the end of the first day, searchers were in the woods. On the second day, multiple parties were combing the mostly roadless and totally uninhabited nearby forest. Bloodhounds were hopefully on Russ's trail. Mac McGinnis had flown up from Minneapolis to help with the search. He flew with the door off the observer's side of the plane for better visibility on low passes over the forest. As Dad knew the area and trusted Mac, he took a turn flying with him as passenger/observer. Misgivings about flying were no doubt overcome by praying for divine intervention in spotting little lost Russ down there somewhere, not to mention safe return to terra firma for himself and Mac. My recollection is the Jensen family was haggard, but not frantic. Everybody was offering or participating in prayers for Russ—all the way to the Twin Cities and the Jensen home in Albert Lea.

Then, late in the evening of the third day, a searcher's friendly dog wandered off from his master's camp three miles from our cabin. He returned with Russ, who had survived the previous few days by eating blueberries and drinking from a creek. He had apparently seen the plane and heard people calling, but had no idea they were looking for him. Prayers of thanksgiving and rejoicing went on late into the night. Newspaper reporters and photographers seemed to be everywhere. In the days remaining, I believe Dad took everybody on boat rides. He may have taken Uncle Curt fishing again, but there were no more hikes away from the cabin with our cousins. The surrounding forest became a forbidding place. The Jensens were relieved when they left for home, and none of them ever returned to experience our friendly Kabekona.

The next summer Dad taught me to run the small Johnson outboard motor so we could go on boat rides during his absences. Soon we had total freedom to live Huck Finn lives on the lake and in the forest. We hiked the shoreline, retracing the route past the trapper's cabin we had visited with Dad on our first visit to the lake. (By this time it was deserted and appeared perhaps abandoned. I speculated the trapper had moved on to other lakes and forest still pristine and beyond the reach of roads and civilization.) Exploring the forest made us Mother's best berry pickers, loading up on blueberries for homemade jam. And one summer we made a crude log raft with a mast and square sail, which we hauled upwind from the cabin and sailed using a boat oar for a rudder.

By the final summer we were trusted twice to take the boat on all-day fishing and exploring trips miles from the cabin. One of our favorite trips was across the lake and up a small river to a feeder lake with hot fishing for northern pike. With no cell phones or other means of communication, we needed knowledge, resourcefulness, and common sense to take off and do the things we did. Mom and Dad forever have my thanks for these gifts they gave us.

Roy Olson and Family at home in Minneapolis circa 1943

BATTLEFIELDS

Father's fight for the common good and his life: 1940–1944

CLEANING UP MINNEAPOLIS

"I believe the churches will have to take the lead waking up the citizenry."
Reverend Roy Olson, March 17, 1941

Minneapolis, Minnesota, was a wide open city in the 1930s and early '40s. A mafia type known as Kid Khan was the city's red-light district rackets boss according to Dad. Mayor George Leach was on the take. Centered along a two- or thee-block strip of run-down low-rent Hennepin Avenue, the district featured two bare-all burlesque theaters, various taverns with gambling, and some number of whorehouses.

A by-product of prostitute patronage were soldiers stationed at Fort Snelling, an army post on the south side of Minneapolis not far from Lake Nokomis Lutheran Church, showing up at the infirmary looking for relief from the pain of gonorrhea. This was not easy for the army doctors to provide before the discovery of penicillin. The situation made the commanding general unhappy, but he lacked jurisdiction to do anything about it. So he talked to Reverend Olson who had found reason to visit the base a few times. Alarmed citizens were also talking and looking for a way to do something about it.

Located a few blocks away from this magnet for sinning were the prestigious downtown churches of the major denominations. Some of these ministers and their lay leaders had already made sporadic attempts to get the city fathers to exercise some control of the district, but without success. This led to a citywide effort of neighborhood church pastors to support a movement to bring Kid Khan to heel. Reverend Olson—fearless and certain he was called by his Lord to help carry this battle from the pulpit to a confrontation with the corrupt city powers—was a perfect recruit. He enjoyed meeting and dealing with people from all walks of life. He was a natural at the art of friendly yet confrontational repartee. I recall table talk one time about Dad and an agnostic acquaintance getting into a discussion of Dad's Christian faith. The agnostic friend thought Dad's faith to be more or less foolishness. I heard Dad's response was "Well, I guess I'm God's fool—whose fool are you?"

Making Sunday news were dignified recurrent ministerial sermons on the illegal and immoral doings down in the red-light district and the Christian mandate to drive the hoodlums out of Minneapolis. Reverend Olson was among those providing more provocative quotes for Monday's newspapers. By early 1941 they had enough support to force Mayor Leach to give the ministers a hearing. The ministers presented their case. The mayor claimed it was all hearsay; he wanted eyewitness evidence. He had a moment of satisfaction as the downtown ministers sat speechless looking to each other. Then Mr. Leach got a surprise. Reverend Olson's hand went up and he took the floor.

Not satisfied with the accounts of the downtown preachers, and always curious about the lives of other human beings, in late 1940, Dad had exchanged his clerical garb for work clothes and with like-minded friend and church member Jim Swanson spent an entire afternoon going to performances of the Alvin and Gayety burlesque shows and ducking briefly into a few other shady-looking establishments to find out for himself what services were available.

At the hearing with the mayor, attired in clerical garb and collar, Dad described in detail the shows and other particulars. There was no denying him! The mayor had no choice but to rescind the licenses of the theaters. The next day Reverend Olson was the feature story in the *Minneapolis Tribune* and *Star Journal* newspapers. It was bad news for the mafia and Mayor Leach was in trouble.

The downtown ministers wasted no time deciding their next move should be to challenge Mayor Leach's reelection by drafting a reform candidate of their choosing. But who? Possibilities were limited, but the talk of the town was Reverend Roy Olson himself. I remember Dad being blown away by the first talks with the ministers committee. He discussed the idea at home—flattered by the proposal, intrigued by the challenge, but uneasy about how he could take leave from his congregation to run for political office, serve if elected, and return to a calling and church he loved. He quickly told everyone, if he ran and was elected, he'd serve only one term. He talked to everyone—preachers, politicians, bishops, members of his congregation, the press, and his family.

One morning he even talked to a couple of mafia soldiers who accosted him outside his church office to discuss why it would be most unwise for "Father" Olson to run for mayor. Dad came home for lunch to tell us about their visit, including reassuring us they didn't threaten personal physical harm but just wanted to warn him of the problems he might encounter if he pursued the agenda discussed in his speeches and sermons. As soon as they were gone, Dad said he'd called Mr. Bakken, a police captain and friend who advised him. To Mom he surmised they must be Italian Catholics because they addressed him with much respect as Father Olson. There was nothing to worry about, but Ken and I should tell Mom if we noticed any strange cars lurking nearby on the street. We were the lookouts. This made us little players in the unfolding drama.

Dad only wanted to run if he could count on enthusiastic support from a broad spectrum of interests beyond the ministerial association and a reasonably certain indication he would win. This led to a whirlwind series of citywide meetings and hastily arranged speaking engagements at churches, service clubs, and other events. He also wanted to be sure of at least quiet support across the religious spectrum, including the Catholic and Jewish communities. He was an early ecumenicist when it came to civil affairs. He and our next door neighbor, Mr. Cardozo, who owned a downtown furniture store, were fast friends.

The "draft Reverend Roy Olson" movement snowballed in March 1941. On Sunday, March 16, Dad preached a sermon that was duly reported on the front page of the next day's *Minneapolis Morning Tribune*, headlined "Pastor Warns Against Indifference to Morals":

> Olson said, "Attempting to maintain the doctrine of separation of the church from politics, Minneapolis churches have dodged issues which are strictly moral and spiritual in their consequences. I do not believe there are enough decent people in Minneapolis who want good government badly enough to do anything about it, or we would have it. I believe the churches will have to take the lead in the man-sized job of waking up the citizenry!"

The rival afternoon newspaper, *Minneapolis Star Journal*, quoted Dad in its own story:

> "I have said all the time," Mr. Olson told the congregation, "that if the good citizens of Minneapolis would get together behind a layman who can and will do the job that needs to be done, that's the way the thing ought to be done. As to the possibility of my own candidacy for mayor I have come to no conclusion."

* * *

Three days later, at a March 19 meeting of Concerned Clergy/Laymen, unable to find a suitable layman candidate, this group drew up and executed a proclamation drafting Reverend Olson to run for mayor. "Pastor Urged To File In Mayor Race" was the inch-high headline in the "Alarm Clock Edition" of the *Minneapolis Morning Tribune* on March 20. The subhead read "Roy E. Olson Weighs Plea Of Clergymen" followed by "Laymen Join in Appeal—Minister to Give Answer Later."

Lauded by the overture and intrigued by the challenge, the following Sunday at church Dad distributed a mimeographed statement saying he'd run if the church members approved. A congregational meeting was called for Apri 7 with notices distributed at Sunday services on March 30 and April 6 in accordance with church bylaws. Over the course of those two weeks, the key clergy/laymen who had drafted Dad made at least two or three pilgrimages to the neighborhood of Nokomis Lutheran to meet with influential members and convince them a vote for Dad to run was a vote against "Sodom and Gomorrah" in our city and for the "greater good" of its people.

Meanwhile, Dad could only sweat it out and await the outcome as the meeting was for "members only," excepting Mom and Dad for whom attendance would have been inappropriate. Attendance was very low. Many members apparently found it impossible to make up their minds. They were proud of "their pastor" but many were not ready to see him storming the local civil temple to throw out the bad guys. Counsel sought from the synod bishop seeking support for this proposed aberration of clerical function was not forthcoming. The president of the congregation was an articulate businessman opposed to preachers in politics who did not like the idea of losing a good minister and having to find a substitute for at least the next couple of years—and perhaps permanently. Dad had other member friends as intrigued as he was by the novel idea of having their minister run and perhaps be elected mayor. Apparently it was a long, contentious meeting. The vote was 68 in favor and 108 opposed.

Dad was disappointed, but immediately switched gears to lead fellow traveler reformers in search of a strong layman. They thought they'd found one in businessman Marvin L. Kline who promised a reform administration. They supported him and he was elected. Unfortunately, he turned out to be all hat and no cattle. The streets were cleaner and business-front signs more subdued, but behind those facades the services offered were the same. Dad made the front-page news again in the March 5, 1942, *Minneapolis Star Journal* going after Kline for "not keeping promises." This led to an appointment by Governor

Harold Stassen to serve a term on a committee advising on how to control drinking, gambling, and prostitution in Minnesota. Unfortunately, health problems surfaced for Dad, precluding any further serious interest in pursuing reform politics. The fight wasn't completely over, however.

In early 1944, the crusader-ministers, including Dad, regrouped for talks with an obscure young political science professor and part-time radio commentator from Minneapolis's small liberal arts Macalester College. The aspiring reformer with a gift of gab was interested in trying his hand at running for political office. He promised to "really clean up the city." I recall Dad talking about him because he was intrigued with the man's middle name—Horatio. The Reverends promised their support. He won. He did the job. The rest is history. His name was Hubert Humphrey.[3]

* * *

TROUBLED TIMES

Beginning in early 1941, at the same time Dad was preoccupying our family with Minneapolis politics, all of us, like every American family, were following the news of German and Japanese aggression in Europe and China, respectively. I avidly tracked the success of the German blitzkrieg overrunning France and moving on to the invasion of Norway. My friends and I were fascinated by accounts of the British Spitfires taking on the German Henkels, Stukas, and Messerschmitts—and winning the Battle of Britain. General Claire Chennault's Flying Tigers in their Curtis P-40s dogfighting Japanese Zeros over southern China were our first war heroes. Free China's leadership were Christian and the Japanese, heathen. This made it a religious war. Feature films were always preceded by newsreels of the recent action. We sensed our country was probably headed for war. All of this was very exciting in my young mind.

On Sunday afternoon, December 7, 1941, I was playing "horse" with Denny Buck on a dirt basketball court in an empty lot next to the Buck's home when his brother Don came out to tell us the Japanese had just bombed Pearl Harbor. We were going to war. I took off for home to follow the news on the radio and find out what my family was thinking about it. We all gathered around the radio the next evening to listen to President Roosevelt's "Day of Infamy" speech and the Declaration of War.

---

3   Forever after Dad speculated that if his congregation had let him run for mayor, and he had won, Humphrey's life might have had a different trajectory. As it was, Humphrey went on to a distinguished career in the United States Senate, served as vice president of the United States from 1965 to 1969, and ran for president in 1968. Following his defeat, the aging "happy warrior" returned to his roots and home on a Minnesota lake. He placed at the entrance a modest sign that said "The House That Wind Built."

Impulsive and patriotic, Reverend Olson promptly decided he wanted to do his part to support his country at war. So he went down to the navy recruiting station to enlist as a chaplain. He was fortunately ruled out on the basis of age and situation. Civil defense was soon up and running as scaremongers saw German and Japanese saboteurs on the move. They predicted it was only a matter of time before the bombing would begin—reaching all the way to the Midwest. Volunteer air raid wardens were signed up in every community. Scout troops were contacted to provide assistants in every neighborhood. My scout friends and I were recruited to be assistant wardens to patrol with approved flashlights during practice blackouts to make sure everybody else's lights were out and no one else was out on our neighborhood streets. This was exciting the first time, but boring thereafter. Mother gave Ken and me each a few dollars to start investing in the savings bond program at school. She picked up our allotment of food stamps while Dad got gas stamps for his car to comply with gas rationing. He was able to buy more gas than most people because he was a clergyman.

Jim came home at the end of the school year aware his carefree college days were over. He was with us only a short time while he sweated out acceptance of his enlistment to be a pilot in the Army Air Corps. During that time, a Wisconsin pastor friend of Dad's, Reverend Nesvig, came to Minneapolis for a church conference with his daughter, Helen. They stayed at our house and by the time they left, sparks were flying between Jim and Helen. It was great fun for us, but soon he was on his way to flight training.

Sadness followed with news that Vernon Dinger, Jim's best friend in high school and a frequent visitor at our home while Jim lived with us, had been killed in action. He had been a crew member on an American bomber shot down over Europe. The cruelty and tragedy of war came home to our family that day.

A few months later, on a short leave at Helen's family home in Stoughton, Wisconsin, between flight schools, Jim and Helen got married. They were still grieving the loss of Vernon and knew full well the dangers Jim would soon face himself.

Jim went on to fly and survive fifty missions over Europe as a B-17 pilot. He returned home to finish his education on the GI Bill. From there, Jim moved on to a prosperous career in business while he and Helen raised a fine and successful family.[4]

---

4   Jim died in 1999. Betty and I are still in contact with Helen who believes divine providence led her father to bring her, rather than one of her siblings, with him to Minneapolis back in 1942. I feel fortunate to have known this exemplary couple who were so representative of the "Greatest Generation." I miss him!

Meanwhile, by late 1942, Dad's personal war had shifted to battles with tumors in his bladder leading to two surgeries and deteriorating health. These surgeries involved major abdominal incisions as modern, less invasive, cystoscopic procedures were still in development. Most devastating was the probability more tumors would eventually show up, predicting more surgeries. But Dad was not about to lose his sense of humor. Following the second operation, he was put in a double room with another man already there preparing for his operation. The two compared notes before the other was sent off to the operating room. On his return, while the patient was still recovering from the anesthesia, he said, "I'll bet that damned preacher never prayed for me." Dad never stopped telling the story and, to my knowledge, never confirmed whether the guy was right or wrong.

Dad's third surgery in the early spring of 1944 was devastating. Recovery was slow. He fell back on his love of fishing by taking a late spring trip to Montana with Dr. Herman Preus, a like-minded friend and seminary professor. He returned rested, but not well. Unbeknownst to me, Dad was certainly suffering from depression. He did a superb job of hiding his true condition from his congregation and children, but not his wife. She soldiered on with faith and courage while allowing no hint of what must have been going through her mind. Though he never told us boys until years later, Dad had learned he had cancer and probably didn't have many years left to live. He thought seriously about what he wanted to do with them and considered finding a smaller, less-demanding parish. Finding a way to avoid wasting his remaining years was heavy on his mind.

The Northwest Coast Inside Passage

Chapter 3

ALASKA, HERE WE COME!

I feel fortunate to have been old enough in the early 1940s to experience travel by train and ship during the final days of the post-Victorian age of servant service, hissing steam, and streaming smoke carrying wide-eyed passengers to faraway places.

PROVIDENTIAL DELIVERANCE

The June 1944 national convention of the Norwegian Lutheran Church was in downtown Minneapolis, not far from where we lived. Dad ran into an old friend, Dr. H. L. Foss, bishop of the Northwest/Alaska Synod, at an early session. In jest Dr. Foss told Dad he was looking for a new minister to place in Ketchikan, Alaska, where Dad had helped organize the congregation back in 1926. Was he interested in returning? The bishop said later he had a hard time believing Dad was serious when he said, "I am."

Never slow to act, Dad came home to broach the subject to the family. He brought out the old black-and-white photos from his seminary intern year up there in 1926–27. He told us about the wonderful people he'd met who were still there, the sea, the mountains, the boating, fishing, hunting, and potential for adventure. He asked us to think about it. I suspect he prayed for God's blessing. I'm sure God gave him a green light because that's what he wanted and so did the bishop.

Dad's next day at the convention involved settling details with Dr. Foss. On his return home that evening, he gathered us again and asked for a family vote. Ken and I were all for it. Jerry and Tim were too young to measure what was happening. Mom looked skyward, but she had a keen interest in exploring the unknown and a minor taste for adventure. She knew well the man she'd married and life with him would never be humdrum. I think Dad had already sized up the electorate and knew he had the votes.

The day after the convention ended, Dad and Mom were people on a mission. They went full bore on closing out our lives in Minneapolis for the move to Ketchikan—Dad's resignation without rancor from a large church; selling his car and our home with virtually everything in it; selling our Lake Kabekona cabin, including furnishings, fishing gear, boat, and motor; buying and shipping furniture for our apartment in the back of the church in Ketchikan; getting all our other possessions packed for shipment; and, finally, making travel arrangements for a family of six plus our Labrador retriever. How they got it all done by early August is beyond me.

All of us were excited except Mom. She put up a cheerful front but was unhappy the morning we boarded the Great Northern Empire Builder, James J. Hill's flagship train, bound for the port of Seattle, Washington. Relatives and friends were there to bid us farewell, including some who thought we were crazy. Mom and close relatives, none of whom had ever strayed far from Minnesota, were understandably tearful. I missed most of the tears, though, as I was busy introducing our black Labrador retriever, Rook, to the baggage car attendant, making arrangements for his food, and being clued in on taking him out for exercise at major stops along the way. This was important because he was simply leashed to a cargo ring with a blanket to sleep on and his water and food dishes within reach. He went bananas when I came to visit him.

The train itself really got my attention. A monster iron horse trailed by a line of classic passenger, sleeping, dining, parlor, and baggage cars with a big caboose at the rear. None of us, except Dad, had ever been on a train like that or west of North Dakota. With the final "all aboard," the clanking of the cars, and the feel of the wheels gaining momentum, we knew we were on our way. All of us, including Mom, were on board for whatever lay ahead.

On the Empire Builder the seats in the passenger cars were all upholstered in plush maroon velvet with hardwood trim. All meals in the dining car were served on white linen with cloth napkins and complete place settings. There was no waiting for a table, and I could order anything on the menu. In the sleeping car, the Pullman bunks were made up with crisp white cotton sheets and pillow cases, and the covers were turned back in the evening before we went to bed. Soon after I was in my bunk each evening, the fatherly attendant passed by to see if I needed anything before saying good night. Talk about feeling pampered.

The passengers, engineer, fireman, and conductor were white, but the congenial porters, waiters, and Pullman attendants were all black men. Racial and gender desegregation was still over two decades away on Jim Hill's train. Though Dad and Mom went out of their way to be friendly and Dad enjoyed opportunities for conversation, I never heard either of them mention the obvious discrimination or question its legitimacy. I was clueless with nary an inkling of my luck to have been born a white male in a middle class family, but I would remember my encounters with these easygoing gentlemen twenty years later while living in Virginia, the state of massive resistance to integration.

The endless prairie views were boring until we got into Montana. We anticipated the mountain scenery and were impressed as we passed through it. My time to be awestruck came after waking up in the morning as we were coming out of the Cascade Mountains near the end of our trip. The train stopped at a village surrounded by rugged peaks. For five minutes I had an opportunity to walk far enough from the train in the cool clear mountain air to take it all in. Looking up I knew my life would never be the same.[5]

We arrived in Everett, just north of Seattle, an hour later to a joyous welcome from Dad's brother, Arthur, and his wife, Myrtle. Art and Myrt had moved west years before, leading to a subsequent migration of siblings and their families who followed them to the Pacific Northwest. They had an eye-popping few days planned for us. Uncle Art was as addicted to fishing as Dad. He and Myrt also had access to a cabin on nearby Lake Stevens. Ken and I were turned loose on the lake to catch a few nice kokanee trout (small land-locked salmon) while Art took Dad salmon fishing on Puget Sound to bring back an impressive king. Both told us this catch was nothing compared to what we would experience in Ketchikan. Over king and kokanee for dinner, we all knew walleyed pike would never again be our favorite food fish.

As most of the 650-nautical-mile voyage to Ketchikan would be through Canadian waters, we sailed from Seattle on a Canadian National steamship. We boarded the S.S. *Princess Louise*, a single-stacker, for an 8:00 a.m. departure on a lightly foggy, gray, low-tide morning. I got my first whiff of the heavy salt air with scents of seaweed on the mussel- and barnacle-encrusted waterfront. I stayed on deck, except for a quick tour of the ship, during those first hours underway. We were entering a new life. The ship stopped for an hour in Victoria around noon and then resumed passage for Vancouver. Following a late afternoon arrival, we transferred to the S.S. *Prince Rupert* to continue our

---

5   Today I know the stop was in Index, Washington. The view was up the face of Mount Index, which stands at almost six thousand feet. It blew me away.

voyage under the cover of darkness.

After a late dinner I prowled the deck and stopped star-struck by the hypnotic sparkler show off the stern. I learned later it was just the churning of phosphorous in the wake, but it was still like magic to me. When I hit the bunk, like a kid in love, I can't remember going to sleep. As the thirteenth-century Persian poet Rumi reminds me, "When the ocean comes to you as a lover, marry at once, quickly, for God's sake! Don't postpone it! Existence has no better gift."[6]

The S.S. *Prince Rupert* was an impressive three-stacker, though it looked pretty drab painted in battleship gray as required during wartime. The crew was Canadian, with accents reflecting different parts of the country. Cabin portholes could be opened so one could to be lulled to sleep by a serenade of wake washing against the hull and the occasional haunting cries of sea gulls on the prowl for food thrown overboard from the galley. Other accommodations and services were not much different from the train.

Fascinating new experiences were found in exploring the ship, including visits to the bridge and going below deck to feed Rook; cruising through spooky fog, punctuated by the eerie sound of the horn every couple minutes; and rolling in the North Pacific ground swell while crossing Queen Charlotte Sound. "No admittance" signs were almost nowhere on board. The crew trusted the passengers' common sense to not go where they didn't belong. No one was seasick so everyone enjoyed the ride. Passing through British Columbia's Inside Passage led to port calls in Ocean Falls and Prince Rupert.

Tiny Ocean Falls, located at the head of a beautiful fjord, remains the only memorable stopover. On approach all you could see were white buildings and look-alike white homes seemingly hanging in tiers off the valley slopes behind a huge white dam. We were given four hours ashore to see it all. We soon learned it was a paper mill town with an enlightened management providing an idyllic way of life and promising an illusionary cradle-to-grave security for the mill employees and their families. They even had a heated indoor swimming pool. When Ken and I wandered in to look around, we were given courtesy swimsuits and invited to join a pool full of teenagers. The *Prince Rupert*'s whistle for departure had already blown when we barely made it back aboard.

Two days later our ship entered Alaskan waters with Dad on deck apprising us of where we were, cruising northbound up the approach channels and along the shoreline of Revillagigedo Island toward our destination. Finally, our eager anticipation was rewarded as the serenely beautiful coastal mountain town of Ketchikan burst into view, signaling the end of our voyage.

---

6   From *Essential Rumi* by Coleman Barks.

"Revilla," as the locals call the island, is near the south end of the Alexander Archipelago, part of Southeast Alaska. The scenic eastern side is now part of the Misty Fjords National Monument. Ketchikan is located on the west coast of the island along a four-mile stretch of the Tongass Narrows. Back then gravel roads would take you five miles south and twelve miles north of the town. You could only arrive or depart by boat or small seaplane. Today the city is serviced by commercial air service landing at Ketchikan International Airport, "international" because they have flights to nearby Prince Rupert, Canada.

* * *

FRONTIER ISLAND LIFE

Our ship docked in Ketchikan on a sunny Thursday morning. A welcoming group from the Lutheran congregation waved to us from the pier. Some of them were people Dad had known and worked with eighteen years ago. They encircled us, everybody wanting to talk at once. You couldn't miss some of the lyrical Norwegian accents because they were first-generation immigrants. English was their second language. Dad quickly dispatched Ken and me to see to our baggage and Rook. Our first surprise was walking a half-mile north on a street built of wood planks on timber pilings over the ocean and rocky shore. Our new abode was on the oceanfront, a new world far from the flatland Midwest neighborhood of city blocks and tarred streets.

The tiny apartment, our family living quarters for the next two-and-a-half years, was in the back of the church. On a walk through it, I realized why Mom and Dad had sold almost all the beautiful furniture they had accumulated in Minneapolis to purchase carefully selected smaller pieces for shipment to fit in our new home. All the communal living, including dinner dining, was to be accomplished in a room smaller than our previous living room. The remainder of the apartment consisted of a breakfast nook, cramped kitchen, three small bedrooms, and a bathroom.

Harbor rats, permanent residents in the church cellar, would occasionally come up to visit the kitchen if the doors were open and unattended. Fortunately, Mom's farm-girl youth had given her an early acquaintance with rats. If the broom didn't work, she called us boys to either drive the invader out or kill it. We became quite efficient at either solution.

Nearby church members made sure we didn't go hungry for the first few days. Fresh fish, frozen venison, baked breads and cookies were tasty deliveries. However, as soon as the dishes were unpacked, Mom was on her way to Ferry's Food Store, a small grocery a block away on the waterfront avenue. Mrs. Marie

Ferry was the sole proprietor, and Mom quickly struck up a friendship with her, leading to a loyalty that transcended any price differences between Ferry's and White Cliff Grocery, the larger store a half-mile away. What went through Mother's mind on her first grocery buying experience in Ketchikan can only be imagined. Back in Minneapolis she had been accustomed to shopping at Froyen's Food Market with a meat, cheese, and dairy department; bakery goods and bread section; fresh fruit and vegetable displays; and free delivery. Of those goods and services, Ferry's carried only canned goods, flour, sugar, salt and pepper, hot and a couple of cold cereals, canned milk, butter, white and wheat bread, a few baked goods, perhaps some oranges and apples, maybe some cabbages or root vegetables, and lots of potatoes—with no delivery. Marie Ferry taught my mother the ropes on how to feed a hungry family a world away from Froyen's Market. One rare service Mrs. Ferry did provide Mom—and other preferred customers—was to make sure she never ran out of certain items by holding a small supply of each out of sight under the counter.

Mom lived up to the culinary challenges of isolated island living. She was a good cook and proud of what went on our table. We soon forgot the past to enjoy the present. Besides, whining was a ticket to missing the remainder of dinner—though soft-hearted Mom would make it right after everyone else was finished.

One taste I had to learn to tolerate was canned milk. In Minneapolis, Mom had fresh whole milk delivered to our door every day but Sunday. Since there was no homogenizing in those days, you could pour cream from the top of the bottle on your cereal, adding skim milk from below to suit your taste. Delicious! In Ketchikan, it was usually canned or nothing. Thus, I picked up at school or in the paper a verse from a limerick contest sponsored by Carnation Milk: "Carnation Milk, best in the land, comes to your home in a nice clean can; No tits to pull, no shit to pitch, just punch a hole in the son-of-a-bitch!" It took me a year of breakfasts to phase out longing to fly back to the farm to squeeze tits for the taste of warm fresh milk.

Mom also did a great job of maintaining family harmony. Sibling dustups must have happened as we were exploring and experiencing our new life. In any event, the tiny apartment proved to be ideal preparation for living happily together on small boats in the future.

After moving in, the first purchase was rain gear for all of us. Dad took Ken and me down to Ed Sande's Men's Outdoor Wear for outfitting in traditional sou'wester hats, coats, and rubber boots: "Helly Hansen, Made In Norway." Another acquisition was an L.L. Bean catalogue, the favorite source for other tried and true outdoor clothing and footwear unavailable in local stores.

Ketchikan, Alaska from the air circa 1950
Photo by Dave Olson

Ketchikan had three schools. Two were elementary schools on opposite ends of town. Jerry and Tim went to White Cliff School on the north end where the mostly Scandinavian fishing community lived. Main School was divided with middle school grades taught on the lower floors and high school on the uppers. Ken was a middle-schooler and I enrolled at "Kayhi," aka Ketchikan High School. With perhaps 120 students total, maybe thirty of whom were in my sophomore class, and my father the new pastor of the largest church in a small town, I was a marked student from day one. Nevertheless, I look back with great fondness and appreciation for my two-and-a-half school years at Kayhi.

Most memorable, perhaps, were the daily walks to school with Ken during his early teens. He was the puppy-love crush of his precocious female classmates. Suzanne Beck and her friends would be waiting for us a block from home at Ferry's store. We'd pass and they would skip ahead to look through a shop's front window, appearing fascinated by the display. We'd pass, and they would repeat the process. Ken ignored them and I was merely mystified. Without any sisters, we grew up clueless boys attracted to the gentler sex with no sense of how much fun we were missing not knowing them from the beginning. My existence was ignored by Kayhi girls until they discovered, thanks to my past water sports life in Minneapolis, I was the best skater and only diver off the high board at Ward Lake.

Church was a joy for Dad. He had brought with him his book of old sermons from previous parishes, easily spruced up for his Ketchikan congregation.

No busy calendar weighed him down with obligations. He was free to wander the town and docks calling on members, visiting members' commercial fishing vessels, and introducing himself to the business and professional people. Totally relaxed, maybe his health problems were behind him.

Administering the sacraments, including marriage, was among Reverend Olson's duties. The ingrown isolation of the community encouraged basic human pleasures leading to early marriages. In later years, reminiscing on his ministry in Ketchikan, a favorite quip of Dad's was, "I thought of adding to the information on the sign outside the church concerning ministerial services: 'Marriages performed; babies guaranteed in six months.'"

* * *

WATER SPORTS

Literally every outdoor activity enjoyed by the island people of Ketchikan involved getting there by boat except skiing, skating, and swimming, which we sometimes did by diving off the dock fifty yards from home. Access to the former two sports was by hiking out from town, but in my mind they also count as water sports. Snow is frozen particles of water vapor that fall to earth as white crystalline flakes; ice is water frozen solid by cold. The following is a more complete inventory of how we passed our free time.

* * *

BOATING

Ed Sande owned two salmon trollers. Less than two months after our arrival he sold the older slower one, the *Friada*, to Dad for a ridiculous bargain price. My guess is he sold her cheap because her engine and fishing gear were too worn out and obsolete for serious commercial use. She was a thirty-two-foot-long wooden double-ender powered by a one-lung (single cylinder) gas engine, producing a top speed of possibly five knots. The engine was a brute that was started by priming with a squirt of gas, closing an open hand-switch ignition, and hand-turning the huge flywheel until she fired. (The flywheel could break your arm if she misfired.) There were two bunks, but somehow we expanded the fo'c'sle space to sleep three. A small oil-fired iron stove and a tin sink with a hand pump to draw water from the tank completed the galley. The head was a deck bucket. Ed taught Dad, Ken, and me how to make her go. We were soon cruising the Tongass Narrows harbor waters on our own.

We needed to know a lot more to venture farther. This led to the purchase of the boatman's Bible, Charles F. Chapman's *Piloting, Seamanship, and Small Boat Handling*. Piloting was all about navigating coastal and inland waters.

Electronic navigation was in its infancy and nonexistent on fishing and recreational vessels. We learned to get along with parallel rule, dividers, pencil, tide and current tables, and paper charts. Magnetic compass gave us direction. We consulted the Seth Thomas ship's clock to measure time elapsed at an estimated ground speed in knots to know when we had arrived at a destination point. Soundings were made with a marked and weighted halibut fishing line on a wooden hand reel. I delved deep into study of that book. An incentive was knowing the sooner I knew more than Dad did, the sooner he would trust me to take the boat out without him. My reasoning was soon rewarded.

Soon after selling Dad the *Friada*, Ed, always in the boat market, took advantage of a super boat deal rare in Ketchikan by buying a thirty-six-foot traditional wooden bridge-cabin yacht named the *Audace*. She was powered by a Gray Marine engine, slept six, and looked to be in good shape for small boat passages to Seattle. Within a few months, however, Ed suffered buyer's remorse and wanted to sell her. When he couldn't find a buyer, he approached Dad, who agreed to the purchase if he was able to first sell the *Friada*. Darned if he didn't get lucky and quickly find a buyer. With that Dad was able to cut a deal with Ed and became the owner of the *Audace* in the spring of 1945.

During the winter of 1944–45, Dad developed a close friendship with Al Hannah who taught math and coached basketball at Ketchikan High School. Al also owned the M/V *Helen Hinton*, a forty-five-foot cabin cruiser. After Dad got the *Audace*, Al told Dad of a cruise he would be making to Sitka in June. He planned to tow back to Ketchikan a cruiser hull he had bought in Sitka to work on. His wife and son would be going with him as crew. He invited Dad to take our family on the *Audace* and accompany him, his family, and the *Helen Hinton* on this three-week cruise. As Dad had the vacation time coming, he discussed Al's proposal with the family. Everybody was in favor of taking Al up on this rare opportunity. (Including me, though I didn't end up going because I was later hired as deckhand for the summer on a Ketchikan-based towboat.)

This would be a big trip for Dad as he had never taken a boat more than fifty miles from home, much less ventured into the open ocean not far from being out of sight of land. On the other hand, he had an already experienced hand in Ken to help him handle the boat and share long turns at the wheel. Trusting Al, he said yes. As soon as school was out for the summer, the two boats were on their way.

The voyage did not lack for excitement. Jerry, eight years old at the time, recalls, "During one of the open water passages the engine overheated and Dad totally panicked. Fortunately, someone on the *Helen Hinton* noticed us falling astern and dead in the water. Luckily, Hannah was both a skilled boat builder and engine mechanic. He diagnosed the problem and fixed it." Dad thought Al Hannah "walked on water" when it came to small boats.

This trip was the high-water mark for Dad and Mom of experiencing life at sea, seeing the more rugged islands and mountains north of Ketchikan and visiting historic Sitka.

Our family cabin cruiser, the M/V *Audace*, anchored at the head of Carroll Inlet on a hunting trip in 1945
Photo by Roy Olson

In late spring Dad had learned the superintendent of the Georges Inlet Salmon Cannery was looking for someone with a boat to patrol two of the cannery's salmon fish traps for the coming season. The job was to run between the traps during the night, thus discouraging fish pirates from making deals with the trap watchmen for a cut of the swag for their silence and assistance in stealing fish. The season was from late July to late August. Patrol was required every night, but there was time for Dad to cruise to Ketchikan at dawn on Sunday morning, conduct church services, refuel, buy groceries, and be back on patrol by dark. Ken went with him as deckhand to keep the settle-up cash in the family. The net income was sufficient to cover the annual costs of owning the *Audace*. Talk about a paid vacation!

* * *

FLY-FISHING

Before we were settled, Dad was introduced to the wizardry and artistry of fly-fishing by Arndt Bue, a Norwegian immigrant banker and church pillar. He took Dad as his guest by small float plane up to Punch Bowl Lake on the mainland east of Ketchikan. Dad came home with a creel full of beautiful cutthroat trout. Forever after his first love would be fly-fishing. Soon there were three fly rods in the cellar. We went on some fun trips, but work prevented me from spending any time sport fishing during the summers.

Ken with a big trout caught fly fishing in the Naha River near Loring on the North Coast of Revillagegedo Island, Alaska in 1946
Photo by Roy Olson

* * *

GAME HUNTING

Back in Minnesota Dad had been a duck hunter during the fall months. He had already bought a second shotgun before leaving and taken me hunting. Now he found a bargain for a third somewhere to arm Ken and take us both bird hunting.

On the first week of the 1944 hunting season, Ed, in his better boat, led Dad, Ken, Rook, and me in the *Friada* thirty-three miles up Carroll Inlet into the heart of Revilla Island for our first waterfowl hunting trip. We bagged three geese and a few ducks. We were ecstatic to find Rook naturally took to retrieving. On return from this first hunt, Mom blessed us with our first roast goose dinner.

Since generous church members often left salmon and halibut at our doorstep, Ed advised us to rent a locker at the fish dock cold storage in which to keep the other two geese and ducks for future use. These birds were followed by the regular additions of venison, salmon, halibut, lingcod, and trout that became our main sources of protein until we moved south in 1947. Ken and I bagged three deer our second season. By that time we were old hands at field dressing, skinning, plucking, gutting, cutting, filleting, butchering, and packaging fish and game to fill our locker. When Mom wanted a fish fillet, duck, chops, or a venison roast for dinner, she dispatched one of us boys to retrieve it.

**Goose hunting with Rook at Carroll Inlet near Ketchikan
on Revillagigedo Island in 1945**
That's me sitting on the log.
Photo by Roy Olson

To open the 1946 season, Dad let Ken, friend Ed Williams, and me cruise the *Audace* to Carroll Inlet for goose hunting. The next morning found us on the tidal flat at the head of the inlet waiting for the geese to fly out. Instead, we had a flock of huge beautiful white birds fly over honking like geese. Thinking they were snow geese, we fired away, downing three of them. The flock immediately returned, flying in low, mournfully honking and crying in their sorrow, and continuing to circle at point-blank range. We didn't know, but we guessed they must be swans. You couldn't help but feel and share their sadness. It was a sobering wake-up call alerting us to what we were doing when we went hunting. We quickly loaded the skiff, including the three swans to take home for positive identification. Knowing we had also broken the law, we hid the birds on the boat until we got home. On return we talked to Henry Henn, the proprietor of the hardware store next door. He confirmed our kill and said it was rare for a flock to show up in our waters, but not unheard of. He said our choices were to quietly butcher them for food or put them in large gunny sacks with a couple of rocks so they would sink and take them out to mid-channel after dark for disposal. We did the latter. I've never forgotten the life-changing experience of that sad day. I find no pleasure in taking innocent beautiful life, including fish.

Dad only liked eating venison, not killing it, so the deer slaying was up to Ken and me. Before he trusted us to take the boat on hunting trips, he went with us to wherever we dropped anchor and then stayed on the boat until we returned.

On an early hunt in the fall of 1945, we cruised the *Audace* north out of Ketchikan across Behm Canal to an unprotected anchoring off the mainland reputed to have really easy hunting. Dad rowed Ken and me ashore to hunt and returned to the boat. It was a windless, rainy, misty day with poor visibility. We loaded our rifles and charged into muskeg terrain directly away from the beach. We separated, but not far enough apart to lose track of each other. I saw deer, but not close enough to see horns promising a legal buck. Ken saw next to nothing. Finally, I got an opening with an easy shot at a nice three-point buck. We dressed it out.

When we were ready to pack the meat back to the shore, Ken said the right direction was one way, and I said the opposite. So we checked our compass. It was a cheap model from our Tenderfoot Scout days in Minnesota, full of water and useless. Finally, we agreed to go my way. Sure enough, much sooner than anticipated, we saw water. But when we got there, we saw no sign of the boat and the water was fresh. Ken said, "I told you so!" I was lost. There were no landmarks and we hadn't bothered to look at the chart before going ashore. We reversed and took off directly away from what we hoped was a lake inland from the ocean. After a strenuous hike, taking turns packing the deer, Ken was rewarded and I was chastened, but relieved, to see the ocean and *Audace* lying serenely at anchor.

* * *

DEER MOUNTAIN SKIING

Ken and I had brought our skis with us to Ketchikan. After finding out there was skiing on Deer Mountain behind town, accessible by a good trail, we wanted to know all about it. We found that a strenuous two-hour hike with skis and a Trapper Nelson pack board would take you to a dirt-floor log cabin with a corrugated tin roof and oil drum stove for cooking and warmth. It was called the "Ski Cabin" because you had to go up there with the intent of spending at least one night at the cabin to spend any meaningful time skiing. We packed our camping gear with us, including a lantern, sleeping bags, and our boy scout mess kit with a pot to melt snow for hot water and skillet to bake our sourdough pancakes and fry our meat. The last leg in was a chug through untracked snow deep enough that it almost buried the cabin. On arrival, the first chore was to burrow down to clear the door. The second was to go out with ax and saw to cut firewood and gather conifer boughs for mattresses.

We made friends with classmates, especially Bob Moore and Ron Daniels, who also went up there for the sport. From the cabin, we reached good open-slope skiing by heading north and then east around the north flank of the mountain to the saddle between Deer Mountain and the next peak to the east. This north face is the "mountain view" from Ketchikan, beautiful in any season, but especially in winter. The panorama is a classic treeless, steep, alpine slope creased by rock ribs near the summit. On a clear day the reward is a breathtaking view looking east over Revilla Island and the intervening ocean channel, reaching all the way to the snow-covered mainland peaks on the horizon—making all the hard climbing to get there worth it.

On one of these adventures our ignorance in backcountry safety almost exacted a heavy price. Bob Moore, Ken, and I had awakened to a beautiful clear day with over fifteen inches of new light powder that had fallen on a hard icy surface crust. After breakfast we put on our skis and took off cross-country for the saddle on the other side of the mountain.

We cluelessly skied out onto the steep north slope to cross it on our way to the saddle. I was in the middle, following the leader. When I was about three-fourths of the way across, the slope below our track, from the leader all the way back to the forest on the western edge, avalanched to the trees below in a wild cloud of snow. Why the snow above didn't avalanche, too, and carry the three of us with it to almost certain death, remains a source of wonder.

Needless to say, after a couple of gulps we quickly continued the relatively short distance to complete the traverse. When we made the return trip back to the cabin that afternoon, we went way below the avalanched snow debris, awed by what we saw and thankful we weren't all buried in it somewhere.

* * *

PISTOL PACKIN' PRANKS!

A few of the boys I knew had .22-caliber handguns they carried on hunting trips to shoot, among other targets, grouse and ptarmigan. The latter is a small member of the quail family that turns snow-white in the winter; both were delicious eating. Ptarmigan were common winter residents above the snow line on Deer Mountain. Rarely hunted, you could get close enough to shoot them for dinner at Ski Cabin. When Ken and I found this out during one of our first weekends of skiing on the mountain, we needed to join the action. This led to partnering on an H&R (Harrington & Richardson) .22-caliber revolver.

On one trip, after we hit the sack at the cabin, Bob Moore also introduced us to some fun he had with his .22-caliber Woodsman. There were mice wintering in the shelter that you could hear scurrying around and enjoying the warmth in the rafters under the snow-covered roof. Bob thought it was great fun to spot one with his flashlight and then try to shoot it. He might have hit one. Ken and I tried our luck, but by failing to get a bead on a mouse I never fired a round. And it never entered our minds that almost every shot fired put a hole through the tin roof. There was a reminder of this the following summer from members of the Ketchikan Outdoor Club who had built the cabin. They were not happy discovering those unexpected leaks.

Toward the end of fall 1946, Ken got the go-ahead to invite friends Joe Lewis, John Stenford, John Christopher, and John Aus to join him on the *Audace* with Ken as captain for a three-day deer hunt. After a successful first day they anchored in a secure cove for the night. Ken was soon in the galley making supper while Joe and John Stenford were up in the pilothouse cabin looking for a way to liven up the evening.

Our H&R revolver, with a box of .22-caliber long rifle ammunition and a block of plug tobacco for clearing condensation off the pilothouse windows, were lying idle on a low shelf. One wicked idea led to another. Soon they were busy extracting the lead slug from a cartridge and replacing it with a wad of tobacco. Joe loaded the gun with this modified cartridge. One bound and he was down to Ken in the galley exclaiming, "You're dead!" and shot him.

Ken went down on the cabin floor in pain, thinking it was the real thing. Seeing the wound in Ken's hip, Joe had an instant vision of having made a mistake loading the gun—and shooting his best friend. After a frantic minute of speculation and remorse, inspection revealed that plug tobacco may be light years mushier than metal, but it still packs a punch on the business end of a bullet. Ken soon recovered and proudly showed a small round scar until it disappeared. Joe says now, "It was a dumb kid thing to do!"

Three of the friends with Ken on that deer hunt went on to careers in the fishing industry. John Christopher fished his gill-netter *Misty* out of Ketchikan for decades. Joe Lewis was skipper of a number of larger vessels. As captain of the crab boat *Viking Queen*, circa 1970, Joe and his crew were credited by Sig Hansen, in his best seller *North by Northwestern*, with saving the lives of Sig's dad, Sverre, and crew of the crabber *Foremost*, picked up adrift in the North Pacific on a life raft near Unimak Pass in the Aleutian Islands. They had been forced to abandon their wooden vessel after she caught fire and eventually burned to the water line. Captain John Aus drowned two years later in the capsizing of the crabber *Viking King*. Joe and Ken reconnected in 1988 in Sitka.

* * *

WATER SPORTS EPILOGUE

My only regret about this period in our family life is that our brothers Jerry and Tim were too young to share in these activities with us while we lived in Alaska. On the other hand, by the time we moved back to the Lower 48, family ties and experience with Alaskans in the fishing industry set them up so both could work summer vacations during high school years as paid deckhands on fishing boats in Southeast Alaska. Summer adventure on a paycheck! Both eventually accumulated more summers than me, many more for Tim, crewing on those boats.

**Chapter
4**

CLOSING DOWN CREEK STREET

Cleaning Up Ketchikan

"The reformer in me came to a boiling point."

Reverend Roy Olson

By 1944, greater Ketchikan, Gateway to the Last Frontier, had grown to about five thousand people, including personnel at the United States Coast Guard base. The town claimed bragging rights as the "salmon capital of the world" and record rainfall, averaging over two hundred inches a year. As a wide-open, hell-roaring logging, mining, and fishing town, Ketchikan had its share of saloons and brothels. Saloons were a major contributor to local commerce, and I think not a few of the upright citizens also took some naughty pride in the services sold on Creek Street. This was a row of houses, conveniently located at the southern end of downtown and built on pilings hung out over Ketchikan Creek, where lonely men went to reap sexual satisfaction. The street was actually a boardwalk off Tongass Avenue, a main thoroughfare with streetlamp lighting making discreet visits difficult. To solve this problem, a forest path was available, providing a back channel to the street for local cognoscente. It came to be known as Married Man's Trail.[7]

Balance was provided by churches representing all of the major denominations, plus a couple of storefronts promising deliverance for sinners. Before his family had settled down in Ketchikan, Reverend Olson was out wandering the boardwalks making sure people beyond his congregation knew

---

7   Visiting Creek Street is featured on every present-day cruise ship's list of recommendations for passengers off to see the attractions of historical Ketchikan.

there was a new minister in town. He sought out all the other ministers to make their acquaintance and talk shop. He joined Rotary and Kiwanis, and within weeks he was scheduled to speak at their meetings. He dropped in on the politicians holding town, borough, and territorial offices. He cultivated an early friendship with Al Hannah, the high school basketball coach. For some reason he felt called to attend a school board meeting.

All of his involvement in town soon led to a query, possibly from Bert Houghtaling, proposing he run for an open seat on the school board. He did and was elected. The board was a collegial group of like-minded citizens and membership provided a supposedly noncontroversial way to be involved in local civic affairs.

Rev. Roy Olson in First Lutheran Church office in Ketchikan in 1946
Photo by *Ketchikan Chronicle*

A priority of the board's was replacing the school district superintendent. In those days, isolated Alaska towns like Ketchikan went south to the states to cast a wider net for applicants. The objective was to find a successful superintendent of a district with demographics similar to Ketchikan's and lure him (women need not apply) with the challenge of providing a quality education in the Last Frontier. Applicants submitted resumes for the board to review which included memberships like service clubs and church affiliation. All other factors being equal, Roy Olson was not above noticing the latter. In the end, the new superintendent was a Lutheran, J. E. Danielson, coming from a successful run as superintendent of a district in Montana. J. E., his wife, Cora, and their daughter, Delphine, arrived in Ketchikan in early January of 1945. The Danielsons promptly became fast friends of the Olsons. They filled a gap in the Olsons' friendships, especially for Ida, who sorely missed their lives in Minneapolis. Ida, the retired teacher, gained a friend in Cora who had also gone to college and talked her language. Best of all, Superintendent Danielson was an experienced educator looking toward a tranquil period in the life of Ketchikan schools. This was not to be.

Danielson's arrival coincided with the board dealing with two controversial political issues—one territorial and the other local. Let's let Reverend Olson tell us what happened, from his memoir:

The reformer in me came to a boiling point. Seeing something wrong, I had to try doing something about it. The opportunity was not long in coming. Alaska had no Juvenile Code in the laws governing the territory. There were high-level people who wanted to do something about it. Learning of my background in juvenile delinquency, they found the money to invite me to the capitol, Juneau, to appear before the legislature on behalf of establishing a Code.

On the day before my scheduled appearance I was sitting in the balcony of the House of Representatives listening to the reading of a proposed bill, co-sponsored by hometown Ketchikan Senators, Gunderson and Walker, to change the law to permit a liquor bar within two hundred feet of a church or school. I was leaning over the railing with what must have looked like indignation on my face, when a gentleman sitting next to me leaned over and whispered, "You don't like this, do you?" My answer was an emphatic "No!" To my amazement he leaned over the rail, tapped a member of the House and said with the voice of authority, "Get this man out on the floor to debate the Bill!" Then he turned to me and said, "Apologies for breaking in. Let me introduce myself. I'm Governor Gruening." In nothing flat a page came to get me and I was led to the rostrum to speak against the Bill. This made the Speaker nervous so he sent a colleague over to the Senate to bring Walker down to defend his Bill. The Senator was not accustomed to debating with a preacher. Presto, the Bill failed to pass and the session was over. The good Senator was waiting for me in the foyer. He declared, "Listen you, you are going to land on the horns of eight hundred Elks [the Elks Club, who wanted the bar and needed an exemption to get it] when you get back to Ketchikan."

* * *

Dad's account left out the best part of the story, though. Fortunately, the *Juneau Empire* covered it the next morning, February 15:

The Rev. R. E. Olson, pastor of the Lutheran Church in Ketchikan, had a field day on the floor of the House of Representatives yesterday.

Senator Walker had been drawn into the fray after Representative Peterson declared he had a wire from the Ketchikan church in question (the church closest to the proposed Club Bar) protesting the bill. Walker derided legislation being swung by pressure groups and the visiting Ketchikan pastor took the floor for the second time on the bill.

"My good friend Senator Walker," the Rev. Olson declaimed, "it is the privilege and duty of constituents to wire their representatives," and posed the question, "Who is the pressure group—your benevolent association or all the churches and schools of Ketchikan combined?" The motion for postponement put by Representative Bess Cross carried, sending the disputed Senate Bill 20 to indefinite limbo.

Backed by the Ketchikan Recreational Council, churches, and several downtown businessmen, Dad was soon back in Juneau with the legislature for several days to work with Senator Walker and Representative Krause urging enactment of laws to strengthen the Juvenile Code for the Territory. Productive mingling with the legislators, including a meeting with Governor Gruening, soon led to its passage.

All this success making capitol news made Rev. Olson something of an unusual celebrity among Territorial politicians and pundits. By early 1946 the talk in the legislature and newspapers statewide was of the organization of a "Statehood For Alaska" association. In February, the *Juneau Empire* reported the association had elected as president Mrs. Bob Atwood of Anchorage, who had been active in launching the group. The Rev. Roy E. Olson of Ketchikan was elected vice-president. "The immediate purpose," officers said [in the *Juneau Empire* report], "is the obtaining, compiling, and dissemination of facts pertaining to statehood for Alaska before the referendum vote next Fall."

My recollection is Dad was flattered to be sought out as the best choice to represent the southern Alaska panhandle. I heard the association had high hopes Dad and his obvious debate and speaking skills would be a key player on the committee when they eventually went to Washington, D.C. to plead the case for granting statehood in the U.S. Congress. With this kind of evidence, is it any wonder Dad speculated he would have made a great lawyer, if he hadn't chosen to be a minister?

Shortly before school let out in the spring of 1946, Superintendent Danielson went to his friend and school board member Roy Olson with a problem he'd never had to deal with in Montana. A few of the young studs at Kayhi, flush with earnings from commercial fishing and other employment, had hiked the Married Man's Trail to Creek Street and left with gonorrhea (the clap) or worse. The family doctors in town were upset about having to treat these kids and the cloud it cast on the community. They contacted Superintendent Danielson to see what action he could take to discretely let all the lads know the dire risks they were taking in going down this street to learn the facts of life. Adding to the dismay for Dad, who was an addicted basketball fan and friend of the high school coach, was the revelation that a couple of the young men were team members. This made it personal for Reverend Olson who previously had ignored the presence of the "ladies of the night" as endemic to frontier towns, to be tolerated as long as they kept to themselves on the other end of town. He even told anecdotes to visiting clergy of the old Norwegian bachelor fisherman who had asked, "Ver do you vant me to go for company and be varmed on cold vinter nights?"

Danielson and Olson went to the school board, where a debate ensued. My guess is everyone, except Dad, was unsure of what actions the board and superintendent should take, if any, to raise the issue publicly. What might be the response from the downtown business community? What about retaliation from Creek Street customers? They agreed on taking no action beyond backing any steps Danielson might take to make male students think twice before visiting Creek Street. Dad thought more should be done. It was not just a health issue, but a moral one, too.

Dad decided to take the devil by the horns and organize support to send the "ladies" back to Seattle. Building on his Minneapolis experience, he began his quest for information. He talked to the doctors, especially Dr. Dwight Cramer who had only recently resigned as city health physician, to get a handle on the exact extent of the problem, the weaknesses of the treatments available to cure the various types of venereal disease, and the relevant dangers to the young men of Ketchikan, not to mention the possibility of passing the disease on to the local high school girls. I remember him coming home to tell us about the doctors' unhappiness with the responsibility placed on them to make periodic exams of the prostitutes, knowing full well they only assured freedom from disease through the next trick to follow. He took Ken and me aside to scare the hell out of us by describing the ravages of the various venereal diseases. Thankfully, he never betrayed the identities of the suffering students.

In an attempt to send the ladies packing without a ruckus, Reverend Olson made his first move by showing up at a city council meeting to make his case.

Here he got the brush off. The few men backing him were mostly doctors who didn't enjoy having to deal with the problems impacting the health of the community. Undeterred, he pushed on with a one-on-one recruitment of supporters—almost all women, mostly mothers.[8] He distributed information and petitions to them for gathering supporting signatures. The women formed the Committee of Mothers, but everyone knew it would take more than that to wake up the town.

Reverend Olson had the answer. He put a special notice in the *Ketchikan Chronicle* advertising his church service sermon to be preached the next Sunday:

First Lutheran Church
THE WHITE CHURCH BY THE SEA
1200 Tongass Avenue

Roy E. Olson, Pastor

Morning Worship – 11:15 a.m.

"The Prosperity of Fools"

THIS SERMON WILL BE AN ALL-OUT INDICTMENT OF, and appeal to, Ketchikan's community conscience. There will be no beating around the bush. Pastor Olson believes the time has come when the conscience of the community needs to be faced with its responsibility in language no one can fail to understand, regardless of the personal price to be paid. There will be no generalizing. Pointed suggestions will be made for formulation into a definite mandate to our city officials—IF the people feel the time has come to do more than talk.
Church School – 10 a.m.
Bus Transportation on Water Street – 9:30 a.m.

The *Ketchikan Chronicle*'s Ward Shori reported the story on September 29, 1946—edited, excerpted, and quoted as follows:

An estimated 275 people filled the auditorium of the First Lutheran Church to hear the sensational resignation sermon of the Rev. Roy Olson, an outstanding pastor of the church for the past few years.

In his sermon, entitled "The Prosperity of Fools," he said he hated to

---

8   Dad recognized early on the power of women, organized and marching, and how critical they were in pressuring the city fathers to enforce the law. He never ever hesitated to support women's rights. He had good reason to do so.

do it as a dirty job. And felt as though he had been assigned the task of cleaning out a barge-load of dogfish that had stood too long. He stated that drunkenness and prostitution were against civil and God's law and no such thing as legalized prostitution. He laid down the challenge to the people of Ketchikan to do the job that needed doing. He said those who condoned the conditions did it because it was "good for business and prosperity." He emphasized this as a prosperity of fools, a false prosperity, and the way to hell. He urged that a committee of citizens be formed with the backing of the community to force the council and police to enforce the law to clean up the town.

Following the sermon Reverend Olson descended from the pulpit to speak from the rostrum, saying the people could return next Sunday and hear the gospel preached as he had gotten his message off his chest. It was now up to the people of Ketchikan.

On the same Sunday the Committee of Mothers distributed this announcement in Sunday papers and at services in their respective churches:

ATTENTION!
MOTHERS of KETCHIKAN
Mass Meeting of Mothers at
First Lutheran Church
This evening at eight o'clock
Opportunity will be given to sign the following petition:

TO THE HONORABLE J. E. JOHNSON, MAYOR, AND MEMBERS OF THE COMMON COUNCIL OF THE CITY OF KETCHIKAN:

We, the undersigned mothers of the community of Ketchikan, being genuinely and sincerely alarmed by the spread of drunkenness and prostitution and their attendant vices in our community, desire to voice our protest against the policy of non-action which has characterized our constituted authorities. For our right to speak, we claim nothing more nor less than the God-given and time-honored right of motherhood. With one voice, we protest that not one or all of the imagined or real benefits accruing to the city in any form are worth the price of one single son or daughter

*for whom we have paid the price of motherhood. We call upon you
now, without delay, to take all necessary steps to bring drunkenness
and prostitution to the lowest possible minimum and exert all
possible vigilance to the end that our present disgraceful conditions
may not be allowed to recur.*

*This advertisement and this meeting sponsored
by the Committee of Mothers.*

* * *

Following up Reverend Olson's bombshell sermon earlier in the day, loads of
women showed up to rally, sign petitions, and organize presentations to the city
fathers. The mayor and Common Council had little choice but to take action,
ordering the city police and attorney to initiate action forcing the Creek Street
madams to close up and leave town. Reverend Olson, basking in the notoriety of
this success, soon had the pleasure of going down to the dock to personally see
some of the Creek Street prostitutes and madams board the steamer for Seattle.[9]

The *Minneapolis Star* followed up with its own story on October 13, 1946,
by staff writer William Thorkelson:

Town Now Pure As Snow, Ketchikan Mayor Says

*Take it from the mayor of Ketchikan, that far-off city in Alaska is
almost as pure as the driven snow which often fills the streets and by-ways.*

*And all because the Rev. Roy E. Olson, former pastor of Lake Nokomis
Lutheran Church here, decided things were a bit rough in Ketchikan and
resigned his pastorate there.*

*Mr. Olson, in a public announcement in Ketchikan, had said that
vice conditions were so bad he believed the city was "practically beyond
redemption." He said that prostitution was allowed to flourish because of
public apathy and with official approval. But Mayor J. E. Johnson of
Ketchikan, in a long distance telephone interview said it was "not true"
his city had "legalized prostitution." He said prostitution existed by
"sufferance" in Ketchikan.*

*Asked what had been done about Mr. Olson's charges, the mayor
replied: "My view of prostitution is the same as Mr. Olson. My method as
mayor was to wait until public opinion crystallized to the point where
people would follow us. The time arrived as a result of Mr. Olson's charges.*

---

9   The notoriety washed over me as well. My skipper in 1948, Harry Diamond, a Ketchikan character, took pleasure
introducing me to locals who came aboard as the son of "the preacher who kicked all the whores out of
Ketchikan a few years ago."

We have already closed several of the places."

The mayor reported, "Mr. Olson plans to leave Ketchikan about January 1 to become pastor of a church in Tacoma, Washington. We're all sorry to see him go."

* * *

Dad told our family that one of the reasons he was accepting the move to Central Lutheran in Tacoma, and thought a new pastor would be a good thing for First Lutheran Church, was because he felt part of his future, if he stayed, would be providing unavoidable leadership to keeping the ladies of the night from sneaking back into town. Unfortunately, Dad was right. Creek Street prostitution was back and thriving within a year after he left town. It stayed that way until the cruise ships started showing up, making the street more profitable to its landlords as a tourist attraction.

* * *

AN AFTERMATH—RETURN TO THE LOWER 48

By fall of 1946 Reverend Roy Olson was wrestling with doubts concerning his future in Ketchikan. The congregation had more or less maxed out its market share of the church-going community, precluding much foreseeable future growth. There were undercurrents of grumbling in the congregation from some parishioners who didn't approve of their pastor making controversial waves in local politics. His job was to quietly pursue saving Lutheran souls.

A few others had grown up in and remained loyal to the pietistic fundamentalist Lutheran tradition Reverend Olson had moved away from in his adult faith. As a member of the school board, their pastor had to take his turn chaperoning high school dances. They voiced their disapproval when they heard about it. Good friend Ed Brakke and his family left the church.

Territorial Governor Ernest Gruening, impressed with the Ketchikan preacher/politician's oratorical skills previously demonstrated in testimony before the territorial legislature, had been responsible for drafting Dad to serve as vice president of the committee to seek statehood for Alaska. Dad continued to be flattered by the prestige of the position, but he pondered how the congregation would respond to absences caused by performing duties beyond the pale of being a pastor.

At the end of the day, closing Creek Street had been a one-man crusade. Though many Ketchikanites supported the closing, none of the town's lay leaders or politicians had surfaced to share Reverend Olson's passion and reformist vision by standing up to help him make permanent the accomplishment. A keen disappointment had been learning the president of the congregation, businessman Roy Johnson, was one of those owning Creek Street rental property. Dad had been puzzled by the disappearance of Mr. Johnson at the beginning of the crusade. Clarification didn't make him feel better.

Reverend Olson started to feel restless. Again serendipity had come into play in mid-September as the same Bishop Foss who had offered the Ketchikan parish to his friend in 1944 found he had a prestigious pastorate to fill at Central Lutheran Church in Tacoma, Washington. The friend he had sent to Alaska to die was reporting apparently miraculous recovery from cancer and return to good health.

Bishop Foss asked, "Roy, would you accept this call if I get it for you?"

Dad responded, "Would I consider it? Of course!"

A couple of weeks later the bishop called with a question that was not family friendly. "Can you and your family get packed up and down here by year-end?" Thoughtless, and caught up in the challenge of going back to a big church, Dad replied, "Sure, no problem."

Dad told the rest of us that evening. No votes this time, just discussion about logistics and targeting departure dates. He announced his resignation to the congregation the following Sunday, September 29. A congregational meeting was held the following Friday. The *Ketchikan Chronicle* reported on October 5, 1946, that members voted unanimously to reject the resignation and asked him to remain there. Dad replied that he would give it further thought, although "in God's economy of things, it might be that some other man might be in that plan for the church here and for Ketchikan at this particular time." Dad was moved by the plea, but the die was already cast. Mom must have been thinking, "Here we go again!"

An early call was made to Governor Gruening's office resigning service on the statehood committee. This led to a quick visit by the governor. He took a morning float plane to Ketchikan, had lunch in our family apartment at the back of the church, and tried to talk Dad out of leaving. No such luck.10

Dad was soon on his way to Central Lutheran in Tacoma to meet with trustees, deacons, related organization officers, and church staff. His other responsibility was to rent a house and buy a Buick, his favorite car. Arrangements

---

10   In early 1965, I participated in the first organized demonstration in Washington, D.C. against the Vietnam War. The principal speakers were Senators Wayne Morse and Ernest Gruening, the only two senators who had voted against the Tonkin Gulf Resolution, expanding U.S. military involvement. Afterward I approached Senator Gruening to express appreciation for his speech and ask him if he remembered my father, Reverend Roy Olson. He replied, "I sure do. A good man. He made a significant difference in Ketchikan and Territorial affairs. I was disappointed when he didn't stay to help us achieve statehood."

were made for us four sons to get early releases and grades reflecting completion of the school semester even though it wouldn't be over by the time we bid our farewells for the trip south. The remainder of our time there was a blur. Parting ways with the *Audace* wasn't easy, and I vaguely remember Ken and me going down to empty out our family's cold storage locker and give away the four deer still there. It had been a good hunting season. We had gotten better at it each year. This subsistence sport had become a part of living in Alaska we would miss.

Packing began the day school let out for Christmas vacation. We were on the next steamer, the same S.S. *Prince Rupert*, shortly after Christmas. Why I wasn't disappointed leaving a small high school, where I was happy, to get lost in a large school midway through my senior year remains baffling.

As soon as we were settled in our new home, Ken and I talked Dad into spending a morning exploring used car lots. We drove home in a clunker 1934 Dodge sedan. Fortunately, the church had an active Luther League for the youth with a marvelous youth minister, Leone Ingman, on staff to keep its kids, including Ken and me, busy and happy.

Among the outings soon after our arrival was a ski trip to Paradise Valley on Mount Rainier. The area had three newfangled rope tows—a new and welcome experience for Ken and me. We quickly got caught up in determination to join with the high school hotshots working on the tows, skiing between shifts and enjoying the overtures of the star-struck Stadium High "snow bunnies" anxious to learn to ski and snag a boyfriend. We were on our way to paradise to ski almost every weekend for the remainder of the season, singing, "Two boards upon cold powder snow, yo-ho, that's all a young man needs to know".

Knowing only a few guys and literally no girls, I had no interest in participating in high school graduation festivities. So I checked to assure my diploma would be mailed to my home and signed out after my last test. Meanwhile, Dad was in his glory returning to pastoring a major congregation in a city. Mom was happy to be back to all the conveniences and cultural opportunities she had missed during her years in The Great Land. My guess is Jerry and Tim had the most trouble adjusting to transfer to a new grade school in the middle of the year, but they survived.

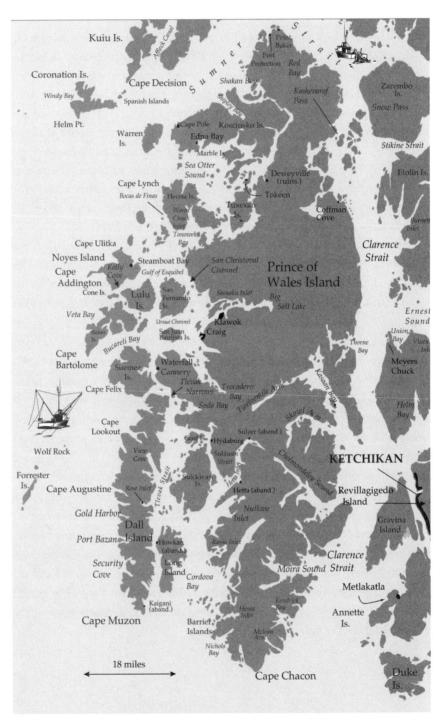

Southern Waters and Islands of Southeast Alaska

PART TWO

WATERMEN OF SOUTHEAST ALASKA

"I really don't know why it is that all of us are so committed to the sea. Except I think it is because, in addition to the fact that the sea changes and the light changes, and ships change, it is because we all came from the sea. And it is an interesting biological fact that all of us have in our veins the exact same percentage of salt in our blood that exists in the ocean. And therefore, we have salt in our blood, in our sweat, and in our tears. We are tied to the ocean. When we go back to the sea, whether it is to sail or to watch it, we are going back from whence we came."

John F. Kennedy, 1962

Nakat's Cape Addington Salmon Trap on a stormy day
Severin Hildre and crew standing solid on the spiller plank
Photo by Tim Olson

HARKY AND SELMA

Two ordinary people who lived extraordinary lives.

"DECKING" ON THE *LOUISIANA II*

During World War II all the healthy qualifying young men who had grown up in seaport towns volunteered or were drafted to serve in the armed forces. This led to a shortage of crew to man the various small commercial vessels operated from those ports. High school boys were eager to take the jobs. During my first year at Ketchikan High School (1944–45), I heard from classmates about their adventures and paychecks working on mostly fishing boats. My mind was soon set on finding work on the water even if I was still only fifteen years old. I asked everybody, "Know of a boat job?"

I was lucky. My friend Harold Silene had decked as the sole hand on the towboat *Louisiana II* the previous summer. He had planned to go back, but in May he got an offer to deck on the bigger, plusher salmon cannery tender *Wyoming*. Looking for a more romantic experience, he took it. As soon as he told me, I was knocking on owner/captain Harcourt (Harky) Tew's door.

The *Louisiana* was a sixty-foot multipurpose workboat. The bulwarks above the guardrail and lower half of the house were painted bright orange, making her a one-of-a-kind boat plying local waters year-round. The scuttlebutt around town was that Harky had southern Cajun roots. I'd hear people say, "How else could you account for a name like Tew with a boat named the *Louisiana II*?"

On the boat Harky was more instructor than commander, and I couldn't have had a better teacher. I soon learned to quickly tie a foolproof bowline knot while blindfolded and tie up a floating log raft in the dark. To be worthy of the dependence that goes with operating a boat like the *Louisiana II* with only one crewman, I had to do my best. Boat maintenance was also done Harky's way and was most of my job when we were in port.

Harky had equipped the boat to handle small barges and tow log rafts, boomed up at outlying logging camps, to the Spruce Mill in Ketchikan. These camps were isolated operations, often located at the head of some inlet, within a radius of perhaps eighty miles from Ketchikan. On log raft tow jobs, we would almost always carry a cargo of supplies, gear, and fuel on the trip out for delivery to the camp. On arrival we would often be invited to have lunch or dinner at the camp so the loggers and their families could catch up on the news from "outside."

Harky knew the surrounding waters probably better than anyone on the waterfront. He was a master of the art of small boat handling, in the maneuvering of scows, barges, and log rafts in tight quarters. Adverse winds, waves, and currents didn't seem to bother him. Even during snowy midwinter, people scanning the usually empty harbor channel would occasionally behold a visual feast as the solitary *Louisiana* was seen patiently towing a log raft to the mill. That's the waterman he was.

Revisiting my first boat job as deckhand on the M/V *Louisiana II* at Harky Tew's dock on a visit to Ketchikan in 1970
Photo by Gene Dyer

This knowledge and talent proved fortuitous when port towns like Ketchikan were on the frontline during the early days of World War II and the Japanese invasion of Alaska. The underprepared U.S. Coast Guard sought local civilian assistance wherever they could find it. Why not take advantage of watermen who knew the territory to help with marine watch of nearby waters for submarine activity and supply delivery to small outlying bases? Captain Harcourt Tew—with his long experience, excellent safety record, and qualifications as the owner/captain of a multi-use boat—surfaced as immediately useful. This led to a special military assignment in transport of ammunition and explosives by ship or barge. The designation led to a Selective Service draft exemption for Harky, and he colored the *Louisiana* above deck in orange and white to meet the identification requirements of small boat owners continuing to ply those war zone waters. Harky supported the war effort from the deck of his boat. When it was over he retained the colors for increased visibility—blind to the fact it made his boat the only boat commonly recognized by name ("There goes the *Louisiana*.") when passing along the waterfront.

Log raft tows back to the mill could take up to three days running around the clock at two knots and logging zero to four knots depending on tidal currents. This was a good speed to troll for fish. As soon as we were underway with a raft, Harky would set up the gear to catch something. A logger's pike pole was lashed to and extended out from the mast shrouds like the whisker pole on a sailboat. Then he tied a heavy halibut fishing line to the forestay, running it aft to the outrigger end of the pike pole. This was followed by reeling out more halibut line off a heavy wooden spool with a spoon or other end gear attached to catch whatever came along. This was loop-tied to the outrigged end of the pike pole. When a fish hit, the action would wiggle the forestay we could see from the pilothouse. It would be time to hit the deck, haul in the heavy fish line hand-over-hand, and land the catch. I never got drowsy on those boring wheel watches because there was always the anticipation of watching the forestay signaling "fish on." Over those summers we caught red snapper, lingcod, and most of all salmon, including a few large kings. When we got back to town, Harky would sometimes give me a fish to take home to my mom. My parents thought the Tews were as good as it gets—even if they were Methodists and Cecile Tew was involved with the Order of the Eastern Star, a freemasonry-related fraternal organization.

I found Harky and his gregarious and generous wife, Cecile, raising two young children, Nancy and Harky, Jr., in a happy home. His deckhand was treated as a member of the family. When we were in town doing day jobs, I would eat with the family. After supper and going back down to the boat to hit the bunk, I'd sometimes hear Harky on deck checking something. His last check would be calling down to me in the fo'c'sle, "Dave, did you brush your fangs?"

The family also took me along on their annual summer vacation at a property they owned at Scowl Arm on Prince of Wales Island. Cruise time to get there was about three hours on the *Louisiana*. The well-equipped cabin was quite roomy with two bedrooms for the family. I bunked on the anchored *Louisiana,* rowing myself out in the evening and back to shore in the morning in time for breakfast. There was an old-fashioned antique windup gramophone with a stack of ancient records to play for entertainment. To this day I can sing songs like "Jimmy Cracked Corn and I Don't Care" and "Can She Bake A Cherry Pie, Billy Boy, Billy Boy" learned at the Tew's Scowl Arm cabin. Some of the days were spent working in the garden. It was a paid vacation for me, a dumb deckhand oblivious of his good luck to just be there.

Cecile's hardy breakfasts could be memorable because cronies of Harky's, Lloyd "Slim" Balcom and Clarence Payne, would sometimes show up to share it. Slim and Clarence owned a nearby one-line salmon cannery. Each also owned fish traps and captained his own cannery tender—Slim the *Eureka* and Clarence the *Wyoming*. On one particular Monday, all the talk was about how U.S. Fish & Game agents had discovered one of Slim's fish traps open so salmon could be caught over the weekend—when all traps were suppose to be closed. We kidded Slim about his bad luck.

"Slim, how big a share you giving your watchman for leaving the trap open over the weekend?"

"Oh, he did it himself to sell the fish to a pirate."

"Ya, sure, that's a good story."

Whatever Slim must have said in court didn't sway the judge either. The fine turned out to be $1,000, as duly reported in the Ketchikan paper. A week later Slim was back for breakfast, happy as a clam, because he had left the same trap open through the weekend closing. The fishing had been good. He had more than made back the cost of the fine. As for the truth about how that trap happened to be open the weekend Slim was caught, your guess is as good as mine.

In 1946 no commercial fisherman in Southeast Alaska could imagine overfishing would ever be a problem. Fishing was an unpredictable game played by honest men in a competitive environment. Few of them gave any time to movements backing conservation to preserve the future. One of the most talked about fish pirates and creek robbers of the day was the honorable Andy

Gundersen. Andy fished his all-black salmon seiner during the summers. This notoriety did not stop him from winning election to represent the Borough of Ketchikan in the Territorial Senate. That's the way it was.

Those were two memorable summers for a mixed up kid in dire need of some growing up. I stayed in touch with the Tews long after, including a few exchanges of letters with Harky during the years I was working in the Far East— the last of which he wrote from the *Louisiana* while anchored somewhere with a log raft, waiting for better weather to finish a delivery.

* * *

SELMA SUCCEEDS IN A MAN'S WORLD

Decades later, I reestablished contact with Nancy Tew Heacock, Harky's daughter. Sharing stories with her made it easy to decide that this memoir would be incomplete without attempting to do justice to Harky Tew, her one-of-a-kind father, and Selma Swanson, her feisty ahead-of-her-time grandmother.

Since I thought Harky came from romantic French-Cajun Gulf Coast fishermen roots, curiosity prompted me to ask Nancy, "Where from, when, why, and how did the Tew family wash up in Ketchikan, Alaska? What's the success story behind all the various properties your parents had already acquired by the time I decked for your dad in 1945?"

I anticipated a tale of Harky's father's success passed on to Harky. Alaska was a man's world. A woman's place was pretty much limited to homemaking, teaching, nursing, clerking, or prostitution, wasn't it? The only woman I ever ran into on a commercial boat during my seven seasons in Alaska was cooking on the *Chomley*—and she was the wife of the engineer. Nancy's unexpected answers continue to fascinate me.

Harky's mother, Selma Swanson, was born in Sweden in 1879. The Swansons were a seafaring family, her father a merchant ship owner and captain. As a fourteen-year-old she was left ashore while her mother accompanied her father on a voyage. The ship and all aboard were lost at sea. Orphaned, Selma went to live with her grandmother who taught her the skills of Swedish sewing and intricate lacework. Two years later, Selma's work was good enough for her to apprentice to a Paris modiste, doing "personal design, styling, and fitting." Nancy says, "Popularity with customers led to Grandma's termination by a jealous owner." My guess is that "popularity" meant she had too much spunk.

Footloose back home in Sweden with a good education and itching to see more of the world, Selma seized an offer to migrate to America under sponsorship of an uncle in Minnesota. "That's where Grandma met Grandpa," says Nancy.

"He had been Harcourt Mark Mac Tewson from Canada. But at the border, U.S. immigration apparently shortened his surname to Tew. Nobody knows why it stuck, but that's how my Dad and me ended up Tews."

Scowl Arm homesteader Sig Windberg, Selma Swanson Tew Mackensie, and Harky Tew circa 1935 in Ketchikan
Courtesy Nancy Tew Heacock, Tew Family Archive

Harcourt Mark was a handsome, Scottish, journeyman cook. He and Selma fell in love. Marriage followed courtship sometime around 1900. The couple, quickly bored with staid and stable Minnesota, decided to move to the West Coast. For a time, Harcourt was a chef in a classy San Francisco restaurant until he got fired for one too many emotional outbursts. Selma and Harcourt then headed north to Washington, where he ended up cooking in Bellingham. Harcourt Jr. (Harky) made them a family in 1903. Harcourt Sr. moved on to be head cook in the cookhouses of big logging companies.

Responding to a "Cook Wanted" advertisement during the drought of 1908–1910 and subsequent devastating forest fires closing Washington to logging, the Tew family moved from Washington State to Ketchikan, Alaska, where a head cook job was waiting for Harcourt Sr. at a salmon cannery. They lived in cannery housing and Selma made friends with other wives and their families. With young Harky in school, Selma resumed putting her seamstress skills to good use. She designed and sewed gowns along with selling beautiful embroidery and lacework. Among her customers were the wives of the cannery, mill, and business owners in thriving Ketchikan. When she grew tired of Harcourt's tantrums, gambling, and drinking, she divorced him in 1915, undeterred by the social constraints of the day.

One of the buyers of Selma's work was Mrs. Anderson, a wealthy widow who saw in Selma the attributes for success in business. She and Selma became partners. The combination of Anderson's money and connections with Selma's smarts and skills led to ventures in property and the fish business. In a few years, Selma was able to buy from Mrs. Anderson the waterfront lots and buildings south of where she lived. This gave Selma and her son a home of their own.

Soon Harky was a young man working jobs in town and on the boats. He was also old enough to notice Cecile Templeton, a comely adventurous newcomer, toiling as a waitress at the popular Blue Fox Soda Fountain and Café.

"Mom was a Yakima High graduate, hired from an ad, and up from Seattle on a one-year contract that promised her 'a job with lunch at work plus board and room in a Christian home,'" Nancy says. "One thing led to another and they married in 1924. How well was Grandma doing? Well, enough to build the little white house next to the main house to give to my Mom and Dad as a wedding gift."

Along the way, Selma and Mrs. Anderson jumped feetfirst into the man's world of commercial fishing by partnering to purchase and run a salmon fish trap, including the site permit. They were the only women known to have done that. They hired a cannery tender captain to set their trap at the site, brail[11] the catch, and deliver it to the cannery for processing. With an honest operator, the trap produced a generous profit on the women's investment.

Floating fish traps were the most cost- and production-effective method devised for catching salmon. Initially designed and used in Puget Sound, they were soon set along the shorelines throughout Alaskan waters, where salmon would swim by in schools of thousands on their way to their spawning grounds. Each trap was anchored at the offshore end of an underwater chicken-wire fence anchored at the other end to the rocks on the beach. The salmon would bump up against the fence and turn seaward, looking for a way around it. The obvious route was into the trap's confining labyrinth, leading them finally to

---

11 Brailing is the act of dipping a net, controlled by a winch operator on a cannery tender or purse seiner, into or under a school of salmon, and trapping them for loading into the hold of the tender or seiner for delivery to the cannery.

enter a small holding pen. This pen, called the "spiller," could be closed, allowing no escape from delivery to the cannery.

Salmon being brailed from the Swanson Mackenzie trap into the *Louisiana II*
Courtesy Nancy Tew Heacock, Tew Family Archive

The sites, on Territorial government land, were registered to reserve trap fishing rights like mining claims. Productive sites could be sold and resold at considerable, sometimes impressive, profit. When national food production companies in the Lower 48, like the Great Atlantic & Pacific Tea Company and Libby, McNeill & Libby, saw money to be made in this industry, they came to Alaska with big bucks to build canneries. They also established nets of salmon fish traps near each cannery to be serviced by fleets of duel-purpose towboats with holds for hauling fish, called cannery tenders. The result was jobs, but most of them went to people coming north each summer to work, only to turn around and take their earnings home to spend in the states. Most cannery profits ended up on the balance sheets of stateside public company owners. Many Alaskans thought this wasn't fair and voted to abolish fish traps as an early exercise of state rights.

But business was not to be the only interest in Selma's life during those years. She caught the eye of another Scotsman, the business manager of a salmon cannery, Angus MacKenzie. Nancy says, "He was a handsome dude, always in a suit topped with a bowler hat." They married after a long courtship in 1925. He proved to be another ideal partner for the entrepreneurial-minded Selma until his untimely death in 1935.

Over the decade of their marriage, the acquisitive MacKenzies successfully accumulated more property. Most notable was the summer vacation and fall hunting cabin and acreage at Scowl Arm Inlet.

In 1934, needing a boat to service and fish the trap, Selma and Angus spotted an ad for a new boat berthed in Seattle whose first owner had christened her the *Louisiana II* and then had to sell her. "Grandma, after buying the boat for $35,000, didn't think it worth thirty-five dollars more plus the paperwork to change the name," Nancy says. "Besides, II is "Tew," isn't it? So she just sent my Dad and Angus off to Seattle to bring her back to Ketchikan. Angus died soon after their return, leaving Grandma a widow."

Fish Trap for salmon set on site near Ketchikan circa 1936
Courtesy Nancy Tew Heacock, Tew Family Achive

On Angus' death in 1935, Selma owned prime waterfront real estate on Tongass Avenue, including a house, garage, separate warehouse for gear storage and boat maintenance, and private dock across the street, in addition to a salmon fish trap on a superior site claim, the *Louisiana II*, and the property at Scowl Arm Inlet. Her house was too big for one person and the house next door had become too small for Harky and his growing family. Selma was fifty-seven years old, in good health, and still full of life. She wanted to move on from

Ketchikan, so it was time to make a family deal with Harky. The bully bargain they reached has Selma's business acumen written all over it.

First there was mutual agreement on Selma selling the fish trap and site to the highest bidder—which she did at a handsome profit. Harky favored this decision because he had already determined he could make more dependable income than was probable in the fickle seasonal fish business by working the *Louisiana* year-round, mostly towing log rafts from logging camps in the region to the Ketchikan Spruce Mill. Subject to the same agreement, Harky bought the *Louisiana* at a fair price. With that accomplished, Selma moved to Portland, Oregon. Harky, Cecile, Nancy, and Harcourt III moved to the big house. Their former home, the small house next door, became a rental. All of this, plus Harky's success selling the services of the *Louisiana*, soon made it possible to agree on purchase of the remainder of the real property. Selma's last sale to Harky was the cabin at Scowl Arm. Nancy says, "Dad always called it their port in a storm if they ever needed one."

Thereafter, Selma showed up in Ketchikan for a visit and vacation every summer. I vaguely recall, in fact, must having met her over the course of the summers I was on the boat. Sadly, Cecile passed away too young from cancer in 1952. Nancy and Harcourt III grew up and moved away from Ketchikan. Selma spent her final years in California and died in her late seventies. She may have lived her life in virtual obscurity, but I believe she belongs high on the short list of liberated, independent, entrepreneurial women who materially contributed to settling Alaska and left a legacy to prove it.

* * *

THE DAY HARKY DIED[12]

May Day, 1975, was Harky's last day on the *Louisiana*. The morning began with Harky and a green deckhand running the boat out about eighteen miles from Ketchikan to nearby Gnat Cove in Carroll Inlet to tow a log raft back to the mill. After tying up to the raft, Harky shut down the engine and returned topside feeling ill. He made it to the head and collapsed. He died sitting on the toilet at age seventy after skippering the *Louisiana* for forty years. The deckhand

---

12   This is Nancy's story as told to her by Harry James (Jimmy) Diamond III, a lifelong Alaskan who had, in his youth, also deckhanded for Harky on the *Louisiana*. Nancy reported she had only recently stumbled onto confirmation of Jimmy's story by retired U.S. Fish and Wildlife Agent Robert E. Wood. Coincidentally, receiving this account was a reconnection for me with the Diamond family. Jim's father, Harry II, was once my skipper when I was mate on the cannery tender *Chomley* in 1948 and at the beginning of the 1949 season. The Diamond family home was a block from the cannery. Jim and his siblings were regular visitors to the boat when we were in port. He was along for the cruise north in 1949. He personally vouches for this yarn as recounted here in a telephone conversation we had in March 2012.

got on the radio to call for help. Then he flagged down U.S. Fish and Wildlife Agent Bob Wood passing by on Alaska Fish and Game's Boston Whaler.

Bob says:

> *I checked and found Tew dead on the pot. We carried him out of the head and laid him on the deck. Leaving the deckhand on the Louisiana, I took the Whaler over to the nearby logging camp to report the death and seek help to get Tew and his boat back to Ketchikan. Over at the camp I found this guy who said, "Ya, I know Harky Tew. I used to work for him. Hell, I can run that boat." I took him back to the Louisiana where he took over. I left to go about my business."*

Jimmy Diamond, also decking at the time, covered the body with a quilt. He called the coast guard to report the death of Captain Harcourt Tew. The call was acknowledged and he was told, "Message received, stand by..." Jimmy waited a half-hour, called again, and got the same acknowledgement. On his third call, Jimmy said, "This is the *Louisiana II* calling. Captain Tew is dead! I am Harry James Diamond III, a personal friend, and we are taking Captain Tew home."

Then he went down to the engine room and says, "I prayed: 'Well, Hark, you always started her up yourself, and I watched you, but you better help me now if I'm going to get you home.' The old reliable Cummins diesel came alive and I said, 'Thanks.'"

With Jimmy at the helm, he and the deckhand cast off from the raft and headed for town. Soon they were approached at flank speed by three coast guard vessels. These boats roared past them on both sides to come abreast a few feet off on either side. A uniformed officer with a bullhorn stepped out on deck booming, "This is Captain...of the U.S. Coast Guard. Heave to and prepare to be boarded!" Jimmy stayed at the wheel looking straight ahead. The officer turned red-faced and repeated the order. Jimmy ignored him. On a nod from the officer, two sailors appeared on deck with weapons. Jimmy opened the pilothouse window and calmly called out, "Captain Tew is dead. You acknowledged my report over two hours ago. Where the devil have you been? I am Harry James Diamond III, a personal friend of Captain Tew, and we are taking the Captain home. We are not heaving to and permission to board is denied. You may respectfully escort us to the *Louisiana*'s berth at Captain Tew's dock." Jimmy closed the window, ending the exchange.

At a loss as to what action to take next, the officer humbly retreated to his pilothouse to do, more or less, as told and provide an escort. He also called ahead to arrange for two ambulances, a couple of Ketchikan police officers, and a fire truck to be at the coast guard base awaiting arrival of the *Louisiana* and escorting vessels. This was followed by a call to Jimmy on the *Louisiana* citing these arrangements and insisting on first landing at the base. Jimmy reluctantly said okay. Word spread in town that Harky Tew had died, and a few people were already on hand to help transfer Harky's body to an ambulance.

By the time Jimmy was released to run the *Louisiana* from the base on the south end of the Ketchikan waterfront to Harky's dock near the north end, the grapevine was busy. Jimmy found another somber group of Harky's friends waiting on the float to tie up the boat. He had succeeded in bringing Harky home with due honor and homage.

Since Nancy was married and living in Haines, Alaska, and the same was true of Harcourt III living in Anchorage, Alaska, they soon sold all of the estate, including the *Louisiana*. The buyer worked the boat with little interest in more than minimum maintenance. An attempt was made to sell her in 2000, but no buyers surfaced. Seventy years old and worn out, she was ignominiously scuttled in a nameless cove a few miles west of Ketchikan. Old boats never die, they just sink.

Captain Tew's Terminal Cruise

The Ketchikan boat everybody knew,
A colorful craft in the harbor view,
Painted black, white and orange trim too,
Plying Alaska waters whither winds blew,
The Louisiana II, Captain Harcourt Tew.
Though Harky's business had no name,
Work boat charters were his game,
Towing and freighting were jobs that came,
Four season services just the same
Till Harky passed to local acclaim.

–Dave Olson

A LATTER-DAY VIKING

*Thoughts of challenge, tinged with tension, raced through my mind.
I'd be deckhand for one of Southeast Alaska's legendary fishermen.*

DECKING FOR KNAPLUND ON THE *BELOIT II*

By early spring of 1947 my dreams were concentrated on going back to life at sea. My goal was to return to Alaska and work on a boat. My former Alaska skipper, Harky Tew, replied to my inquiry and invited me to come up to Ketchikan and hang out at his home while I found a job. Immediately after my last school exam, and skipping high school graduation, I hurried over to Fishermen's Terminal in Seattle to shop the fleet for a working passage to Ketchikan.

Success came quickly. The captain of a tug preparing to tow a supply barge to Nome said, "Yah, I can use you to ease the wheel watches while I train a green hand. We'll drop you in Ketchikan." I moved aboard the next day. Two days later we were on our way north.

Not long into our journey, while I was on watch, all hell broke loose between two crew members. Fortunately, the captain was in the pilothouse when we heard streams of foul language coming up from the deck below. One crewman with a knife was chasing another out of the galley toward the bow. The seasoned old captain quickly retrieved his handgun from his cabin behind the wheelhouse. Then he calmly stepped out on the bridge deck, leaned over the rail looking down on the foredeck scene, and yelled, "STOP!" in a voice to freeze a waterfall. Somehow he forced a truce between the brawling men, but the tension was palpable for the remainder of my days aboard.

As soon as my seabag was dropped at the Tews' home in Ketchikan, I was off to the docks to visit cannery offices and go from boat to boat asking, "Looking for an experienced deckhand? Know of any short-handed boats?" After a few days of nothing but an offer of a cannery job until a boat job surfaced, I was getting anxious. Then somebody let me know the fish packer *Beloit II* was in town down at the cold storage. The skipper was looking for a deckhand. I learned the boat had docked that morning in Ketchikan to unload part of the iced salmon cargo on board and planned to continue on to Prince Rupert that evening to unload the remainder the next day. After landing, the deckhand had walked off the boat. The owner and captain, John Knaplund, needed a new deckhand by the end of the day.

Knaplund was said to be "tough as John Munson," the legendary skipper of the halibut schooner *Atlas*. Rumormongers said Knaplund overworked his son Carsten as a boy, leading to his crippling by his mid-twenties. They said he skippered the *Beloit II* shorthanded, without the third man customary on fish packers. Deckhand turnover was high because few young men could survive or put up with the relentless workload.

But Dad knew John Knaplund really well. In family gossip about Knaplund, I remembered Dad saying, "Yes, people say he's tough, but there's respect tinged with admiration acknowledging Knaplund's success." He was the developer and owner of a major fish buying station, located 120 miles northwest of Ketchikan at Kelly Cove on Noyes Island. During the annual four-month salmon fishing season, up to ninety commercial trolling boats fished the rich nearby waters, selling their daily catch at the station. Knaplund's buying operation was one of the most popular in Southeast Alaska with many of the same fishermen showing up year after year. The company's income came from the difference between the on-the-grounds price paid to the trollers for their fish and the price the Knaplunds negotiated on delivery to the market buyers in Ketchikan and Prince Rupert, B.C. The Knaplunds were sharp, but fair, businessmen. At church, the family was looked up to as "devout and honest people."

We need to go back to northern Norway, though, to really grasp John Knaplund's roots. Paul Knaplund, John's younger brother who had become a professor of history at the University of Wisconsin, eventually wrote a history of coastal Norwegians and their migration to America, titled *Moorings Old and New: Entries In an Immigrant's Log*, featuring his family (and, as it turns out, contributing to my family history as well).

This history for the Knaplunds goes back to the tall fair-haired Haleygr tribe who moved into the coastal area above the Arctic Circle several years before the Christian era and which eventually became known as Halogaland. On the islands and along the shores of the fjords, archeological digs have uncovered many cairns and burial places of people long dead. Artifacts found at old building sites and in refuse heaps bare testimony to the antiquity of Norse settlements in this region. The seas teemed with fish, the forests abounded with plentiful game, and the coastal climate was mild for the growing of crops. By the latter part of the ninth century when Norway was united, the "jarls" of Halogaland were among the strongest chieftains in the kingdom.

The coastal lowlands about sixty miles north of the Arctic Circle and twelve miles in from the entrance to Saltenfjord and nearby Knaplundoy (Knaplund Island) were the home of chieftain Raud the Strong. Raud's grand dragon ship, the *Serpent,* the pride of the northland, later served as a model for the most famous war vessel of the Viking era, King Olav's *Long Serpent.* The saga of Raud's deeds, location of his hall, and his burial place often spark animated disputes to this day.

An old photo of Knaplund Island reflects a setting like much of Southeast Alaska, including climate, flora, and fauna. The arable land was farmed mostly to provide food for the family and forage for the animals. Commercial fishing for salmon, herring, and cod provided cash income. Sons were sent to school to learn to read, write, and cipher, but brought up to expect to make their living farming and fishing.

* * *

John was born in 1881. His early years, shared with brothers, were happy years. His father taught them more than fishing and farming; he gave them a sense of the mysteries of the earth and sea and an appreciation of the beauty, magic, and rhythms of life. Religion played a major role in his family life and as the center of social life on the island. Full-church attractions were occasional visits by missionaries to foreign lands home on sabbatical to solicit support funds by sharing stories of their adventures. This was heady and important stuff to John because, as the fourth and next to youngest son, John knew from an early age he'd have to make his own way in life. There would be no way to do that on Knaplundoy.

Fortunately these young men of the northland were brought up with an inborn restlessness. John was off to his first season in the Lofoten Islands fishery when he was sixteen. By the time he was twenty, a seasoned hand, he was ready to join that band of adventurous Norsemen called to leave home and sail the seven seas. The first five years were mostly on windjammers. Contact was kept with family by letters sent from ports of call around the globe. Naturally born to the sailor's life, he thrived on life before the mast. Ambition and interest led him to learn the seamanship and navigation required to qualify for a master's license on vessels up to two hundred tons. He taught himself to speak, read, and write English, probably by sailing on ships under British flags.

Young John Knaplund crewing on a windjammer (back row, first left) circa 1900
Courtesy Ethel Knaplund Simmons, Knaplund Family Archive

In May 1906, tired of life on windjammers, he signed on with a Norse-Chilean's venture as mate on a vessel fishing off Valparaiso, Chile. The money was good enough to send some home to lend a helping hand to family back in Norway. Within a year he either paid or worked his way up the Pacific coast to the United States and Washington State. He wedded Olga Tvenstrup in April 1911. Son Carsten was born in 1912. Possibly influenced by Olga's family, he filed and qualified for an eighty-acre homestead signed by Woodrow Wilson on May 31, 1913. It was located somewhere in the vast, dry, ranch and farm country surrounding the small town of Prosser in southeastern Washington and over two hundred miles from his first love—the endless sea. Highlighting 1914 was the birth of a daughter, Verna.

Years of sailoring had John ill equipped to work the land. He moved on to try making a living working a regular job for a paycheck. By 1915 he had fallen on hard times. During the winter of 1916, he met an old shipmate on the Tacoma docks with a motorboat ready to go to Alaska. He asked John to join him for the trip up the Inside Passage. When they got there, John knew he was home. He quickly found enough money to buy his own fishing boat.

When the season ended he brought his family to Ketchikan where he built a small home for them. Though their newfound happiness was immediately cut short by the death of Verna, who was tragically run over by the only automobile in town, the Knaplunds persevered.

By 1920 John was trolling the exposed North Pacific waters for salmon off the southwest coast of beautiful Baranof Island, almost two hundred miles northwest of Ketchikan. He was fishing out of Port Alexander, a protected harbor, tiny village, and fish buying station where he sold his catch, bought supplies and fuel, and shared the life of the summer fishing community. Though John didn't know it, he was in learning mode, soaking up valuable preparation for his future.

Fishing his own troller those seasons in Southeast Alaska awakened John's entrepreneurial juices to the business potential of developing fish buying stations at other secure anchorages closer to Ketchikan and other fishing grounds teeming with king and silver salmon. Where and how John developed his business acumen with no background or education to predict success is another testament to Viking determination and intelligence. He also had a knack for charming hard-nosed bankers with predictions of success.

By 1928 or earlier, he had earned and saved enough money to have the *Beloit II* built to his specifications in Seattle, Washington. During or before the building started, he made a trip back to Wisconsin for the two-fold purpose of seeing and meeting brother Paul's family in Madison and to visit the Fairbanks Morse engine manufacturing plant in Beloit. Whether it was at Paul's urging or something he read in a trade magazine, John had come to think Fairbanks Morse had the best engine for his dream boat.

The *Beloit* was a sixty-foot traditional seine boat design with maxed-out hold capacity for fish packing and sturdily built to handle heavy weather. By 1929 John had Carsten and a cousin crewing on the *Beloit*. They were buying troll-caught salmon on the grounds, probably off the west coasts of Dall and/or Noyes Islands, for delivery and resale to a cannery in Ketchikan. The Knaplund & Son Buying Station at Kelly Cove, Noyes Island, was established by 1935.

The site was a natural location for a fish buying operation. It offered secure piling placements and anchorage for the scows and floats providing moorings for the trolling boats plus a good source of fresh water. Most important, major runs of king and silver salmon annually passed along the entire west coast of Noyes Island. The waters off of nearby Cape Addington, at the southwest tip of the island where the Bering Expedition made its first landfall in North America in 1741, were favored by many fishermen coming up from Seattle or out from Ketchikan every spring. They made Kelly Cove their home for the entire season. The legal papers were filed for establishing permanent pilings, docks, and floats in 1940. Expansion to establish a second station at Ethel Cove on Baker Island was contemplated with filings for permits there in 1946. This project was soon abandoned, though, due to the deterioration of Carsten's health. The off-season was spent in a futile search for relief or cure of his debilitating illness.

Opening the season of 1947, Knaplund & Son owned the *Beloit II* in addition to a large buying station scow with a cold storage facility and store selling groceries and supplies on the main deck and a second story providing living quarters for the entire family and other station employees. A small fuel scow was attached to the main scow from which you could walk out along finger floats that provided moorage for the fleet of rafted trolling boats. All of this, plus a few shore cabins and fresh water piped from on shore, had been built starting from scratch by John Knaplund, who also enjoyed enthusiastic support from his son who embraced his father's way of life from an early age.

When I approached him that fateful season, John was alone on the boat. I found him to be the same soft-spoken man who had taken Dad, Ken, and me on the *Beloit II* for a brief fall deer-hunting trip perhaps three years prior. He wasn't a big man—medium height, but muscular with the chiseled and weather-beaten face of a Norseman who had spent years at sea. He offered me $200 per month, a competitive rate. On acceptance, I ran the mile back to the Tew home to say thanks for their hospitality and grab my seabag.

As soon as my bag was stowed in the fo'c'sle, John and I were off to the Ingersoll Hotel restaurant for an early dinner. He told me he'd detoured from going to Prince Rupert with the *Beloit*'s hold full of salmon to stop in Ketchikan and replace his deckhand. Now that he'd quickly found me, there was no need to sell in Ketchikan. He could still deliver in Prince Rupert. He said, "That's where we're going as soon as we finish dinner."

On return to the boat, John fired up the immense direct-reversible Fairbanks Morse diesel (an engine that was stopped and then restarted in reverse to go astern using compressed air) and we cast off for Prince Rupert, seventy miles away. As soon as we were underway he showed me how to operate the autopilot, how to stop the engine, and where we were going on the chart, including point-to-point running times and compass courses (electronic navigation tools were nonexistent). John expressed compass courses in esoteric "points," rather than degrees, reflecting his early learning as a sailor on windjammers. Then, assuming I had learned my lessons well during the previous two summers decking for Harky on the *Louisiana II*, he asked, "Dave, can you take the wheel to Lucy Island so I can get some sleep?" The run would be about six hours through the night crossing Dixon Entrance into Chatham Sound. I said sure and enjoyed the time to ponder what I'd learned so far. It was one of those beautiful peaceful nights with a moon, northern lights, and a calm sea. Life on the *Beloit* would be a new experience.

John was anxious to sell his salmon to the Rupert Fish Company for a better price than he could find in Ketchikan, but there was more to it than that. Prince Rupert, on the mainland, was the terminus of the railroad. The company was on a siding so salmon taken off a boat at the company dock could be transferred directly to special refrigerated freight cars for through-transit delivery to Boston and New York seafood wholesalers. This was probably the beginning of marketing to provide fast delivery of fresh salmon to upscale restaurants and fish markets. The only difference today is fish are flown from the grounds to global markets. I suspect those East Coast retailers also sold products at high markups with snob-attracting labels implying superior quality and flavor.

The Rupert Fish Company unloaded our hold the next morning. Soon we cast off for return to Ketchikan and by nightfall the *Beloit* was tied up at the dock for a night of unbroken shut-eye.

The next day was spent loading the hold with ice topped with groceries and other store inventory for the salmon trollers and crews. Included in John's routine was a visit to the bank to pick up a paper bag containing upwards of $10,000 cash to pay the fishermen for their catch. After the loading, he casually left this bag in the pilothouse, in plain sight, door open, while we were off the boat having an early dinner.

Departing Ketchikan we stopped at the oil dock for fuel, and then we were off to Kelly Cove. Running time was nineteen hours at eight knots unless we ran into bad weather crossing long stretches of open water. Two hours short of Kelly Cove we made an early morning stop at the Waterfall Salmon Cannery oil dock. There we loaded the deck with fifty-gallon drums of fuel for resale to the fishermen.

By the time we arrived at Kelly Cove, just in time for lunch, I thought I could make it on the *Beloit*. John must have thought so, too, and earlier passed the word to Carsten on the radio. How could I not feel good arriving to a warm welcome by John's wife, Olga, Carsten and his wife Viola, and their young children, John and Ethel. Nephews from Olga's family, Paul and Sig Hauglund, hailing from North Bend, Washington, completed the buying station crew. Both were needed as "hands and legs" for Carsten, who could still get around but was valiantly fighting a losing battle against a debilitating disease that would take his life too soon.

After lunch we unloaded the fuel drums, groceries and supplies for the store, and most of the ice, which was to be saved for icing the salmon held on the scow while the *Beloit* was away on delivery. In late afternoon the first troller tied up to the scow to unload its catch. A steady stream of boats followed, one at a time, into the early evening. The fresh salmon, after being weighed in, were passed to the *Beloit* for icing and storage pending delivery in Prince Rupert. So, instead of a nap, I found myself putting on oilskins and boots to join Sig in icing salmon, which became my job every afternoon into early evening until the side bins in the hold were full.

Then it was time to top off the hold with wooden boxes from scow cold storage—each holding about two hundred pounds of iced salmon—batten down the hatch, load and secure the remaining boxes of iced salmon on deck, and prepare for departure. After a late dinner, I hit the bunk until John woke me too early in the morning to get underway for the twenty-four-hour passage to Prince Rupert.

If the weather was good, we took turns on roughly six-hour watches. We often spent hours together in the pilothouse during the long daylight watches. Talk was spare. Answers to my questions to John could be left dangling, but I learned to trust there would be one eventually. Weather was often the subject at hand because there were no regular receivable forecasts. You could pick up current weather at manned lighthouse locations when you got within radio reception range. In between, John was the onboard weatherman. He'd check the "glass" (barometer) but, like Harky, he'd make decisions based on what he saw in the sky and felt in the wind. Whatever we experienced occasionally led to a comment like, "Ya, the glass vas right (or wrong) again!"

Thus, on a blustery rainy day, just underway out of Kelly Cove bound for Prince Rupert, I might say, "Do you think we'll get weather crossing Dixon tonight?" Interrupted only by the tolling of the bells on the Seth Thomas clock, approximately one hour of silence later came John's reply, "I t'ink so." This might be followed by an account of some remembered passage dredged up from his seafaring past or a short lesson in sailor's ways of forecasting weather. I never tired of listening to him tell these tales in his gentle Norski-accented English.

John did the cooking. Oatmeal was the customary breakfast. Boiled humpy belly (pink salmon) with boiled potatoes and canned peas was John's favorite dinner, topped off with canned fruit and Olga's homemade cookies for dessert. For lunch in Prince Rupert after unloading our cargo of fish, John would often give me some Canadian "loonies" and send me to the nearby Chinese restaurant. As soon as I returned, we'd cast off for the eight-hour run to Ketchikan.

* * *

VIKING WAYS

On a late June trip we arrived from Prince Rupert in Ketchikan one morning. In the afternoon as the loading of ice, store supplies, and money was being completed, I could see the weather to the southeast was deteriorating. Once loaded, though, there was no delaying in shoving off for Kelly Cove. I made the usual deck check and cleared the lines and fenders, but I made no special preparation to expect serious gale conditions as neither John nor I saw any cause for serious concern.

At nightfall, clearing Dall Head for the twenty-mile run across Dixon Entrance to Cape Chacon, we continued to neither see nor sense evidence for further preparations. Then, perhaps fifteen miles out and totally exposed to the open ocean's fury, a gale was on us with steepening seas and we were taking waves on our forward port quarter.

Close to midnight, on a sharp lurch to starboard, we heard a racket of wood hitting the cable rigging with enough force to feel a shuttering of the boat in the pilothouse. Leaving the wheel on autopilot to maintain course and keep from broaching, John and I went to investigate. We found the boom and port guy line wildly swinging free, totally loose from moorings and gyrating with each wave in a wide arc to slam against the starboard shroud on the heel to that side and back amidships as the wave passed. The boom was held there momentarily by the starboard guy still secured at the rail. The block at the end of the loose port guy passed over the deck about three feet above the deck and out over the ocean with each wave.

John quickly rigged a stopper line to resecure the port guy. At the next opportunity, jumping on the hatch cover, he grabbed the lines running down to the swinging block and, on the next wave, hanging on with both hands, he went aerial out over the ocean at least four feet beyond the rail to swing back aboard, land on the deck, pick up the stopper line, thread the end through the lines above the block, lead it back, and cleat the guy to the port side rail. (All this at sixty-seven years old!)

Back in the pilothouse John immediately took the wheel, and at the first favorable opportunity he came about to put the weather on our stern quarter, meanwhile explaining we couldn't risk clearing Chacon with the temporary fix on the boom and needed to head for shelter. He spotted an opening to one of the inlets along the Prince of Wales Island coast off to port. He said, "Dafe, vatch out your side, look ahead for any sign of reefs or rocks." Seeing none, we literally surfed into calm waters to shut down the engine and drift. Out on deck

John looked around for any familiar signs of where we were. Then he told me, "Go to bed and get some sleep. I'll call you when ve have daylight." He did. The storm had already abated. Underway again, John had me on the bow checking for any reefs as we eased out of the inlet.

Back at sea I asked, "Where were we last night?"

"Not sure," was the laconic reply. He never noted a place in the log either.

* * *

THE LONGEST NIGHT

In late July we were leaving Kelly Cove once with a full hold of iced salmon and three layers of fish boxes, each holding perhaps two hundred pounds of iced salmon, topped by a canvas tarp and crisscrossed by lashings tied to securing ringbolts on deck. The full load made for sluggish steering with the guardrail barely above water for the passage to Prince Rupert. Casting off from the buying scow early that morning, I was tired and hoped we were on our way to a routine delivery. As we passed Cape Chacon on the southern tip of Prince of Wales Island in the early evening, there wasn't a zephyr of wind, but we already had a rising sea on our bow forewarning us of a gale we knew was coming. This led to storm preparations, including lowering and tying down the boom to rest on top of the deck load, doubling the lines securing our deck load, and rigging a safety line leading aft from the mast over the top of the deck load along the boom so we would have something to hang onto while checking lines and adjusting or adding to them if needed. John calculated the course adjustment he hoped would compensate for the wind and sea conditions that would be driving us to leeward and off course on the sixty-mile run to Triple Island Light and safety in Canadian coastal waters.

Knaplund's fish packer M/V *Beloit II* with deck load of empty fish boxes circa 1947
Ethel Knaplund Simmons, Knaplund Family Archive

There was not a lot of room for error because if, due to poor visibility, we missed seeing the prominent lighthouse on Triple Island in the morning, we would make landfall not knowing exactly where we were. Even I knew this would be a stressful outcome because we were sitting on a boatload of fish that wouldn't hold another day for delivery in prime condition at a profitable price.

There was no sleep that night. John and I took turns at the helm. By midnight, waves breaking hard over the pilothouse were squirting water through the windowsills. The well deck was awash with water up to the rails in the trough (over knee-deep when stepping out on deck). This revelation had us taking turns checking the deck load and visiting the engine room to make sure the bilges were okay. The night got complicated on the second of my rounds when I opened the hatch to check the engine room and was met by a plume of smoke smelling of burning rubber. At the bottom of the companionway ladder was the bilge pump stopped cold and the V-belt powering it smoldering. It took seconds to go below, stop power to the pump, scramble back up the ladder, open the sliding door to the deck, and get violently seasick for the first time in my life. John calmly called from the pilothouse, "Vat's wrong Dafe?" Between upchucks I told him. On recovery and a mouth rinse with seawater, I was soon back at the helm so John could go below and see if repair was possible. It wasn't.

The multiple leaks through stressed seams of plank and deck caulking were too much to ignore for long. The auxiliary bilge pump was an old-fashioned cast-iron rubber diaphragm affair mounted in the well deck between the main cargo hatch and the stern poop deck. It was equipped with a five-foot angled steel pipe handle extending out from the diaphragm for a crewman to work up and down in a two-foot arc, powering the suction of water from the bilge to the deck and overboard. You could sit on the poop deck with the pump between your legs and pump from that position. Since our deck load was three feet high you had to climb over the top of it while hanging onto the safety line to get to the pump. Next was tying in there on the safety line so you wouldn't be washed overboard while working the pump.

John worked the first shift on the pump. We took turns every hour for the rest of the trip to Prince Rupert. For some reason I recall no fear or sense of cold as I sat back there on the poop pumping away wearing woolies under my oilskins with just sneakers for shoes (hip boots would have filled with water). When the stern reached its low point in the trough of a wave, the pump disappeared and the water level rose to chest height a few times, but never high enough to force me to stand up. I recall sensing a wave of relief on my return to the security of the pilothouse—and equally when John returned safely from being out there.

At the helm at about 5:00 a.m., already over four hours overdue for normal arrival at Triple Island, I had the joy of the first sighting of the lighthouse almost dead ahead. Totally calm and collected through the entire ordeal, John broke into a grin from ear to ear. "Ya. Dafe, ve vere lucky. I vas vorried for our safety. Novhere to go for shelter."

I should have been worried, too, but John was so cool I didn't know it. I know now that the history of commercial fishing disasters is replete with lay down founders and capsizes caused by overloading the deck. The many lives lost in the capsizing of crab boats in the Alaska Gulf and Bering Sea during the 1960s through the 1980s was the rationale for the TV serial *The Deadliest Catch*. Carrying that kind of load that night, we knew that any attempt to come about to run before the sea would have put us broadside in the trough at the mercy of the next wave to lay the boat down with slim chance of recovery.

* * *

FAMILY VALUES

John had a friend named Eigil Buschmann, general superintendent for many years of all Nakat canneries and son of legendary Peter Buschmann for whom Petersburg, Alaska, is named. One of Eigil's practices on visits to Waterfall Cannery each summer was to take the *Fritzie*, a speedy cabin cruiser berthed at the cannery, on swings through the surrounding waters to count salmon jumps and visit traps to come up with a estimate of the potential fish pack.

On one of those cruises he stopped at Kelly Cove to check on the troll-caught pack and gossip with John about life in the fish business. The *Fritzie* tied up alongside the *Beloit*. John and Eigil promptly got to gabbing on the *Beloit* deck just above where I was in the hold icing salmon. After greetings, an exchange of family news, and fisheries scuttlebutt, they got down to business. I heard Eigil ask, "Everything working out okay on your pick-ups of fuel (for the trollers at Kelly Cove)?"

John said, "Ya, ve come in too early for your man, but he takes good care of us."

"So how has the fishing been?"

John, pleased to be asked, replied, "All the boats are doing good. The king pack to Rupert was almost 500,000 pounds. The silvers are running big and ve are going loaded on trips so far. Got over eighty boats landing now."

Eigil said, "John, I hear the *Rustler* came in a few days ago and sold a few fish."

With that I stopped icing. I'd heard while John and I had been away on a delivery trip, this Nakat seiner out of Waterfall had quietly come in with some bright gutted silvers they wanted to sell as troll-caught fish—and Paul, who did the buying on our scow, had bought them.

John casually replied, "Ya, my Paul said they reported a good set vere they picked up a few nice clean fish they thought we could buy. They were looking to have a little cash for the crew to share."

Then I learned something of Eigil Buschmann's predatory family values as he responded, while heartily clapping John on the back, "John, you know my boy Bob is on that boat. He's a Buschmann who's going to amount to something—stealing fish from the old man!"

Nobody's fool, John also heard what wasn't said, saying, "Ya, Eigil, don't vurry, ve won't be buying fish from all your boats!"

* * *

TYING UP LOOSE ENDS

By mid-August, most of the trollers were gone. The season had been a success. It was time to beach and secure the small fuel scow and floating docks for winter storage, and shut down the buying station for tow to winter storage on a protected tideflat at nearby Waterfall. Those last two weeks were fun. Sometimes, as we were coming in for a landing, John would say, "Dafe, you vant to take the boat in?" What teenage deckhand wouldn't?

Old John Knaplund circa 1949
Ethel Knaplund Simmons, Knaplund Family Archive

Settle-up for me was at the dining table on the scow the night before the tow to Waterfall. I'd been on the boat for almost two and a half months. Knowing John's reputation, I expected a check to cover that. Much to my surprise, though, the check was for a full three months with the good wishes of the Knaplund family. Little did I know, due to the deterioration of Carsten's health, the family business was for sale. The family bought a store in Clinton, Washington, and settled there. John came north in the spring to help with transfer of the business to the buyers.

John suffered a heart attack and died in 1951. Dad answered the call to conduct the funeral. He had probably met John in 1926 during his year in Ketchikan as chaplain of the Lutheran Seamen's Mission and organizing a congregation, and he had been John's pastor in Ketchikan from 1944 to 1947. During those years he had taken at least one short trip on the *Beloit II*. As my father, he had heard my stories on my return home in early September of 1947 from an unforgettable season as John's deckhand. I wonder how he was able to say good-bye to a storied legend he had known for a quarter of a century. I'm good at holding back tears, but if I'd been there that day? Hard to say if I would have.

TRANSITIONS AND A COLLISION

*I think more than one boat captain would second what happened to
Captain Jason G. Ellis:
"There, but for the grace of God, goes I."*

MY SEASON

In late winter of 1948 I drove to Seattle to shop the corporate headquarters offices of Nakat Packing Corp., the salmon cannery subsidiary of the Great Atlantic & Pacific Tea Company, seeking a job on one of their cadillac cannery tenders. Past experience quickly netted me an offer to go mate on the M/V *Chomley*. I liked the sound of the promotion from deckhand to mate, and it still sounded impressive after I found out the pay was only twenty-five dollars a month more than for a deckhand. For those peanuts you were expected to stand solo wheel watches from midnight until 6:00 a.m.? But, how could I not like being trusted to do my own navigation.

Following my last final exam, I packed my seabag and headed for Maritime Shipyard in Seattle to meet my next boat. I found her to be a classic tender design recently rebuilt from the deck up, including an all-new yacht quality pilothouse, captain's and engineer's staterooms, and roomy galley and heads—a floating castle aft of the original crew quarters in the fo'c'sle. She was one of the tenders working out of Sunny Point Cannery in Ketchikan. Captain Harry Diamond II, an experienced tender man from Ketchikan, quickly put me to work helping ready the boat for the cruise up the Inside Passage.

Meanwhile, my brother Ken was busy working the fleet for a ride to Ketchikan where he had his first deckhand job waiting for him. When he dropped by the *Chomley* to say hi to me, he met Diamond who quickly offered him a bunk. Justification came easy as Ken brought experience, whereas the *Chomley* deckhand was a middle-aged landlubber cousin of Diamond's needing training on the way north.

There was soon good reason to be really glad Ken was aboard. The captain was dead drunk by the time we cleared Ballard Locks into Puget Sound. Unable to stand, he soon lurched to his cabin. We had just enough sea crossing the Strait of Juan de Fuca to propel a green deckhand to the rail to feed the fishes and head from there to his berth in the fo'c'sle. This left Ken and me to navigate the next one hundred miles of inland waters through the evening and night into mid-morning of the next day. We shared those six-hour night wheel watches for the rest of a beautiful trip. The entire crew wished Ken well when he left us to locate Captain Sevrin Hildre and his boat to report for work as deckhand for the season.

The rest of the summer was good except for the times when Diamond got drunk and the rest of us had to step up and get the job done. Fortunately, the deckhand, nicknamed "Babe," turned out to be a friend and sort of father figure, guiding me through the hoops of dealing with his alcoholic cousin.

Late in the season, after acting as skipper for an afternoon brailing a load of salmon from three traps while Captain Diamond was too drunk to get out of his bunk, on return to the cannery I asked for a meeting with Assistant Superintendent Bud Friele. I poured out my frustrations and said, "Bud, I've had it! I either want to go to another boat here or go roam the waterfront for another job."

He calmly replied, "I know of the problem. I'm trying to do something about it. You know his family lives just up the hill from the cannery. If we fire him, who will feed his family? Is he a competent captain when he's sober? How about hangin' in till the season is over?"

What could I say except okay? In retrospect, Bud just wanted to kick the can down to next year, but for me it was a learning experience. Babe's dream summer in Alaska had not been what he'd signed up for. One season crewing for Captain Diamond had been enough for both of us.

* * *

KEN'S SEASON

Ken's first stop on leaving the *Chomley* was the home of the Hildre family to find out where the *Rap III* was docked in Ketchikan awaiting his arrival. A day or two later they were on their way out to the grounds to get their gear down and start catching salmon.

Sevrin Hildre on the M/V *Rap III* trolling off East Cape Addington, Noyes Island
Photo by Tim Olson

The *Rap III* was a sturdy offshore forty-three-foot fishing vessel owned and captained by Sevrin Hildre of Ketchikan. Sevrin was a classic, intrepid, devout, Norse immigrant, commercial fisherman cut from the same cloth and part of the same seafaring community as latter-day Viking John Knaplund. In late winter and spring, he fished off the Gulf of Alaska coast for halibut with an experienced hand aboard on shares. When this fishery closed he hired an eager teenager as crew for the remainder of the season. Knowing the Hildre family from the years our family had lived in Ketchikan, Ken had written to Sevrin asking for a job on the *Rap*—and got it. This would be his first season on a fishing vessel. June and July found them trolling for salmon off Noyes Island and selling their daily catch to Yates & Kram, who had bought out Knaplund & Son at Kelly Cove. Sevrin was a well-known and respected member of the fishing community there, too.

Ken's job was learning and then doing anything Sevrin thought applied to being his assistant operating the boat. Handling lines, steering, boat clean-up, helping in the galley, and eventually being trusted to land and clean fish—all were part of a deckhand's work on a two-man boat. The workday began when starting the engine at daybreak and ended after delivery of the catch at the buying station and tie-up at one of the floats. This might be as late as seven o'clock in the evening for a fifteen-hour day. It could be a seven-day workweek depending on the fishing and work ethic of the captain. Fortunately, Sevrin was tough but not a hard-core driver. You couldn't help but like him.

He was also something of a character, or maybe it was just his boat's engine that gave him some notoriety. It was a monstrous single-cylinder diesel workhorse made in Norway by the Rap Engine Company. Its sound was a poop', poop' poooop, turning a heavy big-torque variable pitch propeller so slowly you could watch it turn under the stern. It was built to run forever. With throttle wide open, the boats it powered would never win a race to anywhere.

While other veteran fishermen with boats originally powered by heavy low-RPM engines of one or two cylinders had converted to multi-cylinder engines, Sevrin was as slow as his engine to see any compelling reason to convert his boat. Sevrin and his engine had become partners. For example, knowing the time it took for the prop to reverse to stop his boat, he enjoyed coming into a dock alone (no one in the pilothouse), shuffling out on deck to pick up a landing line, and saying to the engine, "You can stop now." And the boat would stop dead at the dock while taciturn Sevrin casually passed the landing line for tie-up. Dock bystanders would look on dumbfounded by the performance. That was Sevrin.

Come August Sevrin had a singular coveted contract with Nakat Packing during the fish trap season to maintain and watch the highliner Cape Addington Fish Trap, the only floating fish trap ever to my knowledge to be sited totally exposed on the open ocean. It was custom-built and reinforced to hopefully survive the onslaught of open ocean storms. This trap caught obscene numbers of salmon—over 100,000 in one day more than once! It was serviced by boat because it was too dangerous to put a customary trap watchman's shack on it—the shack would be washed away by any serious Alaska Gulf gale. There was no safe escape, even by lifeboat, from a storm. You would have to leave against a breaking head sea with the nearest shelter miles away. A separate buoy on cable to a heavy trap anchor was set off to the side, behind and clear of the trap, and a safe distance out from shore, to provide secure moorage for the watchman's boat to tie to when not working on the trap. A seasoned trustworthy skipper with a seaworthy boat was needed to tend this trap. Sevrin was the man. The *Rap III* was the boat.

I don't know of a more starkly beautiful or foreboding stretch of coastline in Southeast Alaska. Storm waves over the centuries have carved caves in the shoreline's desolate rocky cliffs. The incoming breaking groundswell compresses the air in the caves. On release these giant compressed air bubbles sound off with eerie sounds of cannon "booming" on the too-close and threatening rocky shore. This was Sevrin's summer office.

Ultimately Ken, followed by our younger brother Tim, spent almost three summers with Sevrin on the *Rap III*. Tim subsequently published a fine memoir of his experiences commercial fishing. He includes a moving celebration of Sevrin's stoical Viking ways:

Blow at Addington Trap

Severin's stubby finger pointed out the wheelhouse door
Toward two rocks forming a cradle for the Rap.
"Timmy, if the trap should break up and come down
on us, ve vill put the Rap right between those rocks."
I tried to make out the crack in the rocks,
invisible in the falling darkness.
"Ya, Timmy, ve vaited too long to round the Cape.
Ve vait it out."
Sevrin sits stolidly in the wheelhouse,
A stub of a cigar held easily in his mouth,
Idling dead slow ahead in the blackness,
Bow to the sea; stern to the foaming rocks.
I go below, roll the night away in my bunk.
In the morning, I lurch from my bunk
To the deck, stare into the stinging spray,
My ears aching from the pounding surf.
I greet a grey dawn without a horizon, the sky
reaching swells overpowering the falling clouds.
"Ya, Ya, Timmy, you go put on some mush and coffee,
Ve have breakfast. The veather is coming down now."
Adapted from *"Salmon Summers"* by Tim Olson

The pilothouse on the beach at nearby Kelly Cove is all that remains of one troller and his boat lost on that shore. I wonder what Mom, a friend forever of the Hildre family and trusting Sevrin, would have thought had she been apprised of the risks of life off the Addington coast. Almost every commercial fishing community began spring with religious services to pray for the safety of the fathers and sons about to cast off for another season. No summer went by without the loss of lives at sea. Every major commercial fishing town had and has a memorial to those lost at sea. I'm thankful Mom's prayers were answered.

By the end of the summer, Cape Addington's enchantment had cast its spell on Ken Olson. He was hooked on life at sea. He eagerly learned from Sevrin all about living and working on a workboat and all there was to know of commercial fishing for king and coho salmon. He loved the excitement of landing a big king and the camaraderie of Kelly Cove fishermen answering to names like Tonto Bill and Merkur Mac. Perhaps he was already dreaming of fishing his own boat off Addington. I never heard him mention seeking another job on another boat anywhere else in Alaska.

* * *

COLLISION

Occasionally calamity,
Begins accidentally,
To end as comedy!

One of the biggest events of the 1948 season while Ken and I were both fishing Alaska waters was the collision of two vessels in Kaigani Harbor. News of the accident spread like wildfire through the Southeast Alaska salmon fishing community:

Boats collide near Kaigani Harbor[13]

Two fish packers, the M/V Kiska, Captain Jason G. Ellis, and M/V Mayflower, Captain John N. Garner, collided last night in the darkness of the channel entrance to South Kaigani Harbor, seventy miles southwest of Ketchikan, on the southeast coast of Dall Island. Following the impact both vessels sank in shallow water. Both crews and one passenger aboard the Mayflower are safe. A tug and barge for flotation is being dispatched from Ketchikan to raise the boats and bring them back to Ketchikan for assessment of the damages.

The owner/managers of the two fish buying stations in Kaigani are seeking replacement vessels to service their operations supplying food and fuel to a fleet of up to seventy salmon trollers fishing out of Kaigani as well as provide transport for the salmon catch from these boats to Ketchikan.

The incident got my attention because I knew Captain "Jay" Ellis of the M/V *Kiska*. In early September 1947, the *Beloit II*, my home as a deckhand that season, dropped me on the dock in Ketchikan to find passage back to Seattle. Toward the end of the first day I boarded a small freighter loading the canned salmon pack of a one-line independent cannery for shipment south. To my delight, the mate was Jay Ellis who had begun his own seafaring some summers

---

13   I had to recollect this front-page feature story of the *Ketchikan Daily News* from July 24, 1948, as best I could because the *Daily News* archives don't go back that far.

previously as deckhand on the same *Beloit II* where I'd spent the season. Jay soon told me if I would work in the hold loading cases of salmon for two days, I was on my way home. Within a week of getting off the *Beloit*, I was in Seattle with new friends.

Perhaps two weeks after the collision I ran into Jay in downtown Ketchikan. I asked what happened. This is Captain Ellis's story as I remember it:

It was like a crazy nightmare. We were mid-channel on our way out of Kaigani after loading fish at the scow for delivery in Ketchikan. Though I didn't know it—heck, who expects another boat to be showing up there at three in the morning—the *Mayflower* was coming in. I'd already sent my deckhand back to his bunk to get some sleep. The engineer was still in the engine room. After setting on a straight course, I'd stepped out on deck to take a pee when I spotted the running lights of another boat. Turned out to be the *Mayflower*, bearing down on us on a collision course. I jumped back in the pilothouse and saw no way to avoid a collision. Instantly my thought was of the *Kiska* and the best way to minimize damage to her. As the stem is the strongest point, I decided, "The hell with the *Mayflower*," and to take the *Mayflower* on my bow before she hit us. So I turned my wheel hard over and rammed her.

Since the *Kiska* was still set up without pilothouse control of the engine except for throttle RPM, I was dependent on the engineer to answer bells from the pilothouse for forward, neutral, and reverse. Thinking we had no problem on the *Kiska*, I rang for neutral and stepped out on deck to call to the *Mayflower* and ask how we could render assistance. Confirmed, I saw the best way, as the boats lay, to go around to the other side of the *Mayflower*, take her alongside and to shallow water for beaching. So I dashed up the ladder to the flying bridge (for 360-degree visibility), rang the engineer for forward gear, and added some speed to get around the *Mayflower*. Meanwhile, I saw two guys on the *Mayflower* already back in the well deck setting up to man the on-deck bilge pump.

So here we were rounding the *Mayflower* a little fast with plans to take her in. What I didn't know was the stem of the *Kiska* was totally stove-in. Water was pouring in through the fo'c'sle and flowing to and through the engine room. This so rattled Fred, my engineer, he panicked, forgot all about us being underway, and abandoned the engine to scramble up the companionway to on-deck safety. I didn't know that either!

So now we were coming at the Mayflower from the other side. I rang bells for neutral and reverse with no response. Unbelievable! By that time it was too close to turn the wheel hard over and miss her. Just before impact, leaning forward over the flying bridge, I looked down at the closing with the *Mayflower*, helpless to do anything about it. Seeing us bearing down on them again, the two shocked guys on the *Mayflower* abandoned the pump to watch us. Just before the hit, I heard one holler at the other, "Shit, Ernie, JUMP! He's going to hit us again." And off Ernie went headed for the stern and, I guess, into the ocean.[14]

At that point, there was nothing I could do above so I went down on deck to find my engineer and deckhand on deck and okay. It was obvious we were sinking. So I went to the pilothouse and grabbed my logbook. We all ended up on the flying bridge as we settled to that depth in the shallows. While waiting for rescue, I wrote up an account of the collision as favorable as possible for me and the *Kiska*.[15]

* * *

Both boats sank in the fortunate shallows at the entrance to the harbor. A tug and barge with pumps was dispatched from Ketchikan to temporarily patch the wrecks, float and secure them to the barge, and bring them back for shipyard inspection and repairs. The *Mayflower* was back in the water within a couple of months. Declared a total loss, the hulk of the *Kiska*, lashed to a scow to keep her afloat, was ignominiously paraded up the harbor channel the short distance from the shipyard past the Sunny Point cannery dock, where my boat, the *Chomley*, was tied up, to be beached at high tide inshore near the north side of the cannery. I took a melancholy self-guided tour of the stripped and broken derelict a day later. Thereafter, the wreck served for years as an attraction for Ketchikan kids to explore and speculate on her past life and sad end.

In a January 8, 2012, telephone interview of Jay's widow, Marilee Ellis, Marilee said:

> *Jay and I met after the accident with the Kiska. He was a deckhand on a towboat. Soon after we married, he gave up on boating and moved on to work for Uncle Bob Ellis at Ellis Airlines in Ketchikan. He stayed with the airline through the merger with Alaska Coastal and eventual merger into Alaska Airlines where he worked until retirement. We lived in Ketchikan after our marriage, raising our family, until "Alaska" moved us to Juneau in 1969. Jay never captained another boat after the Kiska. Occasionally, after going to work for Ellis, he worked part-time decking on towboats for the Ketchikan Pulp Mill. Not a lot of boating. He lived a good life and*

---

14 The young deckhand must have been the "jumper" because Harold Cowan of Ketchikan was the passenger, according to Clyde Cowan who recalls brother Harold's account of the collision, as told over the years, being something like what's written here.

15 This is the tale I've been telling and retelling for sixty years in classic confirmation of Murphy's Law, "When one thing goes wrong, everything goes wrong!" If you don't believe it, I'd love to tell you of someone who could confirm it. Sadly, Jay has passed away. None of the other witnesses are still alive, with the possible exception of Ernie Garner but, if so, where he might be located now is unknown.

died here in Juneau at age eighty-six.

I hope Jay was able to eventually put the *Kiska* fiasco behind him and find satisfaction in his career with the airline. In retrospect, the collision was an accident waiting to happen. I crewed on vessels similar to the *Kiska* in the same waters, and experienced and witnessed the compromises to safety on fish packers and other boats running marginally equipped, and sometimes shorthanded, in an era of loose laws and rare inspections. The District Court for the Territory of Alaska, however, found Jay's version of the collision faulted in such terms as "fabricated and incredible." As losers in District Court, OAKSMITH et al., owners of the *Kiska*, appealed the verdict. Substantiating Jay's account to me are a few excerpts from the appeal of the original decision dated May 26, 1953:

> *On the night in question, the two vessels collided in the channel inside the harbor. Neither ship blew any whistle signal. There were two impacts. The first occurred when the Kiska headed directly for the Mayflower and the Kiska's stem struck the Mayflower portside. The Kiska backed away from the port side of the Mayflower, passed around the stern of the Mayflower, and while the Mayflower was "lying dead" in the water, the Kiska proceeded along Mayflower's starboard side, and under engine power, struck the Mayflower puncturing her hull below the water line, with resulting serious damage to her to such an extent that she sank in shallow water. The Kiska, having sustained serious damage was beached and became a total loss.*
>
> *Other than Captain Ellis, the only other member of the crew of the Kiska, giving evidence in the court pertinent to the collisions per se was Fred Lind, engineer of the Kiska. He was in the engine room before and when the first impact occurred, and consequently his testimony throws no light on the principal factor in an ascertainment by the court of what the trial judge found to be the proximate, efficient and predominant cause of the collision, namely, the absence of the master of the Kiska from the pilothouse and ship controls at the critical periods of her navigation while proceeding outbound along the channel inside of South Kaigani Harbor and to the precise point of the first impact.*

There you have it. Note the engineer of the *Kiska* "was in the engine room before and when the first impact occurred." The appeal includes no mention of where he was when the second impact occurred. Thus Jay's story, to me, including his candidness about what he'd written in the *Kiska* logbook, holds water in accord with the legal findings. As appellant and loser on the appeal, OAKSMITH et al. were stuck with paying damages and the cost of repairing the *Mayflower* to GARNER et al., plus all their own legal costs, plus writing off total loss of the *Kiska* since there was no hull insurance of the vessel.

LADY LUCK DELIVERS

FROM HELL TO HEAVEN TWICE

In the late spring of 1949, I drove to Maritime Shipyard in Ballard, where the Nakat Packing fishing boat fleet was berthed in the off-season, to check in with Port Captain Henry Gunderson and find out where I was on the boat crew lists. Imagine my surprise to find I was back on the *Chomley* as mate under Captain Harry Diamond. My next move was to call Bud Friele and ask for reassignment to another boat. Persuasive as ever, Bud said, "Dave, I've talked to Harry. He says he's off the bottle and promises to stay off. His oldest son will be with you going up. I want you on that boat. How about it?"

"Okay, I hear you," I said. Harry was sober as a judge going north and stayed that way.

In late June I got my second surprise. Yates & Kram, the buyers of the Kelly Cove Fish Buying Operation and *Beloit II* from John and Carsten Knaplund in early 1948, had ended up without a captain for the *Beloit* in the middle of the king salmon run. They needed a skipper; somebody suggested me. They were desperate enough to take the gamble and offered me the job. Nevermind I was nineteen going on twenty, had only decking experience on the *Louisiana* and *Beloit* plus the previous season as mate on the *Chomley*, and zero other experience qualifying me to be a captain. Cliff Yates, the *Beloit* co-owner, found me on the *Chomley*. I was too blown away by the offer to ask why me. I didn't recall the scary stack fire I'd once witnessed to ask if engine repairs had been made to prevent recurrence. I didn't have sense enough to ask a single question that might have given me second thoughts about taking the job. I didn't know I was still just a kid being offered a man's job. Before the day was over I was on the *Beloit* with two young teenagers as crew on the passage from Ketchikan to Kelly Cove.

It didn't take long before I realized I was in over my head, and the two crewmen soon figured out I was in no way prepared to be their captain. The boat was run down from poor maintenance. Worse yet, no long overdue repairs had been made to the cranky old Fairbanks Morse diesel engine. Underway, the beast was still loading up the exhaust stack with oil-laden soot until it got hot enough to burn, throwing out a rain of fire and sparks, and black smoke threatening to burn us to the waterline. Fortunately, though I was either too dumb or too proud to go to the owners with the problems, my crewmen weren't. On perhaps the third delivery to Ketchikan, Mr. Yates met me at the dock. He told me they had chartered another packer and were tying up the *Beloit* to replace the engine.

Then I got my third surprise. Yates told me, "I know you did your best. Now go pack your seabag. Then head over to Ellis Air Lines where they have a ticket for you to take the next flight to Waterfall where they have a job waiting for you on one of their tenders."

Nakat Packing Corp. cannery at Waterfall, Alaska
Tender on left is the Golden West.
Photo by Dave Olson

The man had contacted a Nakat Cannery superintendent who had apparently shopped the canneries to find a slot for me on one of their boats. It turned out to be going mate on the tender *Quaker Maid*—a beautiful big boat I had admired close up during a couple of coincidental channel passings two summers before while working on the beat up old *Beloit*. My reprieve from the *Beloit* was euphoric escape on the *Quaker*.

Cannery Tender M/V *Quaker Maid* underway near Waterfall
Courtesy of Pete Franett, Franett Family Archive

* * *

MORE SURPRISES!

The *Quaker Maid* was the last wooden "seiner design" cannery tender (launched in 1935) custom-built for Nakat service. She was eighty feet long and powered by a 235 Washington diesel with a hold capacity of thirty thousand salmon. The pilothouse, galley, fo'c'sle crew quarters, and heads all seemed double the size of the cramped quarters I thought were fine until I boarded the *Quaker*. Yacht-quality brightwork, polished brass, and varnished hardwood rails and trim also set her apart as one of the prides of the Nakat tender fleet. The crew was different, too. The captain was twenty-four-year-old Norman Buschmann, private school-educated son of Eigil Buschmann, general superintendent of all Nakat canneries.

The crew character was Pete Ekern, the chief engineer. He had been an engineer on Nakat boats forever. When the *Quaker* was built, Pete was there to influence layout of the engine room, equipment, and bench arrangements. Paintwork was top-of-the-line sparkling white enamel. Brass was polished to a high shine. The engine was painted green with red side levers and pumps. At the top of the companionway ladder down to the engine room was a small platform with a Dutch door to the deck. Squat and rotund, Pete spent a lot of time standing in this doorway observing the passing scenery and crew action on deck. I quickly learned, or maybe someone told me, that success on the *Quaker* depended on getting along with dour and taciturn Pete.

There was obvious bad blood between the captain and engineer. Young Norman, probably already an alcoholic, was destined to fail staying dry on the job while trying to survive working on the wrong side of Pete. I soon discovered he was taking nips almost daily, often beginning early in the morning.

Perhaps a week after my boarding, the *Quaker* was sent out to Noyes Island to help tend the setting of the Cape Addington trap. On the way out, I saw Norman have a brief, angry exchange with a stoical Pete visibly leaning out over his Dutch door as Norm passed on his way to the pilothouse. When he got there, he went directly to a bottle in his cabin to quell his rage. He was drunk by the time we reached the trap site. He misjudged speed and angle attempting to make a landing alongside the trap. The slight ground swell was just enough to raise the boat so when we came up on the head log, our guardrail came down hard, breaking the rail loose from the hull at the port quarter. Nobody was hurt, but damage to the *Quaker* was sufficient enough to know it would require shipyard repairs. By the time we got back to the cannery, Captain Buschmann had his seabag packed. He jumped off the boat and headed for the next flight to Ketchikan. I heard he was drunk for a week. That's the last I ever heard of him—ever!

The cannery bosses were also waiting for us at the dock to check the damage. An hour later Assistant Superintendent Don Franett came down to the boat looking for me. He knew I'd just come off a few weeks skippering the *Beloit* on the same passage to Ketchikan.

"Dave, do you think you could take the *Quaker* to Ketchikan for repairs?"

"Sure," I replied calmly as if I did it every day, while my heart raced a mile a minute.

He called the crew together for briefing, including my appointment as temporary skipper for the trip. We cast off at daybreak. We ran into pea-soup fog approaching Ketchikan early the next morning. Fortunately, those were waters I knew well so we had no problem finding the Sunny Point Cannery to tie up behind the *Chomley*. The tender crews like to have died when they got up to discover the *Quaker Maid* at their dock—and me the skipper. Most of all Captain Diamond, my recent captain, flabbergasted by the news, who soon found me to ask, "How the hell did you get this job?"

He returned to earth when I told him, "Heck, it's only temporary till they settle on a reshuffle of the skippers of the Waterfall boats. But it sure is fun!"

The week on the ways at the shipyard was mostly a mini-vacation for the crew. The return trip to Waterfall was uneventful. Though I got along fine with Pete, I was delighted to turn the boat over to veteran Captain Henry

Gunderson and move back to the fo'c'sle. Pete was happy, too, because Captain Buschmann was off his boat.

Captain Gunderson suffered from intermittent back spasms that caused him to occasionally take a day off. On two of those days during the brailing season, I got the high sign to take the *Quaker* out to collect the salmon catch from its quota of traps. All the stars had lined up that year to produce salmon runs in the jillions, leading to a record-breaking pack. Bringing in capacity loads was a daily affair for a couple of weeks for all the tenders. Trips back to the cannery with the well deck awash and the bow up were heady stuff! Even old Pete was impressed.

Ken had been fishing with Sevrin Hildre on the *Rap III* through July when they surfaced, as usual, tending the Cape Addington Trap. We were able to chat briefly a few times during that season when the *Quaker* got the call to brail Addington Trap. We would find the *Rap* already tied up at the trap on our arrival. Sevrin and Ken would have it ready for brailing the thousands of thrashing salmon into the cavernous hold of the *Quaker*. After hearty greetings they worked with our crew loading the salmon aboard.

To my knowledge Sevrin and his *Rap III* tended the incredibly profitable Addington Trap from its first to last season, over two decades. The end came with the advent of Alaska statehood and the abolition of fish traps. This marked the close of an era as the salmon canneries ceased to be economically sustainable and one-by-one closed operations. Sevrin continued to fish a few more years before moving on to a well-earned retirement.

* * *

KEN JOINS ME CREWING ON THE *QUAKER MAID*

Following the season-ending brail of salmon from the Addington Trap, Sevrin and Ken closed the trap and headed for Waterfall for settle-up with the cannery, refueling, and return to home port Ketchikan. They docked the *Rap* in Waterfall on a day when my *Quaker Maid* was also tied up at the cannery, which led to a meet-up with Ken.

"Hey, Don Franett (assistant superintendent) is looking for a second engineer for the *Quaker* to finish our season. How about joining us?" I asked.

Soon we were on our way down the dock for Ken to meet with Pete. The next stop was the cannery office. Franett hired him on the spot. By suppertime he had moved aboard and was down in the engine room with Pete getting squared away on his new job.

We enjoyed a profitable first month (read: lots of overtime) doing a variety of towing and scow handling jobs. By that time almost all of the cannery employees and all of the boats were gone except the small vessel kept there for the winter watchman's use. There were two more laid-back weeks, mostly at the dock, interspersed with a few small jobs for the *Quaker* closing up the deserted cannery. Since Capt. Gunderson had already returned to Seattle to resume his off-season job as the Nakat fleet port captain, another senior captain was assigned to be our skipper for the trip south. I'm glad Franett didn't decide to roll the dice and ask me to try my luck skippering the *Quaker* for the trip south. I wasn't ready. We both knew it.

On the cruise down the Inside Passage we had a damaged rigging scow in tow that slowed us down, and we ran into every kind of fall weather, ranging from CAVU (ceiling and visibility unlimited) to pea-soup fog to storms. The bad weather forced us into pristine secluded British Columbia anchorages none of us on the boat had ever previously visited to wait for clearing. It was pleasure cruising on a paycheck.

There was satisfaction all around as we tied up in Ballard, home again, and looked back on a "big catch" season. Cranky curmudgeon Pete had turned out to be a pussycat working with Ken.

"What's the secret of working for Pete?" I asked.

"It's easy," he replied with a grin. "Just do what he's taught you to do when you're suppose to do it. That's mostly sticking an oil can up your ass and lubing the engine every thirty minutes!"

* * *

CAPTAIN "COOL"

For Those in Peril on the Sea
Third Verse
O Sacred Spirit, who didst brood
Upon the chaos dark and rude,
And bad'st its angry tumult cease,
And gavest light and life and peace:
Oh, hear us when we cry to thee
For those in peril on the sea!
—From the hymn "Eternal Father Strong To Save,"
William Whiting, 1860

All things considered, the most enjoyable of my seven summers at sea was probably the season of 1950. Don Franett asked me to go mate on the tender *Frances E.* The *Frances* was a big heavy-built boat with John (Jack) Hagueness as captain. Jack was a young navy veteran finishing his education in the off-season. He had worked his way up from decking to an acting-skipper slot on another Nakat tender the previous season. This was his first full-season assignment. He was a born skipper with a happy crew. So what made the season so memorable?

Cannery Tender M/V *Frances E* lying at salmon trap
Photo by Dave Olson

The events culminating in what came to be called the "morning of mourning" began for me, and the crew on the *Frances,* on the previous afternoon. For some reason we had been diverted to Port Bazan on the west coast of Dall Island to pick up the catch of Nakat seiners. Near the end of the five-hour run from the cannery, we were met by a forecast of serious southeast gale and growing seas. On the way into the anchorage, in falling darkness, we were passed by the heavily loaded packer M/V *Vermay* on her way to Ketchikan. Perhaps an hour or more after we anchored, we were visited by the skiff man from a seiner to tell us a Mayday was being transmitted by the *Vermay*, with a crew of three on board, reporting foundering in the heavy seas.

As we had the biggest, most seaworthy vessel in the harbor, Jack put our crew to work immediately battening down hatches and otherwise preparing the *Frances* for heavy weather so we could go out and hopefully render assistance. As we were about to fire up the engine and raise anchor, Jack, listening to the radio, called out to let us know the *Vermay* had stopped transmitting. This was soon followed by a message from another vessel, just arrived at the scene, reporting the *Vermay* was already inside the surf line, precluding any attempt at assistance until the storm passed and daylight came.

Following a fitful night, we raised anchor at daybreak and proceeded south to cruise the coast on what turned out to be a sparkling clear day with a northwest breeze. A few miles out we found the wreck of the *Vermay* lying mostly upright but lodged among the monster rocks on the boulder-strewn shore. We spent an hour scanning the coastline through binoculars looking for signs of survivors and saw none. This was reported to the coast guard who reported dispatching aircraft for surveillance and the cutter *Citrus* to the site. There was nothing more we could do so we returned to Port Bazan to load salmon for delivery to the cannery. To my knowledge, there were no reports of survivors.

The *Frances E* burying bow in a big wave, Gulf of Alaska, off Cape Ulitka, Noyes Island
Photo by Dave Olson

In addition to this sad event, I experienced a hellish half minute after the actual fishing season was over. All the tenders were busy visiting the traps to pick up watchmen and, following the raising of the anchors holding the traps in place, tow them to a protected tideflat for winter storage near the cannery. We were on our way back to the cannery on a dark evening with heavy rain and poor visibility. I was alone in the pilothouse as the rest of the crew had a hot pinochle game going in the galley. We were proceeding north in Kaigani Strait between Dall and Long Islands. Approaching Channel Islands the course called for rounding the easterly island close with the shore on the port side until you could look south from the pilothouse port door and see the narrow gap between the islands, and then resume a northerly course to pass safely between nearby reefs on either side. Bear in mind, those were the days before radar, GPS navigation, or even depth sounders, and there were no lights or other navigation aids in the area. I knew the route and the location of the reefs, and Jack knew it, so his concentration was on the card game.

Rounding the island I looked for the view back through the gap just as heavy rain reduced visibility to nothing but gray. Immediately reducing speed to drifting so Jack would know he was needed in the pilothouse would have been the right move. Instead, I guessed the remainder time on course and then turned north. I turned too soon. A few minutes later we slammed into the submerged rock reef. The time was about eight o'clock.

The bow went up about twenty degrees. The boat lurched forward a few yards, then the engine died, the boat stopped, and we listed to port about fifteen degrees. There was an eerie silence. I was shocked. Jack came to the pilothouse door.

"I'm sorry!" I moaned.

He quietly responded, "Calm down. Where are we?"

"On the reef we take to starboard after clearing Channel Islands."

"Okay, you go forward and I'll go aft for a quick look."

We both grabbed flashlights. A quick scan revealed no visible leaks. The depth was six feet amidships—not good for a vessel with an eight-foot draft. Back in the pilothouse, we checked the tide table. We had grounded on an ebb tide with about two more hours to low water. Best of all, the flood tide calculated to rise high enough to float us off by about four in the morning. Jack said, "Just to make sure, Dave, you and Sig (our deckhand) take the flashlights and check the bilges from stem to stern for leaks."

Jack radioed the station at the cannery, manned 24-7, to calmly report our grounding and location. Don Franett was soon on the mic to tell us he was dispatching a tender to our location. Closing, he said, "Jack, good luck and call me every thirty minutes to let me know how you are making out."

Then Jack went back to the galley, asked the cook to make a fresh pot of coffee to replace the pot spilled in the grounding, and talked the card players into resuming their game. With nothing to be gained, hating myself, I divided some of the time between making the rounds of the boat continually checking for leaks and shining my flashlight overboard to wonder at the spectral images of tidal life on the reef. Meanwhile, the depth continued to shallow as the tide went out, and the port list of the hull increased accordingly to perhaps thirty degrees, with water on the slanted lower port side deck. On a subsequent radio call, this development led Jack to say, "Well, major problem now is keeping the cards on the galley table." Even I had to laugh. If we had hit that reef at low water, our *Frances* would probably have been a season-ending wreck instead of an affordable grounding. We had been lucky.

As predicted, when the flood neared high water, we floated free, the engineer started the trusted Atlas diesel, the propeller turned, and we were on our way to the cannery. A diver's inspection revealed a nasty ten-foot gash in the keel and surface damage to the hull—all reparable at the shipyard in Seattle. I have no idea what Jack wrote in his account of the accident. All he told me was, "Dave, don't worry about it."

I wish I'd appreciated the wisdom of his advice. Seven months later I realized in a surprise call what he must have done for me in that report. We moved on to finish the season and return to Seattle. If I could locate him, I'd call him today to say thanks, but he disappeared from my life after the 1951 season, probably to pursue a career ashore. In today's vernacular, he was "Captain Cool."

A REMARKABLE SEASON

Commercial fishing is an emotional seasonal business of highs and lows.
Every season is different. A successful season feels really good!

During the 1950–1951 school year, I continued living at home in Tacoma and commuting to Pacific Lutheran College in nearby Parkland. It was just another late winter evening when a call came from Don Franett, still assistant superintendent at Nakat Packing Corporation's Waterfall cannery in Alaska. He was lining up cannery tender crews for the 1951 season. He needed a skipper for the *Golden West* because Walter Smith had been promoted to captain of the new tender *Eigil B.* Since I was only twenty-one and, as mate, had managed to run the *Frances E.* aground by myself on a dark and stormy night late the previous season, Don's call was a total surprise. When I found my voice, I'm sure I thanked him and promised to do my best.

* * *

KEN GOES FOR BROKE IN THE FISH BUSINESS

As I geared up to skipper the *Golden West*, I discovered Ken had been sneaking over to Seattle between college classes to chew the rag with commercial fishermen he had come to know while working for Sevrin Hildre on the *Rap III.* Their hangout was at the home and boatyard on Seattle's Lake Union of legendary trolling boat builder and fisherman Bill Ingraham, aka "Tonto Bill" (for his fishing boat named the *Tonto III*) or "Whispering Willy" (because he was notorious for spreading the word on the airwaves as to where the fishing was hot, when it was not). Tonto Bill only fished out of the buying station at Kelly Cove, Noyes Island, leading to informal recognition of his prerogatives, including the primo moorage location and a title as mayor of Kelly Cove.

Cannery Tender M/V *Golden West* docked at Waterfall
Courtesy of Don Franett. Walter Smith

In these conversations, Ken caught a vision of catching salmon from his own troller.

"Why wait—why not buy a boat now? Never know I can't unless I go for it!" he'd say, neverminding that he was only nineteen going on twenty with less than $2,000 in savings. He would quietly visit Fishermen's Terminal, the commercial boat harbor in Seattle, unable to resist the urge to check out "For Sale" signs.

He took me with him on one of his boat hunts. All I really recall is our first stop to check in with Tonto Bill on leads to boats. The morning was over by the time Bill had shown me his yard and shop and talked boat buying business with Ken over two or more cups of coffee. I can still hear Bill telling me, "Ken can do this—he knows the trip to Kelly Cove and Sevrin taught him trolling. Bet a boatload he'll catch his share." I believed him.

Pretty soon Ken found the *Lady Fay*: thirty-two feet long, Chrysler-powered, and fully equipped for $3,500. Since he would need some of his savings for minor repairs and maintenance, not to mention covering expenses for the 750-mile cruise from Seattle to Kelly Cove and the fishing grounds off Noyes Island in Southeast Alaska, he was $2,000 short of the minimum needed to buy the boat. He needed a high roller to back him because in those days there was no such thing as insurance on small commercial fishing vessels.

The natural first step was to discuss his vision with family. So Ken brought his dream home to the dinner table. Dad listened with lots of questions and a gleam in his eye. Mom was mum, showing visible reservations. The next morning Dad and Ken went to the bank to find out what Dad probably already knew—no bank was about to loan any kind of money in those days to a nineteen-year-old kid without a co-signer/guarantor.

While they were gone, Mom said, "I hope Dad and Ken know what they're doing."

"Sure, it'll be okay," I replied.

Sure enough, though little was ever left from Dad's salary after paying the bills and savings were peanuts, the incurable romantic in Dad had left prudence at home when they went to the bank. Also, since the bank president was a personal friend of Dad's, I'm sure Dad simply signed the note with no questions asked about capacity to cover if the boat was lost. They soon returned with a certified check. Ken was quickly on his way to Seattle to buy the boat. I'm sure Mom said a few prayers for safe passage and return home in the fall. If Dad, our preacher father, prayed at all I'm sure it was simply for all the king and silver salmon off Noyes Island to find their way to the *Lady Fay*.

My pleasure for the remainder of that spring was to spend most weekends helping Ken get the *Lady Fay* ready for the season. For shakedown he ran the boat to the Port of Tacoma to be closer to home for final fitting out, gear testing, stocking, and fueling. For the cruise north to Alaska, he recruited our cousin Jesse (Jake) Thompson to share the wheel watches and galley chores until they reached the fishing grounds.

Ken's troller M/V *Lady Fay* coming in for a landing at a Nakat Salmon Trap
Photo by Dave Olson

I'll never forget the family going down to the dock to see them off with Jake sitting on the hatch cover strumming his guitar and singing some sailor's ditty. But commercial trolling for salmon is a lonely, strenuous occupation. Fishermen leave their overnight anchorages at daybreak for the run out to the grounds. If the weather is cooperating, and even if the fish are not, it may be near dusk before the hang-tough highliners[16] tie up at the fish buyer's station to unload catches. Ken's days were spent fishing the open ocean waters off Cape Addington, Noyes Island. There was time between bites for the poet to say it all in this paean to fishing kings off Addington:

Alone Near the Breakers

Have you heard the sound of the sea
off Cape Addington?
Where the great mother ocean
heaves her breast out
And the stellar lions splash
under the August moon?
Running fast and deep,
following a trace,
Twenty fathoms down, bright
golden-backed king salmon
weight thirty pounds.
I dizzy and delighted hear
The song of my lines.

–Ken Olson

* * *

ROOKIE CAPTAIN

While Ken was going north and catching salmon, I was busy, too. My *Golden West* lured me over to Seattle where she was docked at Maritime Shipyard next to Fishermen's Terminal, where Nakat Packing Corp. moored and serviced its fleet between seasons. I was warmly welcomed by my former captain on the *Quaker Maid* and now port captain, Henry Gunderson, who was responsible for the fleet and eager to get one more boat turned over to a skipper and sent to sea. The *"Goldie,"* a sturdy unpretentious fish hauling towboat, was already freshly painted with annual maintenance completed on the engine, winches, and other gear. Assistant Superintendent Franett had already hired the remainder of the crew—

16 "Highliners" were the hard-core experienced fishermen who perennially caught the most fish.

mate, deckhand, first and second engineers, and cook. My first job was starting the galley stove to make coffee in preparation for welcoming visitors and crew. Checking a myriad of details—like charts, lines, sea stores (duty/tax free booze and tobacco desired by crew), signing captain's papers, and just getting to know my boat and crew—all made for active, fun days. This was followed by a short cruise to swing compass and refuel. Last came loading groceries.

Me conning the *Golden West* on a warm sunny day
Photo by Dave Olson

June 6, 1800 hours (6:00 p.m.), found us underway for Alaska. Within two hours our engineer and cook were drunk. The engineer managed to get a nasty burn off the engine from the rolling of the boat during the crossing of the Strait of Juan de Fuca. The cook was too hungover to make breakfast the next morning. I told a green hand to relax as it was almost expected and traditional. The rest of the crew just laughed—pleased neither man had fallen overboard.

* * *

FISH TRAP PIRACY

For many Alaskans, stealing salmon from fish traps owned by Lower 48-based fishing and canning operations like Libby, McNeill & Libby and Nakat Packing Corporation, a subsidiary of the Great Atlantic & Pacific Tea Company, was considered to be an admirable accomplishment. A fish still in the water, even one trapped in a fish trap, wasn't caught yet. Additionally, there were tales of the early exploits of legendary players like Eigil Buschmann, general superintendent of Nakat Packing operations, and the Brindle brothers, owners of the Ward Cove Cannery near Ketchikan, doing whatever it took to maximize the catch and pack. Territorial Senator Andy Gunderson, a seiner out of Ketchikan with an all-black boat, was a talk-of-the town trap and creek robber during the forties.

In late July I heard Ken and the *Lady Fay* had been hired to patrol the Nakat-owned Pt. McLeod and Cape Muzon fish traps set near the south end of Dall Island, about forty miles south of the cannery. This was a good deal for Ken. The silver salmon runs would be dwindling for reduced catches by trollers during the fish trap season catching the pink and chum salmon runs. He could make more certain income easier on trap patrol than he would probably make trolling. His job was to cruise between the traps during the night and keep pirates from stealing fish from them. He was to be the Nakat company cop. I thought this was really neat as we had not seen each other since Ken and the *Lady Fay* had left Seattle almost three months earlier. Surely our paths would cross sometime during the season. Then by coincidence, or because Don Franett was a thoughtful boss who saw an opportunity for Ken and me to meet up, Don dispatched the *Golden West* on opening day of the trap fishing season to make the first brails of fish from those same traps.

On approach to the Cape Muzon Trap I was surprised and delighted to see the *Lady Fay* coming in, too, with not just Ken hanging out the pilothouse window, but also our younger brother Jerry on the bow handling the lines as Ken's deckhand. So there we were at about 7:30 p.m.—the *Goldie* lying alongside the trap ready to board the fish with the *Lady Fay* on the port side tied to the *Goldie*. Ken, Jerry, and I had a joyous reunion. Ken told me prices had been good, but more importantly, the fish gods had favored him with a fine catch of kings to sell at Kelly Cove. He was in the chips.

We lowered our brailer net into the spiller of the trap churning with frantic fish. We loaded a few thousand salmon, of which almost all were big, bright silver and king salmon prime for sale at the fish buying station a few miles away in Kaigani Harbor. As the brailing ended, I left the deck for the pilothouse to respond to the scheduled 8:00 p.m. radio call from Don at the cannery to each of the tenders. His primary purpose was to get updates on boat locations and estimates of the fish counts to be unloaded from each boat on returns to the cannery. The total count was then passed on to the cannery boss for determination of the crew needed to process the catch from unloading, through the line, to the can for cooking in the retorts, and finally labeling and into boxes.

Ken and brother Jerry on deck of *Lady Fay* lying along side salmon trap
Photo by Dave Olson

Following my report, I returned aft for a surprise. I'd left the crew to clean up and secure the deck before casting off for the run to the cannery, but instead, there was Ken in a happy trance down in the hold of the *Goldie* selecting and pitching up on deck the biggest, cleanest salmon for transfer by enthusiastic members of the *Goldie* crew to the deck of the *Lady Fay*. Ken could take them to nearby Kaigani Harbor to sell under the pretense he had caught them himself during time-off. I had another vision—if this ever got back to the "sups" at the cannery, Ken would be fired and my skipper days would be over. Common sense prevailed. I said, "Sorry guys, throw those fish back in the *Goldie* hold."

The crew claimed they were helping for the fun of it; I have no idea where the trap watchmen fit in. As for Ken, on a subsequent visit to brail the traps he was patrolling, he admitted to me that he'd simply been carried away. It was hard to pass up the dollar signs on all those beautiful silvers and kings that would never be missed at the cannery. Years later, I told retired cannery superintendent Don Franett the story. He laughed, saying, "You did the right thing *that* day."

Following the last brail of the traps Ken was patrolling, he and Jerry set sail for Seattle. He had $5,500 cash from fishing. After adding a check for trap patrol from Nakat, he finished the season with enough net left to settle up with Jerry for his work as crew, pay off the loan on the *Lady Fay*, cover college costs, and write a check for a new Chevrolet. Mom was happy to have him and Jerry home safe. Dad was bursting with pride telling the tale to all who would listen. More than one comely campus co-ed rolled eyes at him.

* * *

THE *GOLDIE* GETS A MASCOT

Franett dispatched the *Goldie* to Craig, Alaska, a small fishing and commercial town twelve miles from Waterfall, on the evening of the July 3. On arrival I turned the crew loose with orders to be back aboard before midnight. Off they went to have a couple beers at one of the local saloons. When they dutifully showed up at curfew, Mate Sam Deniston was carrying a skinny buff-colored three- or four-month-old puppy he had found wandering around apparently lost on the waterfront boardwalk. He said, "Look, he's homeless. We can adopt him for crew-company on the boat. Name him Mr. Roberts [after the title character in the bestselling novel of life on a navy supply ship during World War II]. Promise, I'll take care of him, including boat breaking—no shit on deck! Okay?"

"No way!" I said. "You hustle him off to where you picked him up, and get your butt back to the boat."

Five minutes later Sam reported back and we took off. Perhaps an hour later, Sam gleefully appeared in the pilothouse with the puppy, saying, "Somehow Mr. Roberts managed to follow me back to the boat. Guess somebody put him back on board."

There was no returning to Craig as I already had orders for the boat's movement the next day. Sam wrote in the log, "Mr. Roberts came aboard sober." Sam was forgiven. For the rest of the run my mind was on the story I'd be telling the bosses back at the cannery.

Mr. Roberts was trainable, smart, and took to his new boat life well. He was boat-broke in a week. Later, on arrivals at Waterfall, we were waved away by other tenders who didn't want us tied up along side their boat. The reason was Roberts would eagerly stand at the rail as we came in for a landing. As soon as I eased us close enough, he would leap to the deck of the other boat—and do his duty. His notoriety spread through the fleet and all the way to the superintendent's office.

Golden West Mate Sam and Mr. Roberts relaxing on the bow of the *Golden West*
Photo by Dave Olson

Most of that season was spent making daily runs south from the cannery to pick up the catch of Nakat owned or affiliated purse seiners fishing out of Port Bazaan, a protected harbor on the west side of Dall Island. Our almost daily job cycle was to make the seven-hour run south in the afternoon, anchor up on arrival, spend the evening counting and loading the catches from each of the seiners selling to Nakat, and then up anchor and make the run through the night back to the cannery for unloading the fish the next morning. This return trip could be a bit nerve-racking because there was often a moderate sea with fog to keep you wide awake through the night.

On August 20 we made our routine afternoon run down to Port Bazaan. After anchoring and dinner we were prepared by six-thirty to load fish and finished loading just after midnight. Throughout those hours no one gave a thought to where Mr. Roberts was hanging out. Underway for return to the cannery, Sam went looking for him. He returned to the pilothouse crestfallen with the news that Roberts had disappeared. He wrote in the log, "Mr. Roberts jumped ship 0120–0140 hours."

We were back at Port Bazaan to load fish the next evening. Sam asked the crew of every seiner as they came alongside us if they had seen or heard anything of a dog swimming in the harbor the previous evening. One reported seeing a seiner crew (not on one of our Nakat boats) pick up a lost dog either swimming in the harbor or barking on the beach: "They have taken your Mr. Roberts with them to Hydaburg, their home port." All of us were amazed and ecstatic to hear

Roberts was alive, but realism more or less dictated Roberts beginning a third life in Hydaburg, a small out-of-the-way native village, perhaps three to four hours from Port Bazaan where no Nakat tender ever had a reason to go.

Or so we thought. During lunch while docked at Waterfall on August 25, Bill Funken, the cannery superintendent, decided he needed a tender to take him down to the Nutkwa Trap, which was owned by the Haida, an Alaska Native group, but serviced and fished under contract with Nakat. The schedule showed the *Golden West* had the time, so I was told to fire up for us to make the brief trip.

Soon after we were underway, Sam observed the route to the trap location passed within two miles of Hydaburg. The only time consideration was to be at the trap in time for closing before the legal deadline of six o'clock.

"Dave, you know we can stop in Hydaburg for fifteen minutes to see if we can find Mr. Roberts," Sam calculated.

"Yah, if you can sell Mr. Funken," I said.

Mr. Funken was with us in the pilothouse listening and laughing.

"Is it okay?" asked Sam.

Luckily, Funken had previously been introduced to Mr. Roberts on the cannery dock before his disappearance and knew the story. Also, we knew Hydaburg had one pier with one short waterfront road forming a "T" going each way from the land end of the dock. Funken agreed, but a warning whistle would blow after ten minutes, allowing five more to be back on the boat—with or without Roberts.

We had hardly stopped alongside the dock when Sam and two other crew bounded off the boat to split up and make the search. They disappeared shouting, "Here, Mr. Roberts, come on Roberts, where are you?" Before it was time to blow the warning whistle, they all returned carrying ice cream cones for sharing with the rest of us—and Roberts was joyfully running for the boat ahead of them.

Sam wrote in the log, "Roberts returned from five days A.W.O.L." The two became inseparable and Mr. Roberts was major entertainment for the remainder of the season.

* * *

SEA SUMMER FINALE

The *Goldie*'s season ended with a hairy fog-bound trip to Seattle, including a socked-in evening that caused us to overrun our calculated time coming out of Queen Charlotte Strait approaching Vancouver Island. We were lost. I eased our way slowly ahead with lookouts on the bow, eyes focused on black water for kelp warning of shallows and searching for an identifiable landfall. Seeing lights on a dock off to port, we landed and tied up, with two local teenagers taking our lines. Asked where we were, they said we were in Sointula, British Columbia, seven miles from Alert Bay, an island village on the south end of the strait where I hoped we might be. Two days later we gratefully tied up back home at Maritime Shipyard. The next day was spent cleaning up and saying good-bye to crew and boat, saying farewell to friends, vessels, and a way of life I'd loved for seven extended summers.

I'm Going Again

(An internal monologue)

To feel the tarred decks of an honest to god
Working boat beneath my feet. And
Watch the bow carve the sea,
Frothing over into long rolling waves,
Disappearing behind to port and starboard.
To breathe in steep shaded passing shores,
Fragrant with Alaska cedars dipping lower branches
In flooding tide. And be
Cleansed by rain swollen streams
Cascading into the accepting sea,
Spraying the air with misting fog.
To be summoned at midnight to hot acrid coffee,
Wheel watch on top, with only the flying bridge
Giving protection from the chilly air. And
Straining to see black logs in black water,
Blinking lights guiding from point to point,
Waiting for the dawn to spread across the eastern sky.
To sleep in the fo'c's'le with friends, the
Turbo-charged Cat droning and whining
A numbing lullaby. And listen to
The water rushing by, with the
Gently rolling hull creaking, my
Sleeping bag warming me.

–Tim Olson, 1979

PART THREE

FORREST GUMP LIVE

Mrs. Gump:
"Life's a box of chocolates, Forrest. You never know what you're gonna get."

Forrest Gump:
"I don't know if we each have a destiny, or if we're all just floating around accidental-like on a breeze, but I think maybe it's both."

Nationalist Chinese Guerrilla Navy armed motor Junk #74 at anchor
Photo by Dave Olson

CIA OFFSHORE ISLAND OPERATIONS[17]

Featuring Captain Ch'en Yu-Ch'ao

Skippering the cannery tender *Golden West* back to Seattle marked the finish of another successful fishing season in Alaska.

What followed were a few days of picking up the pieces of life on land after three months of an isolated life at sea, and that's all I got before starting classes for my senior year at Pacific Lutheran College. I liked the courses, mostly in history and literature, and my professors, so all went well; however, the call to serve in the military would come with graduation. I'd always dreamed of flying so I tried my luck with the air force first. They promptly flunked me on the eye exam. Next was checking in with navy recruiting for a shot at Officer Candidate School. I was told they were already overloaded with applicants ahead of me.

In early 1952, one morning while walking across campus, Dr. Phillip Hauge, the Dean of Men, stopped me for a chat. He told me he was inviting a few other seniors to meet with a government recruiter who was offering an attractive job possibility with a government agency that would lead to release from the draft if selected. Was I interested? Of course!

On entering the conference room next to the dean's office, though, I almost turned and walked out. All the guys there had big reputations on campus. No room for a nobody like me. But I stayed, filling out the forms and answering questions about employment history. I listed mine from deckhand to captain of a fishing vessel with a crew of six. After some minutes, there was a call for one

---

17 All statements of fact, opinion, or analysis expressed are those of the author and do not reflect the official positions or views of the CIA or any other U.S. Government agency. Nothing in the contents should be construed as asserting or implying U.S. Government authentication of information or Agency endorsement of the author's views. This material has been reviewed by the CIA to prevent the disclosure of classified information.

name after the other into the dean's office and, I found out later, quick departure through his other door. I was alone. Was it my turn? The recruiter wasted no time cutting to the chase: "Tell me, from the beginning, about your experience on fishing vessels."

The next day I was noticed to return to the dean's office. Dr. Hauge said, "Dave, the recruiter told me his people are very interested in you. Go about your business as if nothing has happened. Don't discuss this information with anyone. They will contact you."

After clearing background checks, I was called long distance and informed I'd been hired. I was to report ASAP to their offices at 2430 E Street NW in Washington, D.C.; travel expenses would be reimbursed. When I got there, I read the small brass plate on the door. The Central Intelligence Agency had a job for me.

I was assigned to the Far East Division, but nobody told me why. This was followed by perhaps a week of indoctrination seminars to enlighten me and other new agent trainees on the history of espionage as a tool for implementing U.S. foreign policy and the role of covert activities turning back the communist Cold War menace beyond our shores worldwide. There was some mention of the specific need for paramilitary support of allies in the Far East coping with Communist Chinese expansion. Most of all I watched many old movies of successful spying, sabotage, and other underground operations. Months of intelligence classes learning spy tradecraft followed in Washington, D.C. These were mixed with paramilitary courses at a secret location known back then as "The Farm" and parachute jump training, including two night jumps.

As luck would have it, I was in Washington at the same time as the inauguration of Dwight Eisenhower. A CIA trainee friend and I paired up to take in the festive occasion. The highlight of the celebration was being invited by Senator Henry Dworshak to share the buffet and observe part of the ceremonies on the Capitol grounds across the street from his suite on the second floor of the Senate Office Building.

My training supervisor turned me over to the China Branch in late February 1953. Someone there told me I'd landed a job in the private sector doing some maritime-related work for Western Enterprises, Inc. (WEI), which had its headquarters in Pittsburg, Pennsylvania, shipping offices in San Francisco, and field offices in Taipei, Taiwan.

Years later, back at CIA headquarters, I ran into the CIA recruiter who had found me at Pacific Lutheran College in 1952. He told me he had visited the campus knowing the Far East Division was looking for a person with my background and qualifications. From day one, on successful completion of training, I was slotted for WEI Taipei

The primary focus of WEI was described as providing off-the-record paramilitary arms support for Nationalist Chinese desires to return to the mainland in exchange for their support of our intelligence gathering operations. The military objective was to keep alive communist fears of nationalist military incursions so they couldn't justify having all their forces up in Korea. I was on my way to Pittsburg to spend a day meeting with Charlie Johnson, company president, signing employment papers, and being briefed about the commercial aspects of the company.

The next afternoon I called home from the WEI office to tell my mother to expect me home for ten days vacation on my way to Taiwan for two years. From the office I walked over to the hotel to make myself at home in the company's suite, watch TV, and drink a toast to myself. Two weeks later, on an overnight layover in Honolulu to wait for a Philippine Airlines flight to Manila, I stayed at the Royal Hawaiian Hotel, surfed at Waikiki, and sipped mint juleps on the hotel's beach veranda with new friend Lorraine Kriegel, a WEI spouse with four children also on her way to Taipei. She welcomed my company helping her ride herd on her irrepressibly mischievous kids. It was a trying trip for Lorraine, but fun for me.

On arrival at WEI Taipei offices, called the Guest House, I was turned over to the Maritime Section Chief. His job was to shop me around to all the various sections for orientation, brief me on maritime-related operations, and ultimately figure out what to do with me. The most fascinating section visit was a pass through the offices responsible for covert intelligence with all their color-pinned maps, clanking teletypes, and darkroom/photo lab.

A day later, a driver and Jeep were detailed to take me to the port of Keelung on the north end of Taiwan to visit our WEI shipyard. On arrival I met the manager—an unforgettable, totally British, aging China hand and merchant steamer skipper—the rotund Captain Stanley Barden, and his Chinese wife. I also met Vaughn Sherman and Art Sommer, who both hailed from Seattle and ended up becoming two of my lifelong friends. They all shared in showing me how the yard took low or sail-powered junks, flat bottomed boats ranging mostly from fifty to sixty feet in length, and converted them into a latter-day flotilla of lethal privateers. The refit was installing powerful GMC diesel engines to drive them at eight-plus knots and arming the crews with machine guns and recoilless rifles capable of sinking a ship. When a junk was ready for business, its crew would be flown in by air from their home island base to return the boat for service in the guerrilla navy fleet.[18]

While in Taiwan I stayed in WEI's living quarters for male transients located in a lovely lush valley outside of Taipei. It was shared by more than a dozen single men.[19] All of the employees were Chinese or Taiwanese. Few understood any English beyond what was necessary to do their jobs, and there were also standing orders to limit conversation to trivial gossip in case there was a spy in the group. The cuisine was a mix of western and Chinese dishes. If dinner was native dishes, chopsticks were the only tableware. My tiny single-concrete-walled cubicle bedroom was next to a similar room occupied by another bachelor. I can't recall him spending a single night sleeping alone. This development was not shared in my letters home.

On completion of orientation in Taipei, I was sent to Keelung to work at the shipyard. There wasn't anything for me to do under Captain Barden, who spent most of his time managing and advising Art and Vaughn. Art and Vaughn worked with the yard manager getting things done. I was a floater, treading water, chafing for a Forrest Gump divertissement. Fortunately for me, a WEI-owned navy surplus WWII patrol boat, the *711*, with a Chinese crew, while on duty at the offshore Pai-ch'uan ("White Dog") Station was driven aground one wild night on an incoming tide in a midsummer typhoon. The Pai-ch'uans were two islands, with our WEI station quarters on the rugged west island at the top of the native village built on an oceanfront hillside. A staff of about six Americans and a roster of interpreters manned the station. The wreck of the *711* was high on a protected tideflat beach about four miles by boat from the station on the west side of the east island.

Captain Barden decided to get me out of his hair by having me flown out to Pai-ch'uan to try to salvage the vessel. On arrival I was assigned an interpreter. Arrangements were made for a guerrilla navy junk to taxi me and my interpreter across the dividing channel to the east island for inspection of the wreck. I had a camera to document my assessment of the hull damage and possibilities for eventual refloat and tow back to Keelung for repairs. Initial inspection wasn't promising. The tide was out so I found the derelict sitting high and dry on the sand beach a quarter mile in from shore. I hiked down to the shore and took a picture from there of the wreck, including all the intervening sand in the photo. This was sent back to the Section Chief in Taipei. He must have shown it to the Chief of Station to duly impress him

---

18 Under the circumstances prevailing at the time in Korea, I still think it was a valid creative investment of American taxpayers' money supporting the United Nations-sponsored effort to turn back the North Korean invasion of South Korea.

19 WEI employed only a few women in secretarial/clerical positions.

with the apparent hopelessness of salvage. Though it had taken on water during high tides and was laid over on her port side, the hull appeared floatable with a few repairs and auxiliary bilge pumps aboard.

*M/V 711 a*ground at mid-tide on East Paichuan Island
Photo by Dave Olson

The bad news was there was other obvious damage beyond simple cleanup and the hull had gradually sunk at least three feet into the sand. On first inspection, as an American with no access to power equipment, I was inclined to strip and abandon it to the destructive action of the surf.

Luckily, the commanding officer of the Chinese Nationalist Army forces stationed on the island showed up at the invitation of the *711* captain. He had a better idea. My interpreter passed it on: "During the coming days low water hours while the tide is out, how about me ordering a company of my soldiers with shovels to dig out the sand around the hull and a ditch down the beach deep enough so when the *711* floats, she can be pulled off the beach to deep water safety?"

I was dubious of the plan, but why not? Besides, due to the tidal cycle, this would mean a few more weeks for me to live offshore island life—far more interesting than life at the shipyard. The digging was done manning one hundred GI foxhole shovels. Fortunately, much of the low waters for digging occurred during daylight hours. The boat's two anchors were set as far down the beach as possible. I slept on the beach and ate Chinese chow with the *711* crew at their primitive temporary shore quarters during most of the week of digging and other preparations.

Chinese Nationalist army soldiers digging out sand around the 711 at low tide
This effort led to successfully pulling the 711 free to deep water for towing back to Taiwan.
Photo by Dave Olson

The first effort to refloat the vessel occurred after midnight one night, and I joined some crew members to pull on the manila line going out to one of the anchors. We got close, but failed. On the second try, an observer might have thought the keel was lying on greased skids. The Chinese had a navy tug standing by. I rode the leaking *711* back to Keelung. Col. A couple of Section Chiefs from the Taipei offices and the shipyard people were among the group welcoming the crew and me at the dock.

As later reported in Frank Holober's *Raiders of the China Coast*:

Olson received a commendation for this splendid display of initiative, even though he gave full credit to the effective ingenuity characteristic of the guerrillas in solving problems.[20]

Back at the shipyard I could hardly wait to return to one of those island stations overseeing guerrilla navy logistics and other activities. I hoped it would be North Tachen, two hundred miles north of Taiwan and twenty miles off the China coast, the epicenter of guerrilla navy action. The Tachens were an island

20   Frank Holober, *Raiders of the China Coast: CIA Covert Operations During the Korean War* (U.S. Naval Institute Press, 1999), 99.

group controlled by a hereditary warlord loyal to General Chiang Kai-shek. Fishing and farming were major occupations. As fortune would have it, early September 1953 saw me on the PBY[21] on my way there.

The times, work, isolation, people, and place were all pretty much what I envision is experienced today at one of the quieter Forward Operating Bases in Afghanistan. The group varied from five to fifteen men. Our living quarters and offices were all WWII Quonset huts. We had three or four jeeps for transportation on the one-lane dirt roads to everywhere and nowhere on the island. A diesel-powered generator provided more than adequate electricity.

Each new arrival was promptly introduced to assigned personal interpreters. Mine were Richard T'ien and David Tsai. Both were bright, confident, young mainland Chinese loyal to the Gimo[22] who had been educated in American Christian missionary schools in China. Both spoke impressive English. We had no problem with communication. Richard was already working with the fleet; David's duties were split between me and another guy.

We were armed off station and suppose to carry a lethal pill in case of abduction. Many had already survived the hardships of war. A few had seen hardcore duty on the front lines in Korea. The station chief, Daren Flitcroft, and intelligence guys oversaw planning and execution of all paramilitary and intelligence operations. I was only a witness to those activities on a need-to-know basis. My code name was Perry Irwode. A couple of the jokesters called me "Irwaade" for short.

* * *

Guerrilla navy was only one of my hats. Another was responsibility for liaison with the regular navy captain, and maintenance of our "escape and evasion" Higgins PT boat. I passed training to be able to operate the boat myself, including the engines if necessary. The boat was also used for occasional training missions with the underwater demolition team, as a fast taxi to transport big wigs on visits to other islands controlled by the Gimo's forces, and to standby as rescue boat for crew pick-up of any aircraft that were forced down. I went along on almost all these missions. Taking a brief turn conning a PT at thirty-five knots was a thrill the first time.

Finally, as the junior in the group, I ended up coordinating base supply flights and running the movie projector. A fortunate "plus" was falling into jobs where I was in my element, enjoyed every day, and proved to be good at

---

21   A PBY Catalina was a vintage WWII amphibious twin-engine patrol bomber aircraft used by WEI to fly personnel and cargo from Taipei out to Tachen on an irregular weekly basis. Retired U.S. Navy pilots did the flying. The flights were always an adventure.
22   Generalissimo Chiang Kai-shek

all of them.

The guerrilla navy-armed motor junks' targets for boarding were sailing junks and slow bedraggled motor vessels carrying cargoes between Communist coastal ports. Unable to escape our pirates, the hapless boats were captured and escorted to Tachen. The cargo was unloaded for distribution into the local economy and the officers were subject to interrogation. It was classic piracy coupled with an intelligence-gathering objective. The junk crews shared the booty and we got the intelligence.

Tachen Island harbor and anchorage
Photo by Dave Olson

Before my arrival, I'd heard of the exploits of the Tachen guerrilla navy fleet, especially swashbuckling Captain Ch'en Yu-Ch'ao and the gung-ho crew of the #81 *Linhai*. Thus, the first day after I met my two interpreters, Richard T'ien and David Tsai, we were off on the aptly named *Cyclops*, our inboard-powered twenty-four-foot water taxi, to visit the anchored junk fleet and meet the captains and crews. Liking those agile eager crews was easy. Little did I know smoking opium was a rather common pastime in port. All were happy to have the engines and firepower to do better what they liked doing best—piracy. Besides meeting Ch'en Yu-Ch'ao, another notable introduction was to Captain Su Ming-yun, whose junk, #80, probably brought in more loot than Ch'en's *Linhai*. Months later, Su Ming-yun told me, "If you'll let me take out your PT boat, I'll fill the harbor with communist ships every day!"

From the North Tachen anchorage we made the short passage over to South Tachen to visit the WEI shipyard managed by Col. P'ai. To get to the yard we had to walk through the island village, which felt like stepping back in time ten thousand years. There was only foot traffic on the worn cobblestone paths and women who still had bound feet. All business was transacted on balance scales and abacuses. The shipyard operation was equally fascinating. Their business was the building and maintenance of traditional junks using primitive tools and traditional supplies—like oakum to caulk seams. My job was to coordinate supplies and equipment Col. P'ai could use in the yard.

Captain Chen Yu Chao on the *Linhai*, Guerrilla Navy Junk #81
Photo by Dave Olson

Ch'en Yu-Ch'ao did not hesitate to push for a bigger, better boat. The *Linhai* was the drabbest, smallest, and shortest junk in the fleet. While the others were painted mostly black with white trim and adorned with a dragon symbol on the bow with eyes in red, green, and white, the *Linhai* was all navy gray. Sure, it was the most heavily armed and fastest boat. Sure, moonless night exploits doing agent drops and pick-ups on the mainland coast made the gray a reasonable color choice. Successfully evading attacking communist gunboats with the loss of only two crewmen had made him and his covert agent handlers minor celebrities, but he knew nothing of this. Nor to my knowledge did he know his boat was the way it was because those same handlers wanted it that way for their covert missions. Praise was his bonus pay and he earned it!

During my watch, two escapades stand out. Here's how Frank Holober reported one of them in his book, *Raiders of the China Coast*:

In both agent infiltration and the interception of shipping, whether armed or unarmed and leading occasionally to prizes in cargo and prisoners, Ch'en's boat was the star of the fleet. As tribute to his activist spirit, Bill M. succeeded in requisitioning for him a fifty millimeter recoilless rifle, which clearly delighted the skipper. Admonished to use it only for defensive purposes, he immediately searched out an armed enemy junk much larger than his own. He sank the junk and rescued about thirty crew members. He was considerably miffed that the damn boat would not stay afloat long enough for him to bring it in.

The other happened one night when Ch'en and the *Linhai* were on an intelligence mission taking them a short distance up a river on the coast just north of Tachen. I was in my bunk during the exchange of Morse code radio messages between the *Linhai*, code name "Peter Boat," and our operator, Frank Bigelow, a Chinese interpreter/operator, and the operator on the junk, but I did get to read the translations the next morning. They had found a large ship at anchor in the estuary of the island. On reconnaissance they saw no sign of life on board. No lookouts, no one awake to sound an alarm—nothing! Ch'en instructed his radio operator to transmit those findings. Then he decided to board and loot the ship, or maybe even take it as a prize. The next message from Ch'en is unforgettable: "Attempted to board the ship, but sides too high. Fired rounds at stern. Peter Boat returning to base."

The rounds he had fired were 50 mm from his recoilless rifle—powerful enough to do serious damage. That boat wasn't going anywhere soon. When I visited the *Linhai* the next morning, Ch'en was frowning because he'd had to give up on a pirate's dream. Debriefing of Ch'en after his return led to the conclusion the ship was probably a WWII LST (Landing Ship Tank—built in lengths from three hundred to almost four hundred feet) left behind by the Nationalists during their evacuation to Taiwan.

My most vivid recollection is of one late afternoon when I was visiting an anchored junk as two or three other junks cruised into the harbor towing prizes. Ch'en waved happily from the *Linhai* as his grinning crew threw confiscated tangerines to me, my interpreter Richard, and the crews of the other fleet junks.

Ch'en and Su were among the Chinese invitees to most of the occasional dinners we hosted celebrating our partnership. These always featured many toasts of the native rice wines. The two choices were a mild "gal-yung" and a high-proof hot pepper variety called "by-gar." Few of us, including me, could handle the by-gar, but our guests usually preferred it. Toasts ended with "suey-pien" (as you like) or "gam-bey" (down the hatch). Ch'en loved to "gam-bey." The only time he was ever bested was at one of those parties near the end of my tour. Somebody took him on and they carried Ch'en out. He was ready for sea a day later.

My Chinese interpreter Richard and me at work making visits among fleet junks anchored in the Tachen harbor
Photo by Dave Olson

Life was casual. We all shared Quonset huts as equals, including the Military Assistance Advisory Group (MAAG) representative working with regular army forces on the island that was an army colonel rotated every three or four months. He received no special favors, and he treated all of us as equals. My favorite was Col. Dan Walton because we shared a fondness for an ocean swim after lunch off a beach perhaps a third of a mile from our quarters. We knew bad things could happen where we were stationed, but we lived easily in an atmosphere of knowledgeable denial.

One beautiful Sunday in the spring of 1954 I was assigned to run our outboard-powered supply sampan to an outer island in the Tachen group. The purpose was for Dick Kriegel, George O., and three Chinese counterparts to check out the island in preparation for a training exercise. Frank Bigelow, our radioman, was along to enjoy the outing. While passing another island on the way out, busy running the outboard, I was loudly ordered to turn the boat away from the island shore. I was in the stern. Bigelow was sitting next to me on the bench running to the bow on the starboard side. George was sitting next to him. I saw a scattering of splashes in the surrounding water.

Then George said, "If he gets any closer, he's going to hit somebody."

Bigelow replied, "Ya, he just got me in the foot!"

I looked down and there was a clean bullet hole through his boot. As soon as we were out of range, we were on our way back to harbor for treatment and ultimately evacuation that night by PBY. I spent a part of that night in the same sampan at anchor on station with red and green lights pointed skyward for the pilot, Connie Siegrist, to line up on for his landing. He cleared our sampan with little room to spare, scaring the hell out of Richard, David, and me.

Western Enterprises, Inc. (CIA) quonset hut quarters for men manning the Tachen Island Base off the China coast
Photo by Dave Olson

The shooter was a thoughtless sentry with orders to shoot to kill any passage through his sector of island coast. Somebody had forgotten to tell him about us. A sharpshooter with better aim could probably have killed half of us. Frank Bigelow was the only American wounded by gunfire, friendly or enemy. That is, unless you count the time Herb Rominger, doing night guard duty at WEI headquarters in Taipei after a year as a medic on Tachen, managed to shoot himself in the ass practicing quick draw with his side arm.

The communists finally got fed up with the cost and embarrassment of this enemy presence on their coast. They began a campaign with landings on other smaller islands to the north and south of Tachen manned by guerrilla army teams. On one of these, one of our largest junks, #75, got in a firefight with communist gunboats. Other than bullet holes, the junk returned to Tachen looking relatively unscathed. However, laid out on deck were the bodies of about a half dozen crew members, including the captain. It was my duty to visit this junk, review those deaths, and offer condolences for their loss.

This duty later earned me three more honorable mentions in *Raiders of the China Coast* by Holober. Incidentally, the Americans weren't Holober's raiders. They were the guerrilla army forces who mounted diversionary invasions on nearby communist-held islands, and guerrilla navy junk crews intercepting communist commercial shipping. They were pleased to have us on their side because they dreamed of returning to the mainland and overthrowing the communists.

As for the Tachens island group, serious military action began with reconnaissance flights and a few limited target-bombing missions with single-engine Soviet Yak-11s during the final weeks of my year on the island.

On November 1, 1954, a month after my departure, the air attacks escalated with strafing of our WEI compound. This activity intensified to an all-out bombardment on January 19, 1955, leveling our quarters. Base commander Wayne Sanford ordered evacuation on the PT that night. I was in Keelung to welcome them the next morning at six o'clock. It had been a long night. The U.S. Seventh Fleet soon arrived on the scene to assure a safe evacuation a month later of everyone on the islands.

Among those evacuated were the crews of the guerrilla navy fleet, whom I considered my friends. It is my understanding that many were subsequently conscripted by the Chinese Nationalist authorities as forced laborers on building the Central Cross Island Highway where numerous lives were lost. Were Ch'en Yu-Ch'ao and Su Ming-yun among them? The probability they, and perhaps most of the other able-bodied men from those junk crews, may have come to this ignominious end—and influential knowledgeable Americans may have known about the situation, but said nothing to prevent it—still bothers me.

Back in Taipei in October of 1954 I found myself assigned to be assistant to the Offshore Islands Branch Chief, Ralph Katrosh. This put me in the loop of everything happening on Quemoy and Tachen, the two remaining active stations. My dream desk job.

Among my specific responsibilities were scheduling and coordinating with Civil Air Transport (CAT) on air supply and personnel services to the islands. CAT, ostensibly a Taipei-based civil airline with scheduled flights from Manila to Tokyo, was actually another CIA cover company. Through my job I came to know as friends some of their people, including pilots. WEI and CAT people jointly shared a sort of secure social club in Taipei called the Downtown Club. This brought me to a table one evening over drinks listening in on an unforgettable conversation and contributing years later to changing my thinking and actions regarding war and peace.

As a whole, 1954 was not a happy year in the ranks of the CAT pilots. Many had been military pilots in the Far East during WWII. A couple were Hump[23] pilots who had met Ho Chi Minh, knew of his love of all things American, and familiar with his dreams for a post-war Vietnam free of French colonial domination. Now these same pilots were flying supply missions under orders supporting the French determination to continue their domination of the country they called French Indo China. Already they had lost two of their comrades shot down over Dien Bien Phu. They were larger-than-life Captain James B. McGovern, aka "Earthquake McGoon" from the Lil' Abner comic strip, and copilot Wallace Buford. Together they had the distinction of being the first American lives lost in the Vietnam War. One who had just returned from another hairy supply mission, was noted saying "What the hell are we doing down there saving the asses of the damn fucking French? All Ho wants is for the Vietnamese to get their country back."

Those pilots had it right. Since then, reinforced by similar experiences, I've sought out voices with field knowledge to help me reach conclusions on political issues and movements.

---

23 The Hump was the name given by World War II transport aircraft pilots to the hazardous route flown over the Himalayan Mountains airlifting military supplies from India to Nationalist China.

FLIGHT DAZE WITH HAPPY LANDINGS

With Charlie Paterson and Milt Hefty

Flight is freedom in its purest form,
To dance with the clouds which follow a storm
—Gary Claud Stoker, "Impressions of a Pilot"

My compulsion to fly began with vivid dreams of floating free through the air and awakening in a state of wonder and euphoria. In my senior year of college, applying for pilot training in the air force, I failed the eye exam, but the desire to fly didn't go away.

As if meant to be, in November of 1954, the stars aligned in an auspicious opportunity to realize my dream. My CIA job responsibility coordinating supply flights to the offshore islands required visits to the Taipei Airport with time to snoop around. A sign on a small nondescript hangar got my attention, Taipei Flying Club. The club office was open so I walked in to check it out. Turned out the club existed because two Piper Cubs and a four-seat Cessna 170 in good condition had been noticed in this hangar by some Chinese civilian pilots with connections. This had led to a take-over and organization of the club, making the planes available for pilot training and recreational flying in Taiwan air space.

Chinese air force pilots in their free time provided seat-of-the-pants flight instruction at a rate too low to be true in American dollars. My recollection is those hourly rates, paid in Taiwan currency, equated to about 10 percent of prevailing charges by fixed base operators at American airports. The airplanes were maintained by two airframe and engine mechanic club members in their spare time. The genial fellow in the office took me out and showed me the two Piper Cubs available for training. I promptly signed up for my first lesson.

Much of my dual flight instruction was with Chinese air force lieutenant Perry Lee who had trained in Texas. My most exciting moment was with a devilish instructor buddy of his who got bored with the lesson one nice afternoon.

"You want to do a loop?" he asked me.

"Sure," I said.

"Got your seat belt tight?"

"Sure," I said.

Flight Instructor Perry Lee and me about to take off in Piper Cub at Taipei, Taiwan Airport
Photo by Dave Olson

Next thing I knew, we were at full throttle in a shallow dive to gain airspeed. Then he threw the stick back, and the nose went up, and up. Next, almost stalled inverted, came street dirt raining down from cracks in the cockpit floor, which was now the ceiling, into my face. Then we peeled over—down, down, and around to resume level flight. I can tell you—no way is a PA-11 Piper Cub approved for aerobatics.

There were no flight instruction books available in English. No ground school either. Luckily I already knew the elementary navigation needed to find the airport returning from limited solo cross-country flights. All I had to do was report to the office where I was going and take off. Those were exhilarating mini-adventures. One was flying through the beautiful mountainous Taiwan terrain to the scenic rugged east coast of the island, following this for a few miles, and then returning to the Taipei airport. I told everybody I knew about the club, but somehow I remained the only American student.

A few weeks before my return to the United States in 1955, the flying club was abruptly closed and dissolved because a Chinese pilot who had rented the Cessna for a recreational flight went missing. He was reportedly last seen heading out over the Formosa Strait on his way back to the mainland. By that time, though, I had enough hours to test for a U.S. private pilot license.

Due to go home in May, with three months of unused vacation time, I palled up with Floyd Hillier to travel west from Taipei and complete a circumnavigation of the globe. We had a grand tour in a time when Americans were still revered wherever they went, Americanization had barely begun, and commonplace global travel was still in the future.

When I returned to the states I headed to Detroit, Michigan, and the Dodge factory where I had a loaded red two-door waiting for me. I had ordered it before leaving Taiwan through a sweetheart deal offered by the Taipei Chinese Chrysler dealer to people going home. I drove west to a happy homecoming. While home I went out to a local airport to get checked out for flying solo in America.

Under prior agreement with CIA to qualify me for permanent draft deferment, in September I enlisted for three years in the Army Field Artillery knowing I'd be out in six months. I enlisted not knowing Field Artillery did basic training at Fort Carson in Colorado.

Marching through camp in formation one morning, I noticed a sign outside a barracks office entrance that said Mountain and Cold Weather Training Command—10th Mountain Division (M&CWTC). Opening Gump's box of chocolates, I hustled over there at my first opportunity to find out what was going on. They had trained at Mount Rainier during WWII and, as a ski nut, I had followed their battles in Italy. I discovered I might qualify for transfer after basic to M&CWTC to get training in cold weather warfare to be an army ski instructor at Camp Hale high in the Colorado Rockies. I ended the year checking in at Fort Carson for transfer direct to Camp Hale—the last soldier accepted direct from basic training that year by M&CWTC.

Camp Hale was everything I'd heard about it. Located in a beautiful snowbound valley at 9,200 feet, surrounded by the Rockies, how could I not love it? On arrival I was given an orientation that included getting fitted out with ski gear and clothing. The camp tour included a walk-through of a "Jamesway," an insulated canvas half-dome hut similar to the Quonset I had slept in for a year on Tachen Island off the China coast, but much smaller. I was told I'd be bunking in one of these, on a canvas cot, along with seven other men. Also, two goose-down sleeping bags were part of my gear because the huts were unheated during the night.

I was assigned to the same hut as Corp. Charles Paterson, an enterprising weekend ski instructor in nearby Aspen who had built his own log cabin and had three months left in the army. I joined the last two-week class that winter for soldiers aspiring to be ski instructors the army way. I passed and was soon assigned my first class as an instructor, a squad of ten special forces troopers from Fort Benning taking a three-week winter warfare training offered by M&CWTC. My job was mostly to teach them to ski and, beyond that, just be the guy they turned to who thought it was normal to sleep in a tent or snow cave out in the mountain air with the temperature hovering down to twenty or thirty below zero.

Friend Charlie Paterson and me with my Ercoupe on visit to Vancouver, B. C.
Photo by Charles Paterson

I was in skier's paradise, especially on weekends when I invited buddies to share my car for drives to one of the Colorado resorts for recreational skiing. Aspen was the best. After ski hours with other ski troopers we would gather at the venerable Red Onion for beer, dinner, and merry-making. Charlie Paterson charged us a dollar apiece to roll out our mattresses and sleeping bags on his log cabin floor in front of the fireplace. We slept soundly until Charlie woke us up Sunday mornings before leaving for work at ski school. Army life was a joy, but I knew the CIA would be coming to get me in early April. My plan was, on discharge, to drive home to Parkland, Washington, vacation with family for two weeks, travel on to Washington, D.C., and report back to work.

In early March, in exchange for a ride in my car, I was invited to Denver by an army friend, Bill Kilgore, for a weekend at his parents' home. We didn't have plans for Saturday so I thought I might fly a little. The yellow pages led me to Sky Ranch, a private airport offering flight training. An instructor promptly took me up for a check ride. On the flight he questioned me about my experience and hours. On return he had to fill in and sign off on our flight in my unusual Chinese/English logbook. This made him curious. He asked about my flying objectives. I told him I'd be driving back to a job in Washington, D.C. in a month with plans to get my license there. He suggested I start studying for the written test right then, qualify for my license in Colorado, sell my car, buy a plane, and fly back to Washington!

The next thing I knew I was being shown the possibilities by the airport owner, Don Vest. He showed me an easy-to-fly Ercoupe, radio-equipped, with low wings, a bubble-top cockpit, two side-by-side seats, and a cruising speed of one hundred and ten miles per hour. Its flight instruments were limited to the basics required under visual flight rules. He sent me off with an instructor for a test flight. He would let me have it for $1,260. It seemed ideal to meet my travel objective for a person with limited flying experience and affordability. My next stop was at a Dodge dealer's used car office to find out what my car was worth. I was back at the airport the next day to close the best buy of my life.

Before flying out of Colorado, however, I had to complete my service requirement at Camp Hale. I was able to get down to Denver for weekends of flight instruction along with a last weekend of skiing at Aspen and hanging out at Charlie's cabin. While there, Charlie told me of his wealthy Aunt Kaethe in Vancouver, B.C. Though he could barely remember meeting her when he was a little boy, he wanted to see her and reconnect with her family. I told him about the airplane and my plan to fly home to the Pacific Northwest at the first opportunity. If he wanted to join me for the flight to Tacoma, I'd be delighted. He jumped at the opportunity with no idea I planned to be on my way within a month.

Sure enough, in early April I came in from the field for lunch to find a sergeant waiting with orders for my priority discharge from the army and a car with driver to take me back to Fort Carson that afternoon. Since I was still just another private for special delivery the army way, he gave me an hour to eat, get my gear, and say good-bye to friends. I soon became a veteran, pleased to have been of service to my country but much in doubt as to what I'd done deserving to be honored.

On April 13 I passed my flight examination. Charlie joined me a day later for the flight to Tacoma. Our route took us from Denver to Burley, Idaho, where we decided to spend the night due to weather coming in from the west. Clouds obscured the mountains in the morning, but being inexperienced, daring, and dumb I decided to try to make it to Boise. By the time we were an hour out, we found ourselves in a cloud sandwich with the ceiling above, a layer below, and more clouds closing in behind our fleeing Ercoupe. Sans either instrument flight training or the necessary instruments, I flew into the clouds at one point according to Charlie. I have only a vague recollection of either coming out on the other side or making a one-eighty and out. Luckily, the ground layer broke as we approached Boise. We were able to land in heavy rain to wait for the weather to clear. A few hours later we were back in the air for the remainder of our trip to Tacoma. The weather was CAVU (ceiling and visibility unlimited) and taking photographs was our major occupation, passing close by Mount Rainier at a flying altitude of perhaps ten thousand feet.

Happy I was home again, the Olson family was also pleased to welcome Charlie as our guest for a few days while he firmed up plans to go on by bus to Vancouver to renew relationships with his extended family. With a natural talent for architecture, he had drawn up impressive sketches of a dream lodge he wanted to build on his property in Aspen. He hoped visiting his Aunt Kaethe might lead to financial support for construction, and he desired camouflage for this ancillary purpose of his visit. Knowing I was on vacation, he asked if I'd be interested in flying to Vancouver to share his visit there. This allowed him to casually call Aunt Kaethe, say hello, and tell her he and a friend were barnstorming around the Pacific Northwest. Would it be convenient for them to fly up and see her?

A day later we flew to Vancouver, and shortly after clearing customs, Kaethe arrived with her chauffer, Clarence, all spiffed up in his fancy uniform. Kaethe appeared to be prim and proper in her seventies or eighties, friendly and unpretentious. When she saw our little Ercoupe, she frowned because, I suspect, she thought no one flew any distance in anything smaller than ten seats, two engines, and a flight stewardess. Her car was a silver Jaguar. Charlie rode in back with Kaethe and I was in front with Clarence.

Proceeding up the highway along the Fraser River, passing a large timber operation dominated by a tall chimney emblazoned with the ten-foot-high letters CFPL (Canadian Forest Products Ltd.), Kaethe pointed it all out and said, "Charles," (Kaethe never called him Charlie) "this is one of our mills." It suddenly looked hopeful that the Picks could put up the money to help Charlie build his lodge.

Entering a posh section of Vancouver, Clarence took us up a long circle driveway to the front entrance of a forbidding stone Tudor mansion. A maid showed me to my room. It was bigger than my parents' bedroom at home and had an attached private bath.

After dinner, Kaethe adjourned the three of us to her den to watch television. When the program proved dull, Charlie adroitly pulled the drawings of his proposed lodge out of his pocket to show Kaethe what he hoped to build in Aspen. Expressing no interest, using me as her foil, Kaethe turned to me for review of the TV program guide, leaving Charlie hapless with no move but to pocket his plans.

Motoring by a few of Vancouver's vistas and sights the next morning, Charlie again tried to show Kaethe his plans. But she ignored him by asking me, "David, isn't that a beautiful park and garden over there?" This was followed by a tour of a huge plywood mill managed by Kaethe's son-in-law who acted as our personal guide. Most impressive was how machinery was shut down as we passed by, and the employees bowed to Kaethe as if she were the queen. I brought up the rear in the entourage. The second evening was a duplication of the first—Aunt Kaethe quietly dominating with talk, television, and no time for Charlie to show his plans.

The next morning we were on our own, including preparation to fly out that afternoon. Kaethe took us to lunch at an exclusive jacket-and-tie Vancouver restaurant. After being seated and ordering, Kaethe turned to Charlie and asked, "Charles, what is it you want?" On cue, Charlie began pouring out his account of how far he had come, the future he visualized for skiing and Aspen as a world class year-round resort, and where he wanted to go as a player in that picture. He went over his plans for the first units he foresaw to be the beginning of Boomerang Lodge. He needed financing to proceed with the project. Kaethe gave him her rapt attention. I was impressed with his conviction and determination.

When he had finished, Kaethe gave him a look reflecting regret and desire to support him. She said, "Charles, I'm impressed with your story and progress. I'd like to help you, but I don't have any money." She explained that her side of the family fortune had already been distributed through gifts and trusts so she was effectively living on family support. She would talk to her son-in-law who had guided us through the plywood mill the previous afternoon. If he was interested, it would be fine with her. Neither Charlie nor I needed a crystal ball to know his answer. Charlie did a great job of graciously hiding his disappointment so we could enjoy small talk and lunch.

On the flight back to Tacoma, a somber Charlie's mental wheels were already turning and exploring other options to build his lodge. En route we made a brief stop at Sea-Tac International Airport to clear U.S. customs. On landing we were directed by the tower to taxi and park close in, front and center, outside the main terminal surrounded by major airline monsters coming and going. The tower powers had my total attention. I recall how insignificant I felt sitting there in our tiny Ercoupe waiting for Customs and Immigration to show up and welcome us to the U.S.A. Thirty minutes later we were back in Tacoma.

Charlie stayed an extra day so we could go up to Seattle and he could reconnect with Jim and Lou Whittaker, his buddies from M&CWTC days. We were shown their ratty second floor mountaineering equipment store off Pioneer Square. Then we adjourned to a tavern for a couple of beers. Here the Whittaker twins shared their enthusiastic vision for the future of mountaineering in the Pacific Northwest and their destiny to be players in that picture. I had been witness back-to-back to young men's dreams for their futures. With no vision of my own, I thought none would succeed. How wrong I was as the Whittakers would go on to become world famous mountaineers, the drab little store would prosper to become Recreational Equipment, Inc.—the largest co-op in the nation—and the Boomerang would become the lodge that Charlie built...and built and built.

The next day I took Charlie to the bus station for his return to Aspen. It was time to prepare for flying back to Washington, D.C. Little did I know I was going to acquire a copilot.

It happened while I was taking a nostalgic stroll across the Pacific Lutheran College campus and ran into former classmates Marine Lt. Milton Hefty and his pregnant wife, Luella (Lu). Milt and I had last seen each other New Years Day 1954 on a meet-up in Tokyo. He was there on holiday leave from duty in Korea; I was taking my R&R from work at Tachen Island to visit Japan. Lu and I hadn't seen each other since college graduation. All I knew of the prior two years was they had married in the interim.

Milt said that on return from Korea he had successfully pursued transfer to the Marine Corp's Air Wing to become a pilot and had just completed jet pilot training. He was on home leave. His next assignment was to Cherry Point Marine Corp. Air Base in North Carolina. He, Luella, and their son Karl planned to travel there after a visit with his parents in Portland, Oregon, and a stopover in Arlington, Virginia, across the Potomac River from Washington, D.C., to spend a few days visiting Luella's sister and her husband.

When Milt heard about my airplane he wanted more than a ride—he wanted a check ride. We did it that afternoon. In an hour he knew how to fly the Ercoupe better than me. He was also interested in my plans to fly to the same destination in the same time frame as he and Luella.

Simultaneously the light dawned!

"Dave, if I could arrange for Lu and Karl to fly to Washington commercial on their own from Portland, while you and I partner in the Ercoupe—how would that sound to you?" Milt proposed.

"Let's do it!" I replied.

He called Lu for her blessing. She said okay. He said, "Count me in."

It was a partnership made in heaven. It was to be six days of flying adventure featuring often incredibly stupid decision-making leading to one remarkable reprieve from certain death and a hilarious finale—but I'm getting ahead of the story.

Early on May 1, I soloed down to the busy metropolitan Portland Airport near Milt's family home to pick him up. His family, including Lu and Karl, were there to see us off. With the airport located on the south side of the Columbia River, we got taxi instructions to the east end of the runway for takeoff west. This was supposed to be followed by a climb out to the airport's western boundary, a right turn north exiting the airport, and then another right turn to fly east up the Columbia Gorge. Milt asked to take the controls for takeoff. Hardly airborne before we came abreast of the control tower, perhaps fifty to one hundred feet off the ground, Milt did a steep one-eighty for us to go east. Traffic control immediately called, thinking we were experiencing mechanical failure and expecting to declare an emergency. My negative response led to controller orders to circle the airport and justify our flight show. Only Milt could do that. For the next five minutes I flew the plane while we circled the airport. Milt identified himself and then explained what he had done was accepted procedure at military airports. This was his first takeoff from a controlled civilian airport. He promised it would not happen again. The controller bought his story. He authorized continuance of our flight with relief, I'm sure, to see us up and away from his airspace.

We ended day one in Cour D'Alene, Idaho, as guests of my Uncle Art and Aunt Myrtle. The next morning the mountain pass route eastward was cloud-bound, but we were anxious to move on as Milt had limited time to get to our destination. Fortunately, a Western Airlines pilot with local knowledge was in the weather office. Overhearing our plight, he showed us how to take a circular route north to Lake Pend Oreille, continue twenty miles along the eastern shoreline, turn southeast and follow the Clark Fork River canyon to a valley opening south for landing in Missoula. Flying at an altitude of a few hundred feet, the beautiful canyon was narrow with little or no room for turnaround, but the advice we had taken was good as gold.

A day later, the weather was still unfriendly for flying but we had seen enough of Missoula. We felt compelled to push our luck being already a day behind Milt's desired schedule. We filed a flight plan for Miles City, Montana, and took off. We navigated by following the railroad tracks leading to Bozeman. East of Bozeman the tracks disappeared into the tunnel under Bozeman Pass at 5,750 feet. The ceiling was at five thousand feet, so the pass was socked in. However, solely over Bozeman was a patch of enticing blue sky with cloud tops visible.

We couldn't resist so we climbed in circles to come out on top at just over eight thousand feet. The distance to Livingston, which offered radio communication at a small airport, was thirty miles. We adjusted course hoping to find another break in the clouds that would allow us to drop down to flying below the clouds. But when we got to Livingston, the cover was solid with no sign of breaks to the east. So we did a one-eighty back to Bozeman. When we got there, we found the hole we had climbed up through twenty minutes earlier was closed. We were stuck.

A single mountaintop at 8,200 feet gave us a firm position for return to Livingston. We decided to set course from there for a steep descent, really a dive, through the clouds to hopefully come out of the clouds over Livingston. In retrospect this was a totally foolhardy decision, but we were fearless and heedless of the risk. On the start of the dive I was at the controls. Milt, with his superior jet experience, quickly realized my descent was too shallow to come out over Livingston, so he took over. I watched as he pushed the airspeed to over 170 knots—way past "redline" for an Ercoupe. So I took over pulling the yoke back to shallow the dive and reduce airspeed. When we came clear there was a pasture slope two hundred feet below, disappearing a short distance away into the overcast and falling snow to our right. On our left, for a quick bank to safety, was the snow-white town of Livingston. If Milt had not steepened the descent or I hadn't pulled back reducing it, both in perfectly coordinated timing, we would have died that day. I know I would have if Milt hadn't been there. Only divine providence, or something akin to it, saved us from certain death in zero visibility on a snow-covered mountain outside of Livingston.

We landed in five inches of new snow. The airport manager gave us each a cup of coffee while marveling at our incredibly good fortune. We filed a flight plan to Miles City, but we needed two runs to get airborne. The first was to plow wheel tracks in the snow. The second was to follow and stay in those tracks to gain sufficient airspeed for takeoff. A day later the approach and landing in Minneapolis were flown in a cloudburst of heavy rain with limited visibility. It was fun flying in under tower control, but impossible to climb out of the bubble cockpit without getting soaked. Fortunately, we were hosted by my folks' longtime friends Jim and Patience Swanson who lived near the airport.

On the morning of May 7, we made an early takeoff from Chicago determined to fly as far as possible on a clear day. We made a fuel stop at Phillipsburg, Pennsylvania, as twilight deepened to dusk. We talked about staying over, but Milt was anxious to see his family and his leave time was running out.

Unfortunately, the Ercoupe was almost totally unequipped for flying at night. All we had were navigation lights on the wing tips and tail. There was no instrument panel or cockpit lighting and no landing light. It would be my first night flight. We bought two flashlights and a pack of cigarettes. One flashlight was for general cockpit use. We used the red cellophane stripped off the Lucky Strike cigarette package to cover the lens of the other flashlight and secured it with a rubber band—it would serve as instrument panel lighting. Then we filed a flight plan for landing at Washington National Airport at about 10:00 p.m. Since I knew the layout of the Capitol, with the Potomac River running through it, I was confident we would have no trouble finding the airport. Unknown to us, landing would be during the evening rush hour at the second busiest airport in the nation.

We took off. Airborne, Milt and I took turns—one of us flying and on the lookout for other aircraft while the other was holding the cellophane-wrapped flashlight on the instrument panel and also trying to read the chart and log flight information with light from the second flashlight.

Our route took us to a beacon twelve miles northwest of, and up the Potomac River from, the airport. Over the beacon we contacted the tower for approach and landing instructions. The controller thought we knew what we were doing and where we were going. He directed us on a southeasterly course down the river, to maintain a certain altitude, and to call when we were four miles out from the airport. Scanning the horizon, I could see at least a half dozen descending aircraft in patterns to land somewhere and, complicating the picture further, a few broken clouds. We had abundant reason to be on high alert.

By the time we contacted the tower, we were looking downriver at lighted runways at Anacostia Naval Air Station, Bolling Field (U.S. Air Force), and, across the river, Washington National. It looked like a triangle of choices. For a minute, we weren't certain which was National. We were still over the river and closing in fast with a control tower beacon off to our right. We called hoping it was Washington National. A flight controller immediately asked us to turn on and blink our landing light. Our response was "Negative, we have no landing light."

"Ercoupe 209, what do you have?"

By that time we were almost abreast of the National tower even if we didn't know it. I responded with the clear flashlight blinking out of the cockpit canopy. Somebody in the tower spotted it. The controller told us to blink again and start doing exactly what he told us. We responded affirmative. He came back with course and altitude instructions.

I suspect the tower controllers spent the next few minutes telling at least two or more airline captains to divert, hold, and delay while they got us on the ground. If one or two cussed us out in their cockpits, I don't blame them. Then the controller directed us to a ninety-degree right turn followed shortly by another ninety-degree right turn that set us staring into the array of lights for landing on the main runway. We were directed to land as short as possible, take the first runway exit right, and brake for further taxi instructions. We performed perfectly. Parked on the taxiway, in the moonlight, engine idling, multi-engine commercial planes coming and going fifty yards away, we giggled like giddy kids, until ground control noticed (we only had one transmitting frequency—not used by commercial traffic) and directed us over to the general aviation terminal for registration and tie-down.[24]

We had made it! We had pushed our luck in varying degrees almost every day. Waiting out there on the taxiway, I think the euphoria came from flying blind for a week and landing in what seemed like Camelot.

The next day, I returned to fly out to "Bailey's Crossroads," a small airport in Falls Church, Virginia, to rent tie-down space for my Ercoupe. My first airplane improvement project was adding cockpit and instrument panel lighting for night flight.

---

24   All dates, from/to locations, and flight times in this story are taken from entries in my civil pilot's log.

SAILING FOR LIFE

Like A Sailor At Sea

Moved, by invisible currents,
I have drifted, windless, like flotsam asea,
On the sea of life.
My life at times has been like that.
Swaying to the swell,
I've sailed, catching any wind,
Blowing my way,
For more than a day,
On the sea of life.
My life at times has been like that.

— Dave Olson

SAILING BALTIMORE TO ST. PETERSBURG

With Art, George, John, and Neil

Serious sailing is like flying –
Both promise moments of terror!

On return to work at the CIA in Washington, D.C., I found myself afloat in the bureaucratic limbo of overseas returnees between assignments. Soon I ran into George O. a good friend from the months we'd both spent living on Tachen Island in 1954. He had learned about my interests in boats, and now he told me his brother-in-law, Pete Brown, and wife, Carol, were both avid sailors and owned a thirty-two-foot classic wooden cutter, the *Sanderling*. Pete's company transferred him to St. Petersburg, Florida. He and Carol had managed to sail the boat south from Marblehead, Massachusetts, to Chesapeake Bay where they had run out of time to go further. They had sailed the boat up to the head of the bay to leave it there with a sailing buddy whose name I can't remember, let's call him Joe, who lived on the bay shore near Baltimore, Maryland.

Cutter S/V *Sanderling* off-shore sailing down Atlantic coast with Art Sommer on stern
Photo by Dave Olson

George and his wife, Betty, invited me to go up to meet Joe and enjoy a June weekend of sailing on the *Sanderling*. When I showed keen interest in learning more about the sailing game, Joe took a shine to me. He was looking for a sailing companion. This led to a succession of weekends out on the bay, including learning the ropes of reefing sails, heaving to, and coping with thunderstorms and squalls.

On about the fourth of those weekends, he said, "Dave, Pete can't get away from work to take the *Sanderling* the rest of the way to St. Petersburg and neither can I. I've told Pete, and so has George, about what we've been doing and your background in boats. If you can put it together, you're welcome to sail the boat to Florida."

The time was right. I'd returned to CIA with an undecided future. The Far East Division was eager to keep me, but their vision of my future was some time on one of the Southeast Asia country desks in Washington to be followed by a projected two-year tour overseas in that country. My interest was in finding an American girlfriend, marriage, and having children, which created a friendly conflict between division's interests and mine and caused me to explore opportunities for movement to another division. I had two weeks vacation time remaining—and figured this was stretchable by taking unpaid leave if I didn't get back in time.

The boat's electronics consisted of a Raytheon Marine Radio Direction Finder with reception bands for tuning in lighthouses and commercial radio towers along the coast. So I spent part of that weekend getting the hang of using it for determining position offshore. It was simple and easy. Satisfied, I took the charts and books home for planning and started fishing for friends who might be interested in sharing the venture. Art Sommer, John Sherry, and Neill H., all friends from work, took the bait.

Early Friday, two weeks later, George and I set sail from Baltimore down Chesapeake Bay to the yacht club in Norfolk, Virginia. Flying a Marblehead Yacht Club burgee per instructions from Joe, we casually tied up Saturday morning in guest moorage. Though the Browns currently belonged to no club, Joe said it didn't matter because the boat's home port was Marblehead and nobody would check it out. We spent two days enjoying the facilities. Neill, John, and Art drove down to join us on Sunday. George left to drive the car back to Washington, D.C. On Monday we were on our way.

Our shortcut route on the first leg, avoiding having to round Cape Hatteras, was to motor out of Norfolk down the Dismal Swamp Canal in the dark. About halfway in, we went astray and grounded in the mud in the poorly lighted shallow channel. Neil, a veteran navy scuba diver, swam out to sound with his feet for the channel. Once he found it, with three crewmen out on the bowsprit to raise the stern, we easily backed off and resumed passage. By morning we were in the open, sailing Pamlico Sound with fair winds to refuel at Ocracoke, Virginia, on the Outer Banks at the south end of the Cape Hatteras National Seashore. From there we blithely headed out into the Atlantic for some easy sailing in beautiful weather. While crossing the inviting Gulf Stream, Neil and I took turns diving off the boat and grabbing a line off the stern for refreshing swims. On perhaps the fourth or fifth day, we made landfall sailing into historic Charleston, South Carolina, to feast on local cuisine, tour the city, resupply, and call families to let them know we were enjoying a fine voyage. Art was apprised of a serious illness in his family, calling him home and reducing the crew to Neil, John, and me.

Me balanced on the bowsprit of the *Sanderling* making good time off-shore
Photo by Dave Olson

We cast off in light winds under clear skies for more offshore sailing very late the next afternoon. None of us checked the weather forecast as we expected to be at sea for a week or more. Motoring out the buoyed fourteen-mile harbor channel, and after passing the sea buoy marking the entrance, we raised full sails under a favorable breeze, but soon began noticing the weather rapidly changing with darkening skies and rising northeast winds. I turned on the radio to get the weather forecast of a major northeast gale with winds to fifty knots, gusting to sixty knots. By that time we were over an hour out from the sea buoy with its high candlepower light astern, blinking in the twilight.

Neil and John were all for turning around and hightailing it back to safety in Charleston—a four-hour run minimum under power in the dark. Based on previous reading and experience, what I feared most were the treacherous seas and currents we would encounter as the ocean depth shallowed to a dredged channel the last three miles, with dangerous shoaling on either side.

The *Sanderling* was a full-keel cutter-rigged vessel designed for offshore passages. A cutter is a single-masted vessel with the mast stepped further aft than a sloop. This is so two sails, a jib and a staysail, can be set forward of the mast for a more versatile choice of sails. The sail inventory included a heavy canvas storm staysail for maintaining way and heaving to, if necessary. I was confident the *Sanderling* could survive any gale.

We discussed the routine for heaving to, a sailor's common fallback maneuver to gain safety at sea during stormy weather. It involves bringing the bow of a boat into the wind to stop its forward motion. It is accomplished by lowering all sails except a small foresail and then turning the boat into the wind. As the boat rounds up, the sail loses wind and goes slack. As a result, the boat falls off to windward. The sail then fills again, driving the bow back into the wind so the sail goes slack. This initiates a repeating cycle. I reminded John and Neill of all this while laying out my plan to sail eastward to get as far offshore as possible. We would then put the wind and sea astern to carry us south until the storm abated. Neil saw the logic and sided with me. John graciously gave in, needing no reminder that I was the captain.

We all turned to securing everything on deck and below. Neill and I prepared for shortening sail by setting up for reefing the main sail and securing the storm jib on deck for raising later as conditions deteriorated. Bear in mind all sails were hanked on (set) by hand as roller furling hadn't been invented. Also, there were no harnesses for deck crew to tether into security lines for safety. The clunky cork life preservers were only a hindrance so we didn't bother with them. Lacking two-way radio, we had no way to transmit an SOS. EPIRBs (today's emergency position-indicating radio beacons) didn't exist, and even if they had, modern Coast Guard air search and rescue would have been the only survival possibility. The only crew safety precaution I took was rigging a line across the cockpit for the helmsman to hang onto if we were pooped with a ton of water coming over the stern and filling the cockpit. The other was to insist the hatch to the cabin be kept closed except for necessary crew movement. I also did my best to briefly alert them to my vision of what else we might encounter riding out the gale. I warned them, "You never know when a rogue wave might come along and board us."

I got no sleep that night. By midnight we had reduced sails down to the storm jib on a southeast course. By morning we were surfing before a following sea, doing about five knots on a southwest course. The seas reached perhaps twelve feet. Breakers on the stern drove the bow into the trough with a lot of water on deck. But the stern rose in the turbulent froth and we never took a drop over it. Once I was certain this wouldn't happen, I relaxed to enjoy the show. This was our exhilarating life for the next thirty-six hours. I was glad I hadn't succumbed to returning to Charleston. Porthole and skylight leaks soaked a couple of bunk mattresses, but we weren't cold. Food was limited to bread and cold stew direct from the can. No one got seasick and we were all thankful for that.

By nightfall on the third day the weather cleared, the sea came down, and our *Sanderling* hove to in St. Simons Sound, off the barrier islands near the channel entrance to Brunswick, Georgia, marinas. The next morning about eight o'clock, with a groundswell of about six feet, we entered the buoyed channel under power hoping to find a restaurant serving "Hungry Sailor" breakfasts. We were in for three surprises.

The first shock was immediate and mine. The charted channel appeared more than deep enough; however, going in, the depth shoaled abruptly to a menacing shifting sandbar. The swell steepened and then heightened to break dramatically. Shifting currents contributed to the chaos. One of those breaking waves lifted our stern straight up, like going up a floor on an elevator, and we looked down to see our bow diving into the trough and taking water on deck. The *Sanderling* listed violently, forcing me at the helm to brace and secure myself with my free hand while Neill and John were forward hanging on for dear life to the mast.

No sooner were we into it, me dreading a mistake in navigation and afraid of grounding, when we were over the bar with safe passage restored. I looked around to see where we were going. Directly ahead was an impressive resort with a block-long oceanfront promenade deck. We were dumbfounded to observe the promenade rail alive with guests watching us come in. They waved at us, and we waved back, as I made the left turn to stay in the marked channel and round a point into the harbor.

Once moored in the marina, our first job was getting wet mattresses and bedding draped over the boom for drying. Just as we were finishing, a chauffeured black stretch limousine pulled up at our dock opposite our boat. The driver told us he was from Sea Island Hotel. The management was so pleased with the exciting show we had just provided their hotel guests that we were invited back to the hotel as guests for the day, including room, dining, and evening entertainment. In less than maybe five minutes, we closed the boat and boarded the Cadillac. In a mellow state of astonishment, we heard our arrival being announced on the PA system, leading people to want to talk to us all day. We were stuck out wandering around unshaven in shabby clothes and sneakers, but we were the celebrities du jour.

While we were strolling around the hotel, a manager approached us. He volunteered common local knowledge among boaters that the entrance channel was overdue for dredging, and it was prudent to avoid crossing the bar with storm waves or a high ground swell coming in from offshore. Of course, that was news to me.

The next morning we cast off to motor south down the Intercoastal Waterway. John left us to fly home from Port Stewart, Florida. Neil and I crossed the state via Lake Okeechobee, reaching the Gulf of Mexico at Fort Myers. Carol and Pete Brown had come down from St. Petersburg to meet us. Since Neil had more leave time remaining than I did, I drove the Browns' car back to St. Petersburg to catch a flight to D.C. and Neil finished the delivery with Carol and Pete.

* * *

LIVING LUCKY—MOSTLY

With Major James Lassiter, USAF, and John Morrison

The return to life ashore was brightened by a job offer from an unexpected source. News I had returned to Washington from army duty in the ski troops in my own airplane had been circulating on the CIA grapevine among WEI people I had worked with or met in Taiwan. One of them was Jim Lassiter, former head of the Air Support Section. He was an air force reserve major with flying experience in the Antarctic. Major Lassiter was organizing a small expeditionary group to do some secret aerial mapping of an unexplored section of the Antarctic continent from two U.S. Air Force C-47 aircraft (the military version of the Douglas DC-3). The project would be part of Operation Deep Freeze in Antarctica. The objective of the mapping would be to produce documentation that might be used later to support American claims to territory.

Lassiter sought me out because he was looking for someone to be responsible for supply procurement and records maintenance, as well as cold weather survival if the expedition experienced aircraft failure. Was I interested? Naturally, I signed up.

Best of all, because I had learned to fly and Lassiter had decided to forego a copilot (our crew included the uncommon USAF Master Sergeant Beverly, a veteran C-47 master mechanic who could also fly one if needed), I became the copilot, learning on the job. In early December we took off for Antarctica.

Flying down the west coast of South America at low altitudes with overnight stops in Panama, Lima, Peru, Santiago, and Puerto Montt, Chile, gave me an opportunity to see a little of South America. I liked what I saw. We got as far as our jump-off point to the continent, isolated Punta Arenas, Chile, in the Patagonian region on the Strait of Magellan. The airport was a single concrete runway with a few tie-downs on the apron, one small fuel tank, and no buildings. Sergeant Beverly put me to work helping install skis on the landing gear while teaching me other stuff about C-47s.

Then the unexpected happened. Our Antarctic rendezvous partners, famed polar explorer Finne Ronne and his ships, were stuck in the Weddell Sea pack ice far from land. We were stranded in Punta Arenas. In the nineteenth century, the town had been a major coaling station for ships transiting the straits connecting the Atlantic and Pacific oceans, but it had fallen on hard times and into a time warp after completion of the Panama Canal. Since then it had been mostly a center for sheep and cattle rancheros with one quaint old hotel with dairy products delivered daily by horse-drawn wagon. As celebrity foreigners in a small city, we spent the holidays being feted by our new Chilean friends with golf games, trout fishing, horseback riding gaucho style, and invitations to their parties. We had a ball.

By the end of January, the Pentagon brass deemed it too late in the Antarctic summer to safely fly into Finne Ronne's finally established base. So we removed our skis and flew home. I logged eighty-three hours of copilot time, suggested and signed off by Major Lassiter, although God knows how I would have safely landed the plane if Jim had keeled over in the left seat.

I soon left the project to flounder on an unfortunate desk assignment in the South American Division.

In July my housemate, John Morrison, invited me for a weekend at Rehoboth, Delaware, where he and a few guys had a vacation rental near the ocean beach. For some reason I couldn't go with them by car, so I flew out on Saturday afternoon. Per instructions from John who knew my Ercoupe, on arrival at Rehoboth, I was to fly the beach. He and his friends would be having drinks on the deck of a nearby rental shared by some women, including his girlfriend. They would be looking for me, and someone would come out to the airport to pick me up. The "someone" turned out to be Betty Drummond, a casual comely acquaintance of John's and one of the women sharing the rental. Why Betty? I'm firmly told—only because she had a car. On her arrival at the airport, sporting a tan to die for, I asked if she would like a ride in the Ercoupe to fly the beach. She thought it a great idea. We've been a couple ever since.

Restless after my trip to Delaware, I spotted an article about a home service business in Hollywood that was franchising. Why not organize one in the nation's capitol? Why not combine vacation and business to fly there in the Ercoupe? Looking for a partner, John, also a WWII Liberator navigator, thought going transcontinental in a small plane would be a novel vacation.

We took off on September 12. Home in Tacoma I visited my family while John went south to visit friends in California.

On September 23, I soloed south to Hollywood to check out United Home Services. The owners proposed I buy a franchise for $50,000, unaware I had only $5,000 to invest in a business. After lunch I flew to Walnut Creek to pick up John. We were back in Washington, D.C. three days later—me with plans to leave the Agency, sell my beloved Ercoupe, and become an entrepreneur.

On New Years Eve, both of us three sheets to the wind, I proposed to Betty she do some Gulf of Mexico sailing with me on the *Sanderling*. She liked the idea, but said, "What will people think? Not married? Not even engaged? Unthinkable!" That was the era. So we decided to get married.

I resigned from the CIA in early 1958 to work with two friends, Tom Hillary and Art Sommer, organizing Services Unlimited, Inc. with offices in upscale Georgetown. Betty and I got married March 28 of that year. Through the generosity of Pete and Carol, I was able to borrow the *Sanderling* to honeymoon in the Gulf of Mexico and ran her aground off Sarasota the first night at sea. We limped into harbor, ignominiously motored up the inland waterway to Tampa Bay, and returned the boat to Carol and Pete, marking a disastrous way to begin a marriage. But somehow Betty got pregnant during that week. Daughter Jenifer was born December 30, late enough to be legitimate and early enough to be a tax deduction. From day one we called her "Jef," spelled phonetically.

My venture partners and I achieved a two-line honorable mention in *TIME* magazine in early 1960 and my son Alan was born June 26. Unfortunately, it was downhill from there. My business dream was broke a year later.

For the next two years I failed trying to sell life insurance. During the last of that, on my own, I studied the growing field of corporate pension plans while Betty stoically supported our family on her part-time dental hygienist's income. Most of the following year after that was the worst. Unemployment benefits didn't exist, so to stay above water we leased our house and rented a cheap apartment. Halfway through the year I took a job as night clerk, working from 11:00 p.m.–7:00 a.m., at an apartment tower so I could job hunt during the day.

We never despaired. Four months later I landed on my feet with the

National Automobile Dealers Association Retirement Trust as the first field representative presenting and installing their association-sponsored employee retirement plans in member dealerships nationwide. Every other week or so, I'd fly to a state with a schedule of seminars at various cities already arranged by the association for my talk and slideshow. On arrival, I'd rent a car to travel the state. Small states might be covered in a week. Others, like California, might call for a trip of two or three weeks. I'd make my presentation in the morning, sign up dealers in the afternoon, and usually move on to the next town to repeat the routine the next day. I loved the job and travel. Betty cheerfully accepted raising the family while supplementing the family income continuing to clean teeth part-time, and all of it with me away much of the time. Looking back, I think she was simply pleased to see me settling into something with a decent paycheck and a future.

Shortly after going to work for the auto dealers, with U.S. involvement in Vietnam expanding, I got a call from a CIA headhunter making an appointment to see me. His purpose turned out to be an attempt to recruit my return to the Agency. If I accepted, the plan was to give me a six-week refresher course, then send me to Vietnam to work in maritime-related paramilitary/intelligence operations. He offered hire back at a Civil Service Rating salary equivalent to what I would have achieved if I'd never left, plus a 25 percent hazardous duty bonus, plus full restoration of life, disability, family, and other personal insurance and benefits, plus generous fully paid home leave privileges. The proposal was attractive, but I'd heard no mention of the flag or saving our country or the world for democracy. He said, like an after-thought, "Those are important too." With thoughts of what I'd heard about the roots of our Vietnam involvement while in Taiwan and other information, I told him I'd loved working for the Agency, but, married with children, I wasn't interested in endangering my life unless my country's security was at risk.

These experiences led me to take an extended lunch hour to attend the first formal demonstration against legislative commitment of our armed forces in Vietnam at Lafayette Park in early 1965. When John Ordway, Retirement Trust Director, heard about it, I was asked to his office. He reminded me of the mind-set of the people upstairs favoring the war. He ordered me to never again engage in this activity during working hours or share my opinions on the subject with other employees. I obeyed.

Some of my job travel incurred an added value. After showing Ordway I could travel more flexibly at a savings over commercial air and car rental costs, I was okayed to fly myself between seminar appointments in small leased planes at association expense. Most of those euphoric hours were spent flying low wing Mooney Mark 20/21s, with retractable landing gear and cruising at one hundred eighty miles per hour. I'd take off from Washington, D.C. on Sunday evening for stops to work in states with towns and cities as far west as Chicago, and fly home Friday night. I was on cloud nine.

Betty and me about to take off on business trip in Mooney Mark 21 from Dulles Airport
Photo by Dave Olson

* * *

Two years into this arrangement, on request from the state of Washington for a summer seminar series there, I volunteered for the job. The timing made it possible for my family to go along so I could combine work with family vacation, and the first series led to invitations for two more summers. The timing could not have been more fortuitous, especially for vacationing with Mom and Dad and Ken's family in the Pacific Northwest.

In 1964, Dad had seen an opening he couldn't pass up. He retired from Pacific Lutheran College to become pastor of a small church in Concrete, Washington where there was also a personal incentive. Concrete was on the Skagit River, renowned for steelhead fishing. Trout abounded in nearby lakes looking up to majestic Mount Baker. Though she never said much, Mom missed her friends in Parkland and the winters were long in Concrete. They stayed nine years.

Ken and his family were able to join us for a few days on all three of those memorable summer family vacations. We spent most of our family times together at beautiful Baker Lake, nestled in the North Cascades in the shadow of Mount Baker, hosted by Mom and Dad, who were now Grandma and Grandpa Olson. Ken's family also hosted us more than once at their home in Clinton on the Whidbey Island coast.

My increases in salary, combined with Betty's income, was sufficient for us to take our family to Vermont to learn to ski and me to resume ski jumping, working my way back to jumping the fifty-meter hill at the Middlebury Snow Bowl. The next winter we went up to Greenwich, Connecticut, for a long weekend visiting Betty's parents. I took along my jumping skis because the time provided an opportunity for me to make the short drive over to Bear Mountain State Park, near New York City, the birthplace of American ski jumping and home of the legendary Tokle brothers, Torger and Art, and jump the fifty-meter hill where they had made history. Torger had been in my pantheon of sports heroes since before I'd taken my first jump. He was an Olympian and among the best in the world before World War II, during which he joined the U.S. Army's 10th Mountain Division and died in battle in Italy.

It was a beautifully clear and warm Saturday. My father-in-law, Walter, went with me. On arrival, we found thousands of spectators already there waiting for a competition to begin. The only way I could jump was to join the action. Never mind it was my first jump in a year and I was thirty-seven years old. After a meeting with a jump judge who cleared me, I was entered, given a number, and sent off to take my first practice jump. I got in line with my skis behind the other entrants for the climb to the top. At the bottom, and off to the side of the landing hill, was a black ambulance. On the hike up I learned from a guy in front of me who looked my age that due to the lack of natural snow, I'd be jumping on a hill of trucked-in pulverized ice—so be prepared for a fast ride.

Each jumper was announced over the PA system. Finally, the jumper in front of me was proclaimed: "Our next jumper, making his first jump of the day, Olympic team coach and Bear Mountain's own, let's give a big hand to Art Tokle!" Down he went for a beautiful jump to the accompaniment of more cheers. The next day the Sunday New York Times featured a half-page photo of Art Tokle airborne and reported the crowd at twenty thousand people.

I had never jumped before more than a few hundred people nor with an ambulance closer than the nearest hospital. The next announcement was: "Our next jumper is Dave Olson, unattached, Washington, D.C."

"Unattached" meant I wasn't a member of any club or ski team. By that time, looking down at that crowd, I was stupefied and on autopilot. The acceleration was as advertised. Someone said I looked okay in the air, but lost it on the landing.

The right side of my face came off the crushed ice a swelling mess. A medic looked, gave me a bag of ice, and wished me luck. By the time I regrouped with Walter, vision in my right eye was close to nil. He drove us home. Betty glanced at me and said, "That's your last jump!" Monday I was back at work denying I'd been in a barroom brawl. My skis, made of varnished straight-grain hickory and considered classic heirloom "jumpers," continue service as a treasured bookshelf.

After six wonderful years, Ordway left for greener pastures. His successor, Joe Parren, and I didn't get along well. This was my fault because he did the best he could for me. In 1970 he found a great way to accomplish a business objective and get me out of his hair. Well aware of my roots and desire to live by the sea, he sold the association powers on a transfer of me and my family to the San Francisco Bay area for me to establish and manage a West Coast office. It was a life-changing opportunity for which I owe him eternal thanks.

We settled north of the Golden Gate Bridge in the marvelous Lucas Valley of Marin County. Our contemporary California Eichler Homes community was teeming with active families just like ours. Continuing my Forrest Gump life, two months after moving in, my new friend and neighbor Jerry Raube and I paired up to buy an Islander 21 sloop. We promptly named her *Skol*, celebrating Scandinavian toasts. Back at sea and under sail I went on to enjoy over two decades of sailing adventures, including some racing as crew on many boats.

CLIMBING TO HEAVEN

Certain events have a way of changing everything.

Through the 1970s and into the early 1980s, all of us—Betty, daughters Jenifer (Jef) and Susan, son Alan, dachshund Clovia, and I—thrived on living the Marin County, California, experience. We loved the lifestyle and people we found in Lucas Valley.

We joined the nearby Lucas Valley Community Church where Jef was soon very active in their youth program. We enjoyed the numerous attractions close at hand, especially in the great outdoors. Betty was in heaven playing tennis outside year-round. I shared her fondness for the game, though was never good enough to beat her. The neighborhood pool was open for swimming half the year, and all three children spent at least one season on the swim team. All three also took up learning to play the guitar. Jef's guitar became her bridge for life to friends and fellowship. We all went hiking, skiing, beachcombing, camping, and backpacking. Saturdays were sometimes for family sailing on the *Skol* and exploring San Francisco Bay. Vacationing relatives, including Ken and his family, came to visit us and we reciprocated with visits to see them. There were countless exciting places to explore within a few hours driving time from home.

The summer of 1976 was special. Our family partnered with sailing friends Gene and Joyce Dyer and their children, Marc and Kym, to bareboat charter a bridge-decked diesel-powered forty-three-foot cabin cruiser, the M/V *Charisma,* out of Seattle for a three-week cruise to Southeast Alaska. I was captain. All the older children shared the crew duties—standing wheel watches and learning other seafaring skills transiting the Inside Passage north to Petersburg with memorable stops in Prince Rupert, Ketchikan, and Misty Fjords. Everyone returned elated by the unforgettable adventures and wonders of small-boat life at sea.

**The Dave Olson family in front of Tlingit Totem Pole,
Saxman Village, Ketchikan, Alaska in 1976**
Left to right: Dave, Alan, Susan, Jef, and Betty, during stop-over in Ketchikan on family crewed small boat cruise from Seattle to Southeast Alaska.
Olson Family Archive

* * *

SEPTEMBER 1982

The entire family was drawn to the attractions of the Sierra Nevada mountains. Alan joined the Boy Scouts shortly after our arrival in California in 1970. In 1972 I went along on a one-week fifty-mile backpack hike in the Sierra just south of Yosemite National Park. We came home determined to experience more of the wonders of John Muir's "Range of Light." A few years later Alan took a course in rock climbing offered by his high school. Soon he and his friends had accumulated some personal gear, and I would drive them over to nearby Mount Tamalpais to practice their skills. Naturally, I had to try it too. I loved it.

Later, through neighbor friends, I met Tony Smith, a San Francisco dentist with years of experience doing technical mountaineering routes in Yosemite and along the Sierra spine. When he heard about my newfound interest, he wasted no time inviting me along on his next climb with his buddy, Mike Glogowsky. From then on the three of us managed to get away for two or three climbs every year. We didn't do any of the famous big walls, but we enjoyed climbing many popular climbs such as Cathedral Peak, Mount Clark, Matterhorn Peak, Mount Ritter, Mount Darwin, and Clyde Minaret.

Then came Saturday, September 12, 1982. Jef was home in great physical condition after a year working and playing in Sun Valley, Idaho. She had done some climbing on nearby Mount Tamalpais and in the Sawtooths of Idaho. Alan was home from fishing in Alaska, and a young family friend and experienced mountaineer, Terry Diraison, was living with us. I suggested we all climb Bear Creek Spire, one of the easier climbs in the Sierra, a Class 3–4 climb topping out at 13,713 feet. After checking the guidebook the unanimous response was, "Sure, why not?" It would be a four-day trip, beginning with a five-hour drive to the trailhead and a four- to five-mile approach to establish a base camp for the climb at about 11,400 feet. The second day was a layover day for getting adjusted to the altitude. Day three, the climb. Day four, the hike out and drive home.

The weather was perfect. On the lazy layover day, Jef spent a good part of the afternoon off making friends with some backpackers who had camped not far away. Later, over tea and cookies, Jef read a few favorite psalms to us, breathing life and immediacy into the familiar passages. I will never forget the pleasure and sense of peace and well-being I felt that evening.

Once we were on the climb, Alan and Terry took turns leading the pitches to prudently put in desirable protection, which would limit the distance a leader would fall, allow for anchor belays, and make easy climbing for the followers. I climbed in third position to join them, leaving Jef to enjoy the views while awaiting her turn.

On the fifth pitch, about one hundred feet above Jef, I came to a large rock one step up and to my right. Somehow I nudged that rock enough to break it loose, and it just took off. I hollered "Rock!" to warn Jef. I can still see her now, looking up, gauging the trajectory of the rock. She went left. If she had never moved, or gone to her right, the rock would have missed her.

* * *

TRAGEDY ON BEAR CREEK SPIRE

The rock hit Jef and crumpled her body. I frantically yelled down to her. There was no response. Then I called up to Alan and Terry telling them what had happened and I was going down to Jef. The slope wasn't that steep so they were able to quickly belay me down to her. One look told me she was dead. Alan and Terry were down to the ledge to join me in a few short minutes. The three of us just stood there stunned and devastated by what had happened.

Finally, because it was getting late in the day, we had no choice but to mark the site and leave her body there. The three of us, burdened by unbearable sorrow, had to make our way back down to base camp for the worst night of our lives. When morning came, we broke camp and hiked out to the trailhead and nearby ranger station. Per instructions, we waited there for the Mono County sheriff's deputy to arrive and take notes on the accident and location of Jef's body. The deputy said the county would send a helicopter rescue team up to the site to recover her. Then we were released to go home. I believe Terry did the driving. I didn't have had the fortitude to do it myself.

On the way home I steeled myself to accept any response from Betty as my deserved fate. We arrived after dark. Unable to face Betty and Susan by ourselves, I suggested we go first to see our close friends, Gene and Connie Turner, living just three blocks from home. The five of us then went to our house. When we walked in without Jef, Betty knew instantly something awful had happened. When we explained what had occurred, Susan became understandably hysterical. Betty, speechless, calmly left us to go to the phone.

"What are you doing?" I asked her.

"I'm calling Fil to see if he has anything to calm Susan," she replied. Dr. Filmore Rodich was our family doctor and lived a half a block away. Fil and his wife, Judy, were at our door in minutes. They were successful in calming Susan. I remain in awe at how Betty handled that night. She saw me through it without ever losing her composure. I don't know how she did it.

The next day the sheriff's office called to tell us they had recovered Jef's body, the coroner had confirmed the cause of death, and they were requesting further instructions. After a brief family discussion, I called back approving they turn her over to the local mortuary for cremation and asking that they forward her ashes to our home. Beyond that, the next few days were a blur. All I know is the door was always open and a constant stream of people came and went every day and evening. I also remember Fil and Judy just walking in during the next evening, and every evening thereafter through the first two weeks, to say hello, find chairs, sit, and say little or nothing. They were just there to make sure all was well with us, our family, and our visiting friends. It was an inspiring gesture of human compassion.

Extended family began arriving on Tuesday. Betty's mother, Elinor, flew in from Greenwich, Connecticut. My mother, Ida, and brothers, Ken and Tim, came from Seattle, Washington. The news reached Betty's sister, Bobbie, at a rural town in Switzerland where she was attending a business conference. She spent the next few days frantically doing the best she could, by train, plane, and rental car, to reach our home to be with Betty and Elinor. Thwarted along the way by sold-out flights and exhausted by two sleepless nights, she arrived shortly after the memorial service.

I have little idea of how news of the accident quickly reached relatives and friends from church, school, college, and work in California, Washington, and Idaho. Reporters representing newspapers from Marin County, California, and Wood River Valley of Idaho called seeking accounts and photos.

On Wednesday, September 15, 1982, the *Marin County Independent Journal* ran this story:

She Died In The Outdoors She Loved

By Lindajoy Fenley, IJ staff

Jenifer "Jef" Olson died Sunday in the outdoors she loved—on Sierra Crest, 200 feet short of her destination. The 23-year-old Lucas Valley woman died instantly when a rock crashed down from about 100 feet above her. She was climbing Bear Creek Spire on the Crest between Mammoth and Bishop with her father, brother and a very close family friend when the accident occurred.

"I was down (to her) in a minute. There was nothing I could do," her father, Dave Olson, said. Olson was nearest his daughter with his son, Alan, and the friend, Terry Diraison, tied above him. The four had nearly reached their 13,700-foot goal when the accident occurred. "I just reached up for what we call a flake," the father said, "and it came loose ... it was a monster." Other climbers understand it wasn't anyone's fault," said the grieving father. "It's the kind of thing that happens in the mountains. Rocks are just waiting to fall." The granite boulder hit Miss Olson on the head and back, killing her instantly.

But her companions faced a long and painful hike back to civilization. Leaving her body there, they rappelled down the steep cliff until they reached terrain where they could walk again. It was still tough climbing to their base camp where they spent Sunday night, Olson said. Early Monday they packed up and walked the rest of the way to the ranger's station. Miss Olson's body was recovered by a sheriff's helicopter Monday afternoon.

An avid outdoorswoman, she enjoyed skiing, backpacking, canoeing and sailing. A year ago, she moved to Sun Valley, Idaho, for skiing and other outdoor activities. The family, who had moved to Marin in 1970, lived in Sun Valley during Miss Olson's last year in high school. She graduated from Wood River High School there.

In Marin, she had been active in Terra Linda High School choral and madrigal groups. She participated in a peer counseling program at the school. She also played guitar in folk services at the Lucas Valley Church. She graduated from Whitworth College in Spokane, Wash. in 1981. She was head resident in the dormitories at Whitworth for two years. She also was a counselor and, later, assistant director at Camp Murrieta Sports World—Olympia for two seasons. She was born in Washington, D. C.

Within a couple of days after Jef died, bedeviled by perceptions of inadequacy, I wondered how we could continue and extend what she had done so well in her short life. Literally everyone who called asked what they could do to help recognize her passing. As a family we quickly decided to establish a scholarship fund in her memory at Whitworth College where she had spent four happy, inspirational, and fruitful years. We suggested contributions to the Jenifer Olson Memorial Scholarship Fund at Whitworth. This decision set me to thinking about the financial status of small, people-oriented liberal arts colleges. I pondered the need to preserve these institutions so graduates they produce can fill niches in a society desperately in need of people like Jef. We wanted the awards to recognize students living the life Jef had lived as a student and go toward preparing them for careers in ministry and social service.

Professors at Whitworth, former teachers who had become her friends, welcomed our ideas and promptly went about making arrangements for the fund to become a reality. We were indebted to the fast work by Dr. Pat McDonald, a treasured professor of Jef's, coordinating with Dr. Bill Peterson, Vice President for Student Life, and Rich Matheny, Vice President for Development. Since her major interests had been in counseling and leadership on campus, at camps, and in churches, we wanted to call it the Jef Olson Outreach Award. The Student Life office convinced us a more appropriate title would be the Jef Olson Outreach Scholarship. We found enthusiastic support from that office for grantees to be chosen more on the basis of participation and leadership in service activities rather than academic achievement. Economic need would be factored into the qualification. We had no idea of the support that would be generated for the fund.

A memorial service was held at Lucas Valley Community Church on Friday, September 18th. It was a California summer day. The church was far too small for the number of friends and family who came, so a PA system was put up out in the courtyard so the overflow could still hear the service. Our extended family walked through the thick crowd during the processional into the church. The Sonshines, the Christian folk singing group Jef had belonged to during high school, had been hastily brought back together by her friend and mentor Shirley Blaul to sing songs from the days when Jef had been with them. The pastor, Reverend Dale Nystrom, who's daughter Caren was one of Jef's best friends, preached the homily straight from the heart. My brother Ken spoke for our family as neither Betty nor I felt the strength to talk. Ken's daughter Joanne and Jef had been more than cousins from the beginning, and Ken wove a tapestry of Jef's life as one of faith lived as an adventure. I was unable to control my grief, giving thanks for all these people, and so many others, who inspired Jef to be who she was.

Everybody was invited to an open house hosted by Lucas Valley friends at our home after the service. All I remember is people coming and going for the rest of the day and into the night.

On Sunday afternoon, Gordon Pool, a sailing friend and neighbor, hosted a group of family and friends on his ketch and sailed us out under the Golden Gate Bridge into the Pacific Ocean. There we held a brief moving service committing Jef's ashes to the depths of the eternal sea she loved.

Finally, everybody went their different ways to resume their busy lives. I also had to pick up the pieces of my life; my family depended on it. It was time to return to work. Two weeks after the accident, I was on a long drive down Interstate 5 from the Bay Area to Los Angeles on business and to ease my sorrow I brought along the tape that Jef had compiled as a gift to Betty titled "Awesome Mellow Tunes For Great Moms." Playing those songs, while thinking about the life Jef had lived, I pondered how she would want me to live. How could I honor Jef's life?

Those thoughts evolved into a daily invocation for me, even as I write these words today. While often falling short, I do my best every day to live the life I think she would want me to live—being active in social, environmental, conservation, and political causes; standing up to be counted for mercy, justice and peace; showing compassion for those less fortunate through my actions; damping down my tendency to be judgmental; reveling in the wonders of life and all of creation; expressing my loves without hesitation; and loving God and my neighbor as myself.

I resumed climbing mountains because I perceived encouragement from Jef. During the summer of 1983, my mountaineering companion Mike

Glogowsky joined me to summit Bear Creek Spire to mount this brass plaque on the summit:

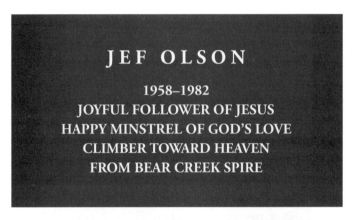

Jef in a reflective moment
Taken on Whitworth College campus in Spokane, Washington
Photo by a friend of Jef.

THE INSPIRED LIFE
OF JENIFER ANN OLSON

Over the last five years of her life, Jef was immersed in acquiring the intellectual and spiritual tools to live a happy, vibrant, and fulfilling vocational life of active ministry. She had chosen to attend Whitworth College in Spokane, Washington, a thousand miles from home, and our family had seen little of her beyond holiday gatherings. She was busy breaking her own trail, and she was good at it. After her death, friends from her past who we knew and a host of strangers surfaced to share stories, anecdotes, and letters to relieve our collective sorrow. In addition, we kept two newspaper articles written by journalists who knew Jef personally and saved pieces about and from grantees of the scholarship we created in Jef's name. This is a collection of those treasured memorials of her life and legacy, capturing the warmth and human bonding power of her character—the essence of who our Jef was.

* * *

ROBERTA McKERCHER, *WOOD RIVER JOURNAL*

The *Wood River Journal* is the daily paper of the Wood River Valley in Idaho, covering all communities in the valley including the Sun Valley Resort. When word of Jef's death reached the valley, Roberta McKercher, a reporter for the paper called to share with us her friendship with Jef. She had met Jef back when Jef had one of the leads in a musical at Wood River High, and had been impressed with Jef's cheerful expression of life. She was pleased when Jef returned to the Wood River Valley.

"I got to know Jef well at my church through her participation in our church activities," she said. "I admired her unusual ability to build meaningful relationships with older people."

Roberta's September 16 article included a photo and the following excerpt describing what Jef was doing, besides skiing and working to cover expenses, during her year in the valley:

Following graduation from college, [Jef] returned to the Wood River Valley in December 1981 because she loved skiing, carried memories of happy times here, and rightly felt she might be useful to local probation officers and in youth work. While here she provided special music at both St. Thomas Episcopal and Emmanuel Episcopal churches, and assisted starting a youth group, and with many special events in the two churches. She had decided to return home to advance her education and had gone to California to make plans for this with her family.

* * *

FUNDING THE JEF OLSON OUTREACH SCHOLARSHIP

Jef was not forgotten by our neighbors in California, either. On November 17 an article appeared in the Marin County *News Pointer*, "Lucas Valley Neighbors to Celebrate 'Jef' Olson's Life," by Marjorie Newton, who lived in Lucas Valley:

The loss of someone very dear is always a tragedy and a reason for sadness. However, in the case of the recent death of Jenifer Olson, her parents, Dave and Betty Olson, are concentrating on the positive aspects of their tragedy. They want to celebrate their daughter's life rather than mourn her death.

The initial newspaper stories said Ms. Olson died in the outdoors she loved. The postscript story is the cumulative testimony of local teachers, pastors, peers and friends telling of Jef's seven years of involvement in life enrichment and helping services activities, Christian outreach programs, voluntary work with juveniles on probation, visiting convalescent homes, peer counseling at Terra Linda High, and directorship of the Marinwood Day Camp.

Friends and family of Jef are building a memorial fund to promote student participation in student life and outreach programs at Whitworth College. The community of Upper Lucas Valley has decided to become involved in development of this memorial fund to extend Jef's short, but significant, life. On Sunday, November 21, the Lucas Valley Racquets, the women's tennis club Betty has been a member of for years, is hosting a mixed doubles tennis tournament and wine tasting benefit. Wine is being donated by Buena Vista Winery. Other donations include items for auction such as a weekend at a Tahoe condo. The public is invited. Prooceeds will go to the "Jef Olson Outreach Scholarship" fund.

A week later, the Lucas Valley Homeowners Association's newsletter *Valley Vibration* featured a "HIP HIP HOORAY…to Marj Hayden and her marvelous committee for raising $2,200.00 for Jef's fund."

With fundraisers like these, the scholarship account soon reached $10,000—enough for an early first award of $1,000 to Kurt Dale, a student walking in Jef's footsteps as a residence advisor, "to determine how he can…increase his opportunities to reach out to others as Jef did to those around her."[25]

The fund would eventually reach over $60,000, offering annual Outreach Scholarships. Representative of the awardees over the years was Molly Hough in 2013. Along with being a resident assistant for two years, Molly wrote:

This year I am the student body president and genuinely love this job. When first elected, I thought about how the Whitworth community could have a year of being a courageous university where our mission statement is truly lived out through our actions. So, I am a dreamer and started dreaming big with other Whitworth students. We were then able to form a movement known as Unite. This is a movement aiming to educate and empower entire communities to act in efforts to reduce the injustice of human trafficking within the Pacific Northwest and across borders. We are now working with nonprofit organizations, churches, high schools, other universities, legislatures, and law enforcement. It has been incredible to work hard on this issue. I am able to do these things because of awards like the Jef Olson Scholarship. After graduation I hope to continue pursuing the fight against human trafficking.

* * *

Betty and I look back on a three-decade history of annual Outreach Scholarships honoring Jef. Soon we will hear from another Molly Hough, and then another—confident this process will continue long after we are gone, Jef's legacy to each grantee who reflects on her life and lives theirs in kind.

* * *

TO KNOW HER WAS TO LOVE HER

So who was the real-life day-to-day Jef who we loved and friends idolized? From junior high onward, her life was a river of friends. We knew those whom she brought home to introduce. Others we knew only through Jef's sharing of stories about them. Fortunately, Jef and many of her friends were saving many

---

25   Letter from Julie Anderton, Ph.D., Vice President for Student Life, Whitworth College, December 9, 1982.

of their letters and photos. Anecdotes and writings Jef accrued before she died, and those of friends shared after her death, would fill a book.

One of Jef's last letters was written to friends from her Whitworth years, the Walker family in Spokane, Washington, shortly before her fateful return home:

Dear Walker Family,

I've been thinking about you a lot lately. My heart is full of thanksgiving when you are on my mind. I'm sure your summer has been filled with activity. What's John up to? I miss your family so much. My life is busy yet I sense a calm gentle spirit. I've spent the summer teaching kids aerobic dance. The kids have been a learning lesson for me—as well as a giving of myself to them. It's funny how teaching is a two-way street.

My job at the Pizza Barn has been trying in many ways dealing with an employer who mistreats his employees. But it's a good learning time too since the boss is giving me more responsibility and I'm learning more about what I have to expect from employees for an employer.

The minister from our church has moved to Tacoma. The congregation has had to pull together and form a more solid sense of direction and purpose. It's been a very healthy process—I think. My role has changed from a youth oriented direction—to music. The spirit moving through his music seems to blossom more and more each week. Sometimes the spirit is so overwhelming it feels like my body can't hold that much joy. It's exciting.

God seems to be pointing me toward graduate school this fall. What amazes and scares me are the tugs to get a double master in social work and divinity. I'd appreciate your prayers as I start the application process. In September I'm taking a trip home to see my family. I can't wait. During that time I'll be deciding if I should move back to San Francisco for the year .

Keep on pressing on—Because of Jesus. –Jef

A card of condolences from a family in Idaho included a moving tribute:

We knew Jef from the Pizza Barn where our Jeff worked with her. When he started working there, he was having a hard time adjusting to his first job. Jef was able to listen to him and help him through a bad time. He finally came to terms with working and thought the sun rose and set on your daughter. She talked to us about the difficulty he was having and helped us be more supportive of him. We want you to know we'll remember Jef's love and thoughtfulness for our family. —Bonnie, Mel, Jeff & Jason Warren, Hailey, Idaho

Like her grandfather Roy, Jef had a propensity for bringing people home to live with us for a while. The first was Terry Diraison. We had met Terry during his and Jef's high school years when they palled around in a loose group whose activities centered on making folk music at members' homes and outdoors in woodland and seashore settings. On graduation they dispersed to go to college. Terry's parents divorced, his mom moved to France and his dad to Southern California, leaving Terry to fend for himself.

On finishing his freshman year, Terry returned to our area determined to reconnect with his friends, find work, and make a go of it. Jef came home at the same time. She soon took off to visit friends where she ran into a homeless Terry. When she heard his plight she returned home to tell Betty Terry's story.

"Since Alan is in Alaska for the summer, how about letting Terry have his room and hang out here for the summer?" Jef said.

Betty couldn't recall Terry so she suggested Jef bring him around after I got home from work to meet us and see if we liked him.

"Gee, that won't work because I've already told him he can move in tonight," Jef replied. Terry only wants to meet with you and Dad to make sure everybody likes each other. Don't worry, it'll be okay."

Terry joined us for dinner. During the dance of getting acquainted, Terry inquired about family rules. Betty and I mumbled that we really didn't have any. Jef said, "Well, there is one rule. No matter what you've done, no matter how bad it is, you always tell the truth. That's it." He moved in to join the family and become an intermittent boarder for the next decade.

Another visitor was the unforgettable, irrepressible, arty and athletic, quirky free-spirit Lisa Lee, a Whitworth classmate of Jef's. Her nickname was "Leeroy." We first met her while she was on a vacation roadtrip with another classmate, traveling south down the West Coast from her family's home in Portland. She and her buddy showed up at our door at Jef's invitation to spend two or three fun days with us. During the next school year she was selected to spend January Term interning with a firm in San Francisco. Leeroy needed a place to live. Jef suggested living with us. And so she did. We all had a grand time as she had already met Terry and other friends of Jef during her earlier visit.

From then on, including after Jef died, Leeroy never failed to stop and see us on any trip taking her near where we lived. On one of those trips she shared this story:

At school Jef struggled with her dream of being called by God to be a missionary in a foreign country. We saw no sign of any talent or interest in foreign languages. My friends and I all thought she was crazy as her incredible gifts working with American youth would be wasted. So one night I took a blanket and sneaked into Jef's room (as a resident assistant she had her own room—never locked) before she showed up for bed. I crawled under her bed to lie quietly while Jef put on her pajamas and laid down to sleep. When I thought she was asleep, thinking she would be too groggy to realize it wasn't a voice from heaven, I said in a loud disguised voice of authority, "Jef, this is God talking. Jef, your calling is to be a missionary to people here, where you are, not far away." To my chagrin, the prompt response I got from Jef was, "Thank you, Lord, and please tell Lisa to go to bed now."

* * *

Betty and I urged our children to seek paying jobs early in life because we thought our early jobs had been important building blocks for our futures. Jef started out with babysitting gigs, but as soon as she was old enough she got a job at McDonalds. Another job during her late teens one summer was working as a gopher in the San Francisco insurance office where I was employed, and under the supervision of Lynda Regan, co-owner of the agency. Lynda later said of Jef, "She was always cheerful, spoke right up, and arrived at the office ready to go to work." It was a special summer as Jef and I were often able to share the world-class ferry commute on San Francisco Bay from San Rafael to San Francisco.

During her senior year at Whitworth, carrying a lighter academic load, she worked as a waitress at The Hindquarter Bar, a cocktail lounge in Spokane. Asked about it, she said she enjoyed the customers, lived for the tips, and felt the experience would contribute to her career vision. Betty and I were selective when sharing this news—our daughter working as a cocktail waitress. I told her I was proud of her spunk and independence; I loved her for it. Betty shared those sentiments.

We have no idea how many boys, and later men, dated Jef over the years of her brief life. My guess is they would fill a room. Paul Gulick was a special friend from the beginning of high school until her death. We recall her accepting dates with one mixed-up broken-home delinquent because she felt his need for companionship and feared for his future if she rejected his overtures. During her college graduation festivities, she introduced Betty and I to a "sort of" boyfriend she was dating. She told us later they were "just good friends." To my knowledge, she guarded against letting a relationship get really serious. In casual conversation, she once confided in me she thought Betty and I married at a good age, twenty-six and twenty-eight, respectively, at the time. She felt secure, valued the freedom of being single, and was determined to wait for the right guy before taking the plunge. That's as close as we got to the men in her life.

Beginning during Jef's teens, and for a long time thereafter, one of her closest friends was Louisa Arndt, the mother of Paul, and someone who remains a close friend of ours as well. Following Jef's death, in sharing our grief and to express hers, Louisa compiled for us a six-page eulogy of quotes from the cards and letters we received from others sharing their sorrow. She wrote, "Laughing and clowning were a part of Jef's life. Weird presents, costume parties, practical jokes, family anecdotes, and crazy camp songs were all in the picture. She loved dancing, but most of all, folk dancing. She became good enough at it to teach classes."

A member of one of Jef's aerobic dance classes said, "I was the oldest member of the class by a good deal at age sixty-five, but Jef made the dancing a lot of fun."

She never took team sports seriously. During grade school she was on the neighborhood community swim team, but her main contribution was cheering for teammates. She reached a high point her last winter as a stalwart member of a ragtag volleyball team playing in a young adults league. Touch football at the beach was another favorite team sport, and she embraced the thrills, skills, and spills that went with downhill skiing, whitewater canoeing, and brisk-breeze sailing. She was a "go-for-it" girl doing what she did. Out on the jogging paths, especially at Camp Murrieta with like-minded staff, she found time to train for, enter, and finish the famous Bloomsday (twice) and Dipsea (hard-core hills) running races.

Music was an integral part of Jef's life as well. She took her first guitar lesson when she was twelve, and her guitar was never far away thereafter. She sang in choirs, madrigals, and musicals, at home, in the homes of friends, beside a campfire, or on a boat deck. She delighted in sharing with those around her the joy she found in music. Camp, folk, and contemporary songs were all part of the fun. As a teenager she sang with a group of Christian folksingers called the Sonshines. They opened Sunday services and entertained at other church gatherings as well as convalescent and retirement homes. She carried on her music through college years and, in the months before her death, she led the folk singing during opening services at churches in Ketchum and Hailey, Idaho.

"Her music—her love of it, her manner of complete sincerity in rendering it, her choice of verses that carried a Christian message—words at my command cannot express how touched and inspired we all were," said Shirley Blaul, Sonshines leader at Lucas Valley Community Church.

"Jef was a motivator," said Vicki Duneman, a counselor at Camp Murrieta. "She encouraged me to finally, after years of putting it off, begin to play the guitar. At camp we spent many evenings playing and singing to wind down from the day's work. She started a collection of songs we sang to be gathered together and given to me as a Christmas gift. I'm sure she left it among her unfinished projects."

"Jef was a tremendous support to my ministry here, as well as a good friend to my wife and me," said Reverend Nick Morrison of St. Thomas Church in Ketchum, Idaho. "I felt we were a team as Jef began each service with group singing, creating a family feeling that was beautiful to see. Her endearing personality and beautiful gift to our congregations through her music will be remembered for a long time."

Anecdotal of Jef's charm as a persuader is a laugher we tell about a ten-day British Columbia cruise Jef, Betty, and I shared with three friends, Jerry Raube, Gene Dyer, and Paul Gulick, aboard a bareboat chartered thirty-six-foot cabin cruiser in June 1981. We all took turns cooking in the galley, but Jerry demurred on his share of the chore saying he didn't know how to make anything—his wife, Grace, did all the cooking at home. So he ended up paired with Jef for a few meals. She mentored a reluctant Jerry into doing and enjoying his share of the cooking and baking. On the way home, Jerry swore us to secrecy so Grace would never know what Jef had coaxed him to learn aboard the M/V *Laissez Faire*.

Jef was fourteen when she attended her first camp. This was the Quaker Meadow Camp of our church. It was here she began her personal commitment to the gospel of Jesus Christ. Thereafter, she said she was a Christian at every opportunity, and she affirmed it by the way she lived.

"Many of the youngsters who went to Quaker Meadow Camp were there because Jef sold them on the idea," said Reverend Dale Nystrom of Lucas Valley, California. "Jef was a gentle persuader rather than a preacher. She was the spark plug of a marvelously successful teenage youth group at our church."

"Her Christian faith was quiet, unassuming, and universal. She belonged to no denomination. I know my faith in God, and the human race, was strengthened through my friendship with Jenifer," said Marji Unsoeld, a friend from Lucas Valley.

Summers continued to be camp time. On her first summer home from college, her Quaker Meadow experience qualified her to be hired as director of the nearby Marinwood Community Center Children's Day Camp. The next summer (1980), Diane Murphy, a teacher at Whitworth during the school year and director of Camp Murrieta in Olympia, Washington, took Jef along as one of her staff counselors. The camp was one of six summer camps operating under national organization sponsorship and located at college campuses from coast to coast. The camps offered a special program for mostly overweight eight- to eighteen-year-old girls, often suffering from low self-esteem. The directors were advance-degreed physical education professionals trained to work with carefully selected staff, mostly college students, to help the campers achieve their goals. Jef loved the work and the challenge. She came home bubbling with enthusiasm over what she felt had been accomplished and looking forward to returning for a second go-around in 1981. That year she was assistant director, and she thrived on the added responsibility. Betty and I had trouble all summer and thereafter hiding how proud we were of her achievement.

Jef Olson and Paul Gulick hanging out with their guitars on bridge deck of M/V *Laisse Faire* on cruise to Desolation Sound, B.C.
Photo by Dave Olson

Somehow the news of Jef's death even reached some of the teenagers who had attended Camp Murrieta while Jef was on the staff:

I met Jef in the summer of 1980 at Camp Murrieta. I was a spoiled, immature brat bent on being miserable for the duration of camp. With her honest, non-condescending treatment of me, I gradually came out of my shell. My parents couldn't get up to see me on parents' day. So Jef and Tim Stall, a colleague on the camp staff, took me and two other parentless girls sailing on Puget Sound. It was a fantastic afternoon despite the fact we had to keep bailing out the boat. Jef kept saying, "The boat's going to sink and we're all going to die!" We laughed about that for days. Whenever something would go wrong, either she or I would say, "Well, I guess we're all going to die!" And then we would dissolve into hysterical giggles and everything would be better. That afternoon that started out with me being homesick and very depressed, ended up being just great, thanks to Jef. So anyway, that's the origin of HAPPY SAILING. Some of what she taught me still rolls thru my head from time to time.—Lisa Svanevik, Klamath Falls, Oregon

I hope I'm not bringing back painful memories of your loss, but I feel I must write and tell you how much Jef meant to me. Your daughter was the most loving person I've ever met. She gave of herself all the time. I had some special problems at camp and when I left I gave Jef a letter telling her how much she meant to me. When I came back a year later, we both felt awkward around each other, but Jef went out of her way to sit with me at breakfast, walk to classes with me, and make me feel good. I had no self-confidence at all. She helped me build it. When I finished the five-mile run, she was the first person to give me a hug. She was the first person to tell me I was special. I'd never believed I was anything until Jef said that. The last day of camp was depressing because I knew I wouldn't be seeing Jef anymore. When we hugged, and said good-bye, she told me she loved me. I knew if Jef loved me, I really was special. —Rhonda Bauer, Woodinville, Washington

Diane (Di) Murphy, professor of physical education at Whitworth, summer camp director, and mother of two children, also found time to be a special mentor and blessing in Jef's life. They discovered each other on campus, something clicked, and friendship followed. Shortly after Jef died, Di suggested to Camp Murrieta staff that each might write a letter to Jef expressing thoughts to her as if she were still with us. In her letter, Di shared memories of Jef's role in her professional and family life:

Dear Jef,

I've been trying to deal with all my feelings since I learned of your death. I'm angry and sad. I have this deep down ache. I grieve for myself, your other friends, and especially for your family—people I don't even know. I've spent a lot of time reflecting on who you are and what you meant and mean to our lives. It seems like you never had "acquaintances," Jef. Everybody you knew was a friend. And you had such a gift of communicating affection that no one was in doubt about your love. I'm so grateful for that gift. It motivated us to share our feelings with you.

I'm grateful, too, for Camp Murrieta and those shared memories. Remember when you wrecked the van? You were so upset. By the time I found out what you were actually trying to say through your tears, I was relieved to know it was just the van and not something really serious. Remember the time you took Karen and Chris [Di's children] ice-skating, and, while at camp, to Tumwater Park on your day off? It was just as much a treat for you as it was for them. How I love you for loving them. Remember the time in the office and the dance tapes you provided? We were so proud of ourselves for establishing that open communication as we worked together as director and assistant director…and aerobic dance instructors! Weren't we terrific? Now, when I see the posters we made and teach the dances we taught, I just have a very hard time. While I'm doing this vital and enlivening activity, I'm remembering everything about how you taught, and danced, and the ache inside becomes unbearable. It doesn't seem right all of this can go on without you. It's so hard to say good-bye to those shared experiences. Occasionally it pops into my mind that you are teaching aerobic dance to the "saints." I have a feeling you have taken heaven by storm. They are experiencing the kind of enthusiasm only you could introduce.

I don't understand much about heaven yet. I think about the concept that a thousand years of our "time" is like a night from the perspective of eternity. I don't understand that, but I suspect it relates to the answers for my "unanswerable" questions. I believe we have much yet to share and some day I will hear you say "Hi, Bud!" I believe you now know God in a way I can only wonder about and I am happy for you. At the same time, I must tell you I miss you and so the loneliness persists. I am grateful for a sense of God's arms about me. I pray for your family and other friends. How fortunate you were to grow up in a home immersed in love, and how fortunate for all of us that you were so loving in return. That makes it harder…and easier now.

Loving you,
Di

Bonnie Lattimore became a close friend of Jef at Murrieta where she served as camp nurse. By the time Jef spent her year in Idaho, Bonnie and husband Dan, and their children, were living in Colorado. They managed a meet-up with Jef and other friends in Yellowstone Park during the summer before Jef came home. On September 13, before Bonnie had heard of Jef's death, she penned this note and questionnaire to Jef; and then, before it was mailed, got a call with the news. She sent the letter to Di, instead, who passed it on to us in a scrapbook of Murrieta days:

> *Still love me? You are such a stinker, and I don't know what to do with you! Maybe you've had great reasons for not writing—just let me know them. We are all fine adjusting to school really well—we had a good visit with Kathy and Tony after Yellowstone. Possible job for Tony in Ft. Collins—flew him in last week. See, you may have more people here [in Colorado] to visit than you thought. We do hope all is going well for you. Please let me know. We have some great pictures of you—will get you copies when I get mine from you!*
> *Love you bunches, Bonnie & Family*

To further tease Jef about her procrastination as a correspondent, Bonnie wrote an addendum for Jef to complete and return. It read:

Jef,
> *Send the below back in self-addressed stamped envelope today—check all boxes.*

Dear Bonnie,
> *Yes No*
> *____ ____ I got a job in California right after I saw you in Yellowstone.*
> *____ ____ I didn't get a job so I am getting ready to go back to Idaho and move home.*
> *____ ____ I still plan on showing you and Danny my town when you come to Cal. in Nov.*
> *____ ____ I am fine and feeling good about all that's happening.*
> *____ ____ I feel lousy, but am accepting what seems to be God's plan.*
> *_x_ ____ Even though I am terrible at writing, I love and care about all of you, and thrilled you feel the same about me!*
> *_x_ ____ I have a beautiful picture of me I will send you when I return this letter.*
> *____ ____ I am sorry for not writing sooner!*
> *Much love, Jef*

We know Jef would have returned the questionnaire with photo and responding repartee.

* * *

Tracy Gibson Williams—an assistant professor in the School of Education and chair of Teacher Leadership at Seattle Pacific University—heard from Di Murphy about my wish to connect with friends of Jef from Whitworth and Camp Murrieta years who might contribute to Jef's story. Tracy didn't hesitate to contact Betty and me. She wrote:

> *Jef was a song-leading sister who arrived at Whitworth ready to change the world, and she did. She was part of a terrific group of girls at college, camp, and once for several days at our family cabin at Priest Lake [Idaho]. Jef was one of the angels in our life and like a real sister to me. I saved a final handwritten note from her in my writing files for years following her death. Now, as I teach teachers, principals, and school superintendents, I ever hope to inspire them to action like I experienced with Jef.*

Jef's closest friend and confidante from day one at Whitworth was Pamela (Pam) Corpron. After college, Pam went on to marry a classmate, Robert Parker, earn her Ph.D. in English and literature, have two sons, and return to Whitworth as a professor. In 2006, I wrote to Pam asking if she would be interested in reflecting on the friend she knew so well. Here are the highlights:

> *I met Jef the first night of my freshman year at Whitworth College in September 1977. I was unpacking boxes in my dorm room when I heard someone singing and playing a guitar down the hall. I followed the sound until I found Jef, and she invited me to join her. I did and we sang in harmony from that point on! If you're lucky, a few times in your life you meet people who immediately become old friends. Jef was one such person for me—a soul mate from the beginning. We never exhausted our topics for conversation, never stopped finding things to laugh about, and never lost our intense connection, no matter how much time we spent apart.*
>
> *Jef once explained to me (in conspiratorial tones) that she came from a long line of staunch Norwegian Lutherans. Choosing a Presbyterian college like Whitworth was tantamount to heresy. But Jef loved Whitworth immediately. She threw her energies into Student Life, the Chaplain's Office, and her psychology studies. She gathered friends wherever she went, and I was always glad to be counted among them. In February of 1980, I wrote in my journal, "Thank goodness for consistent, steady people like Jef. I love her so much! She is one of my most valued friends. Her honesty and commitment is amazing. She listens when no one else will and gives me*

honest, unwatered feedback. She keeps me accountable, but I'm free to discuss my bad attitudes with her without feeling judged."

Jef celebrated life and reveled in her physical existence; she loved to eat, drink wine, wrap her arms around people, and fill a room with music, laughter, and conversation. We took great interest in the male species and speculated endlessly about love, sexuality, marriage, and our latest crushes. Jef and I loved to play together; we shared many happy hours hiking, biking, jogging, swimming, and playing Frisbee, tennis, or racquetball. Like most college women, we worried about our weight and the dreaded "freshmen fifteen." We were dedicated fitness partners.

During that summer [of 1980] at Camp Murrieta in Olympia [Washington], we worked closely together. I wrote, "I'm so glad we're working together [this summer]. I feel confident in our ability to work with these girls and know good things that'll happen with our two heads together."

I found this entry dated July 23, 1980: "I've been moved to another world and feel as if I could stay for days. Right now I'm sitting in a hanging wicker chair on a foliage-surrounded deck. It's quiet and calm, and I can see the pale blue Puget Sound from here. Jef sits on the other side of me, writing also. We are companionably alone with our thoughts. I'm growing to appreciate this friend more and more as I spend time with her this summer. She is a woman of many resources and depths. She is not arrogant about them, but as I spend time with her they are revealed bit by bit. I treasure this friendship and pray that it will be one that can be nurtured in the years to come. It's not often you find someone with whom you can be yourself—unreservedly." Later in the summer, we took off for an overnight of camping. And I wrote, "We slept out under the stars at Millersylvania Park. It was an absolutely beautiful starlit night. Completely romantic except there was no man in it. We giggled ourselves to sleep."

In the year after we graduated, we both found our first jobs—Jef in Sun Valley and I teaching high school English. When the news of her death came to me in mid-September of 1982, I grieved her deeply. I was stunned to realize that life could be so arbitrary, and I mourned knowing we wouldn't grow old together or share those many milestones we were anticipating. During that time, my journal is filled with a sense of unfinished business. In one entry dated September 9, 1983, I wrote directly to her: "But Jef, I never returned your dress. You know, the striped sundress, with the thin straps, that you wore so well? Today, without thinking, I pulled out a burgundy colored blouse you leant to me. Is it mine now? Or will it always seem borrowed? So much of what I am now are things you gave to me, not the concrete objects, the many gifts and notes, we exchanged, but the hours of listening and sorting, crying and running and eating and swimming and telling family stories. These are the gifts that are a part of me, unalterably fixed in my spirit and in yours."

Jef and I journeyed through five of the most intense growing years of our lives, and I still feel their imprint in profound indelible ways—perhaps even more so as I have returned to Whitworth as a professor. Many times when I walk across the Loop, I sense Jef's spirit rising up to greet me in the cool shade of the old growth pines. I often meet students who remind me of her, and I am honored to give out the scholarships you named for her at the May awards ceremony. Honestly, this is always a bittersweet task for me. I am filled with such hope for these students and their futures, but I feel such a longing for Jef at these times. I wonder how her life would have developed in tandem with my own. I miss knowing her at this stage of our lives. Would she have stayed in the Northwest? Gotten further education? Married? Had children?

I'm not sure whether God reunites us with our loved ones after life. I like to think so. For only then, it seems, will we be fully restored to ourselves and made whole again. Perhaps then, this is the promise of the resurrection—a promise of wholeness not only in Christ, but to all those who have been Christ to us in this life. Jef was one of those people to me, and remembering her always reminds me of life's fullness, of its brevity and beauty, and the impermeable gifts of joy and longing, grief and hilarity.

Any significant loss takes years to process, and for me grief and gratitude are always mixed in death. We wouldn't grieve if we didn't love and value to one lost. Our pain marks their significance in our lives, the important place they filled in our hearts and memories. There is no accounting for our loss; there is no "getting over it." Lately, I've been trying to honor this part of living, to receive loss as a gift of sorts, and to acknowledge the fierce bonds that make loss painful. Somehow to diminish the loss (and the pain accompanying it) diminishes the fullness of our love for the one grieved. So, grieve well for Jef, grieve deeply and grateful, celebrating her brief but luminous presence in our lives.

Much love, Pam

PART FOUR

FLOATING FAITH
ON THE M/V CHRISTIAN

Now there are varieties of gifts, but the same Spirit;
and there are varieties of service, but the same Lord,
and there are varieties of working, but it is the same God
who inspires them all in every one.
To each is given the manifestation of the Spirit for the common good.
I Corinthians, Chapter 12, Verses 4–7

M/V *Chistian* on maiden voyage to Southeast Alaska
Ken Olson Family Archive

PROVIDENCE BUILDS A BOAT

There are periods in just about every life when nothing much happens of interest to anyone outside a family. Often during the passage of those years, however, small necessary stepping-stones are laid, eventually setting the stage for the pursuit of a dream. So it was for my younger brother, Ken Olson.

After a profitable season in Alaska in 1951 as a commercial fisherman and captain and owner of his own salmon troller, Ken returned home to Parkland, Washington, a winner. Flush with success, he quickly followed up with buying a new Chevrolet, making the Pacific Lutheran College football team as a linebacker, and netting a pretty girlfriend.

In the spring of 1952, he sold the *Lady Fay* and bought a bigger, better boat, the *Seabird*. With our younger brother Jerry, game for another year with Ken, they took off from Seattle for Kelly Cove as soon as school was out. Unfortunately the season was a bust, and Ken deserted the grounds to send Jerry home early. He decided to stay in Ketchikan to work on a construction crew while living on the *Seabird*. Eventually he sold the boat and returned to Seattle.

Back in Washington, he found Selective Service looking for him. Back in college, sobered by the experiences of the past year, it was time to figure out what he wanted to do next. Not attracted to a two-year hitch in the army, in 1954 he enlisted in the U.S. Marine Corps for three years. This would give him plenty of time to decide where he wanted to go with his life. Earlier he had become fascinated with the migration of salmon and expressed an interest in majoring in biology followed by pursuing a master's degree in marine biology at the University of British Columbia in Canada. By 1954, however, he was also thinking seriously about entering the ministry. It would be a game-changing career choice. He craved a different space and time to think it over; he got both in the marines.

Sgt. Ken Olson, with his mind made up, completed his tour in the marines in 1957. On return, declaring a pre-seminary major, he returned to finish work on his degree at Pacific Lutheran College. His only noteworthy course was in folk dancing, taught by Helen Enger, a comely Pacific Lutheran graduate with a master's degree in physical education. Soon she was Ken's girlfriend. Ken and Helen married in May 1958, and Ken received his diploma in June. The couple moved to St. Paul, Minnesota, where Ken began classes at Luther Seminary in September. They also started a family; daughter Joanne arrived in November 1959.

While doing post-graduate work in theology in 1961, the recently ordained Reverend Kenneth Olson cast about for a call to serve a church and earn a living. It's no surprise he found his first parish close to home on Whidbey Island in the Puget Sound. The parsonage was a short walk from the shore. It seemed he was a waterman simply following in the footsteps of his minister father who found a way over his long career of serving congregations while never living far from water. Ken's parish was made up of two small congregations. One church, St. Peter's, was located in Clinton and the other, Trinity, in Freeland, both coastal harbor villages.

In his pastoral flock were people spending careers in maritime-related pursuits, including commercial fishing. There was a spontaneous bond between them. Another natural enthusiasm was youth ministry. Soon he was involved in the Tri-Conference Camping Association's summer programs. This was a joining together of the Evangelical Lutheran denominational congregations in King, Pierce, and Snohomish counties of Washington, all fronting on Puget Sound. One Bible camp was located on a small coastal island off Port Townsend. Two others were located on lakes not far from Seattle. Ken and the youth in his parish were annual attendees at these camps.

Among the pastoral colleagues at camp was the Reverend Kenneth Daugs whom Ken simply called Daugs. The two Kens discovered they shared a common fascination for waterborne ventures and love of the sea. Olson wondered how the two of them might utilize their interest to provide a more exciting Christian experience than traditional Bible camp for teenagers in their churches. How about taking a small group of high school kids from their congregations cruising in a couple of outboard-powered runabouts on a two- or three-day camp-out in the nearby San Juan Islands? Olson had the ideal partner in "Can-Do Daugs."

Olson borrowed two boats from church members for a shakedown trip. One was an open eighteen-footer and the other a cubbyhole-decked twenty. Daugs, with kids from his church, went in one boat and Olson, with his kids, went in the other. Days were mostly spent letting the kids run the boats. Every night was roughing it on the beach at a different island. As Daugs tells it, "It rained the entire three days, but the campers returned home full of enthusiasm for the experience." The year was 1967.

The next summer the Kens moved up to a twenty-foot Bayliner, along with the original twenty-footer, for a week of boating in the same islands. They spent the days with the teenagers caught up in spiritual reflection, exploring the marine world as God's creation, and sharing the adventure. Writing of a second camp, Daugs enthuses:

> Later the same summer we lined up twelve boys for another week. By that time Ken and I had come up with a pretty funny good guy/bad guy Bible study routine to share over driftwood campfires. The overnight camp at Turn Island, near Friday Harbor, was always a private laugh between Ken and I. Turn Island is a very small, uninhabited island with no facilities. We were alone on a warm summer evening. After dinner on the beach, while almost all the crew were gathered around the campfire for our routine, one of the boys, fittingly named Bottomly, was spotted casually wandering around naked. The kids couldn't pass it up! The crew ran amok chasing Bottomly across the tiny island in the darkness. Bottomly escaped by diving in the ocean. A couple dove in to join him. Then they all gathered, including Bottomly, back at the fire to, as they say, "roast their wieners and buns." We duly noted an account of the incident in the log. Other camps were at Jones, Stuart, and James Islands along with a midweek stop at Roche Harbor for showers and ice cream. Prevost Harbor, Stuart Island, was a popular stop for swimming in the warm waters of a freshwater lake not far from the beach and up to fifty-foot dives off the nearby shoreline cliffs, called "Lover's Leap," led by Ken.

Daugs continues:

> In 1969 and 1970, we bareboat chartered a thirty-eight-foot troller, the Christina Gay, owned by a member of Ken's St. Peters church. Vic Painter, a state highway patrolman and member of my Prince of Peace church, came along as counselor for the growing group of rambunctious teens. We all traveled on the Christina and camped on the beaches.
>
> Early on Ken and I knew we had come up with a new way to work with high school youth in an entirely different environment from traditional Bible camp. We knew we were on to something good. Everyone in our congregations and Tri-C was talking about it by 1969. We realized the program needed its own boat."

Our dad claims, "Divine providence built the boat." Well, sort of. Pluck, luck, and resolve played major roles, too. But nothing would have come together without a flexible, creative boatbuilder, fortuitous timing, and a cast of supporting characters hankering for a share of the venture.

No vessel sized and equipped for the visualized service was in existence; so they had to find a way to finance and build a new boat to suitable specifications. As luck would have it, there in Freeland on Holmes Harbor, a five-minute walk from Olson's other church, was Nichols Bros. Boat Builders, specialists in building small steel workboats. The reverend didn't know Frank Nichols, so he just moseyed in one day in 1968 to look around and introduce himself.

**Preserved façade of Nichols Bros. Boat Builders yard
as it was when the M/V *Christian* was built in 1970**
Photo by Dave Olson

Like his father, the young reverend saw getting to know local business people as an enjoyable first step in pursuing ministry to a community. He walked in with an intriguing icebreaker. He wanted to talk boats. He wanted to explore some cockeyed idea to build a boat for a Bible camp.

They talked long enough to discover they spoke the same language. One visit led to another. Soon Rev. Olson was finding excuses to drop by the yard where business was slow—an excuse for Nichols to hear the reverend and a good omen for what Olson had in mind. Commonly this was near the end of the workday, especially during the cold dark days of winter, when whoever was around, would gather at an old potbellied stove in the yard building to chew the fat. Conversation ran the gamut from shoptalk to island gossip. Sometimes Frank would pass around a cleaned-up oilcan of Teacher's Scotch whiskey.[26]

---

26 Ken and I, and all our brothers, acquired a fondness for an occasional shot of Scotch as a lubricant for good conversation during our seasons of commercial fishing in Alaska.

Would you believe, Ken had stumbled into friendship with possibly the only boatbuilder on God's earth with time to ponder the pipe dream, the boat yard to build it, desire to work with the dreamers, and a creative ad hoc scheme for success?

During my family's Whidbey Island vacation with Ken's family in 1969, Ken took me for a drive by of Nichols's nondescript boat building company at Holmes Harbor. On the way he prattled on about the enthusiastic response from teenagers to going on small boat Bible camp retreats in the San Juan Islands. He enthused about what could be accomplished with a bigger boat. He described the boat and wanted to show me where he hoped to see it built. I saw the same gleam in his eye he'd had eighteen years earlier when he was carried away by the itch to buy his own commercial salmon troller.

Reverend Olson naturally kept his boating buddy, Reverend Daugs, in the loop as his relationship with Frank Nichols bloomed over the months. On Olson's invitation, Daugs ferried over to meet Nichols. Already high on the potential for the project, Nichols loaned Daugs and Olson a wooden model of a boat and a sample construction plan to help drum up interest. Using these props, the Kens teamed up on an informal pitch to a pastoral conference in mid-1969. Daugs moved soon after to a pastorate in Denver, but this setback didn't stop Olson. Promoting Tri-C sponsorship continued. Eventually, over the course of more meet-ups, casual agreement was reached between Olson and Nichols on a game plan.

First, building would begin with a boat hull that was equally suitable for finishing as a purse seiner qualified for the Alaska salmon fishery. This would be for a fallback sale if financing fell apart on the completion of a no-frills passenger-carrying cruising craft. Second, accordance was reached on a practical layout of the space below deck and the superstructure interior to accommodate a maximum number of campers and crew. Third, Ken would canvass his congregations for volunteer help to reduce the cost of completion. Fourth, before the keel was laid, Ken would work on raising start-up money wherever he could find it along with gaining formal commitment from the Tri-Conference Camping Association to support the project and program. After all, his hopes rested on Tri-C buying in as owner/manager of the proposed vessel. In his mind, thousands of restless high school youth in member churches would make the primary passenger pool. What teen wouldn't jump at a chance to go to sea for an exciting Christian retreat experience in a travel-adventure world? The kids' parents would be impressed with the modest cost. The boat would be Tri-C's five-star Bible camp.

Nichols calculated the yard would require an $8,000 down payment followed by three additional payments of $8,000 at various stages of completion of the contract. The balance of costs—including engine, plumbing, electrical, woodwork, paint, electronics, and other gear—would be subject to purchase or procurement and installation by the buyers and qualified volunteers. The final cost projected to add up to perhaps double the total to be paid to Nichols Bros.

Was Olson in Neverland thinking he could pull this off while serving his parish? You bet, but then the unexpected happened. Daugs decided that going to Denver was a mistake. He yearned to return home to the Pacific Northwest. He got lucky with an ideal pastorate in Everett, Washington, on Puget Sound directly across from Whidbey Island. The partnership reunited in February 1970. For Olson it was time for flank-speed ahead. Ignoring the naysayers, the dynamic duo, buoyed by hope and a prayer, blithely embarked on their self-appointed mission.

Their first move was to cobble together a boatbuilding committee of interested church members and friends whose knowledge, expertise, skills, contacts, experience, and enthusiasm would all be called into play to get the job done. Walt Hossfeld, a retired fisherman, chaired the committee. Another member was Ted Hvatum of Seattle Ship Supply, a centerpiece of the enterprises serving the fishing industry at Fishermen's Terminal in Seattle. Roy Peterson operated a fuel dock in Ballard. Rev. Ken Johnson was a Tri-C member sharing the vision. These were the principal doers on a committee of eleven. Olson and Daugs were the ex officios who were in on everything. Ten of them, including Daugs and Olson, put their money where their mouths were by signing promissory notes for $1,000 apiece to help secure bank financing. As for Tri-C support, as Daugs tells it now, "Your brother Ken on the Tri-C Ministry Team worked a lot with Ken Johnson, another team member. Johnson was a key person persuading the Tri-C to get on board." They voted to do it.

Conveniently located in Freeland, near Nichols Bros. Boat Builders, was the Whidbey Island Bank, a small locally owned and operated bank, serving the south island community. It was a typical "good old boy" bank of those days where qualifications for loans were often based on the banker's personal relationships with the borrowers. In this case, two members of the group seeking financing for the project, Walt Hossfeld and Roy Peterson, were also on the bank's board of directors. Matt Nichols says, "It also didn't hurt that Nichols Bros. did their banking there and Roger Johnson, bank president, was a good friend of my dad's, sharing a preference for Scotch." This fortuitous combination solved the underwriting problem.

The bank accepted the ten $1,000 notes as front money and cut a deal covering all financing of the project from day one through delivery. The vessel served as security for the loan with Tri-C as the borrower. The note provided for repayment in installments. Tri-C would hope and pray to cover those with contributions supporting the novel ministry and surplus income from passengers over boat operating expenses. A windfall came their way when Rev. Olson had the pleasure of announcing a "Mr. and Mrs. Weterman of South Whidbey had given a twenty-acre tract on the island to Tri-C. Income from sale of the property, in five-acre tracts, was designated by the donors to be used to amortize the debt on the boat." It turned out to be a win-win for all the stakeholders.

For Nichols Bros., review of the company's records reflected no new boats delivered in the year before the *Christian* was built. Daugs recalls, "During one of our initial meetings, Frank said that if no demand for new boats continued, this would be the last boat he'd build at the Freeland yard. His brother had the family home-base yard in Portland he could move back to if necessary." Instead, launching of the *Christian* was the beginning of a flow of new business that would grow under the management of Frank's sons, Archie and Matt, to become one of the major ship building yards on the West Coast.

Frank Nichols, Ken Daugs, and Ken Olson going over architect's plans for the boat
Courtesy Matt Nichols, Nichols Family Archive

The work contract with Nichols was signed on June 18, 1970, with the president of Tri-C and Ken Olson signing for the buyers. Frank Nichols went to work. Periodic inspections of progress led to more money from the bank whenever the builders needed it. Building progressed with a partnership of good faith.

Frank, in addition to construction execution and management, oversaw the work of volunteers coordinated by Olson. Archie Nichols, still in high school, showed up almost every day after school and weekends to work on the boat and learn the trade from his father. Olson was also a regular, usually showing up around quitting time to check on progress, and sometimes having a nip on the Teacher's whiskey with Frank.

When Cummins Diesel heard about the boat, they signed up to provide at cost an engine package, including drivetrain, and free lifetime maintenance and repairs. Earl Gallagher, a Cummins engineer, volunteered to coordinate with Frank on the installation of the engine and then to finish it in his spare time.

Daugs had a member of his church, Dave Sharp, who also happened to be a master electrician. The boat needed expert wiring, so Sharp, along with fellow member Earl Dutton providing the materials and Daugs promising to be the faithful helper, stepped up to volunteer his services. Daugs says, "We ended up spending six months of Saturdays on that job."

Plumbing was mostly a team project of Sharp, Olson, and Daugs. Bill Smith and Roy Simmons, Clinton carpenters, did the beautiful joinery and other cabinetry. Carl Simmons, Roy's brother, installed the glass. Ted Hvatum and Seattle Ship Supply were a source of at-cost equipment, electronics, fittings, fixtures, paint, lines, and other gear throughout the building period. Walt Hossfeld and Roy Peterson rounded up other costly key parts like the hydraulic hoist and anchor with winch and chain from their commercial fishing buddies. When it came time to ballast the boat with five yards of concrete, the Kens' Luther League kids showed up to happily do the grunt work. Painting and finishing was a family volunteer affair.

All of this off-contract labor and materials was estimated to have cut the cost up to 50 percent. The boat was built at a cash cost of $75,000 and appraised at $140,000 initially—$150,000 on completion. Asked what the replacement value would be today, Matt Nichols replies, "Two million dollars—and that might be low!"

The congregations of Olson and Daugs deserve credit for patience as their ministers surely spent more time on the boat than on their sermons. Wives and families deserve the same.

Outdoor Ministry Gets New Tool

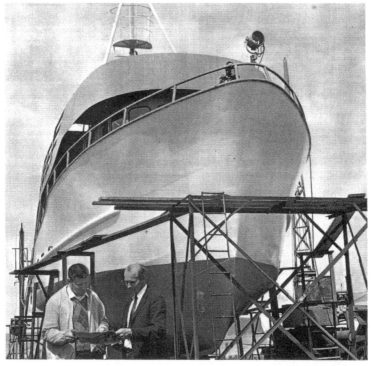

SLEEK SHIP—This is "Christian," the 56-foot steel-hulled vessel which will be used in the camping ministry of western Washington. She was due to be launched in mid-June from these ways at Holmes Harbor on Whidbey Island, Wash. Looking over plans in the foreground are Rev. Kenneth Daugs, left, Everett; and Rev. Kenneth Olson, Clinton. The lad on the fo'c's'le deck is Rev. Daugs' son, Daniel.

—Photo by LOG editor

Ken Daugs and Ken Olson reviewing hull construction progress

As the *Christian* remained nameless during the building phase, suggestions proliferated to give her an identification that would set her apart in the boat world. With no easy agreement in sight, everyone finally coalesced around honoring an unusual gift. Daugs tells the moving tale:

> The Christian *was named by E. W. Wangsnis, a member of my congregation. During construction he was dying from cancer and coming to faith before his death. During an early visit I entertained him with stories of the boat's origins. He was intrigued by the tales. From then on I had to report at every visit because he was eager for updates refreshing his spirit. On one of my visits he gave me a ship's bell with the name M/V* CHRISTIAN *embossed on it. He had paid for the engraving on his own*

initiative. He suggested this as a good name for the boat. He died before we launched her.

The finished boat was beautiful—all white, fifty-six feet long with an eighteen-foot six-inch beam, weighing sixty tons, powered by a three-hundred-horsepower diesel, and carrying 21,000 gallons fuel for a 1,500-mile cruising range at ten knots cruising speed. Accommodations included a complete galley and mess, two heads with showers, and sleeping quarters for thirty including crew. She was licensed to carry up to fifty passengers on day cruises.

* * *

FLOATING FAITH

July 7, 1971, was the appointed day for christening the new boat. A small group of people who had longed for this day showed up for the ceremony with their families. Wives of the Kens, cheerful accepters of their husbands's absence while building a boat most of the past year, were called on to do the traditional honors of breaking a champagne bottle on the hull. Helen Olson, a retired physical education teacher, batted first and failed to break the bottle. So Helen Daugs gladly took a swing at it and finished the job. The launching was successful—until the keel slid into the mud with draft too deep to float.

A small tug failed to pull her free. There she lay like a wounded swan until higher water set her free the next day.

Ken Olson, master licensed to one hundred tons, signed on as captain. Ken Daugs had fun in the engine room. All systems go led to a successful first run for a boatload of friends and families across Puget Sound to a temporary guest berth at the Everett Yacht Club. The next few days were busy.

Dedication Sunday afternoon, July 11, was the next event in the life of the M/V *Christian*. It was much more important than christening because the *Christian* had been built for induction into service of the Lord as a floating church. Religious observances would happen daily at sea, including church services every Sunday. The members of over one hundred congregations were invited along with friends, relatives, and representatives of other parties of interest, including the press. Local newspapers found the novel story of sufficient interest to include articles announcing the dedication.

Hundreds were there, swarming the boat and the dock, including my wife, Betty, and me from California. There was such a large crowd on the floating wooden dock that it caused a surprise sinking, briefly holding up the initiation of formalities. The throng scrambled to clear, but not before those in the center of the dock were in water over their ankles. Kids of all ages lining the rail on the *Christian* looked down on the hapless guests and laughed uproariously at the comic scene. Being stoic Lutherans used to wet feet, nobody was upset.

Reverends Daugs and Olson took turns conducting the dedication service. Walt Hossfeld, who had played so many roles in the project, including chair of the building committee, was involved as well. Somebody provided music. Reverend Roy Olson, Ken's and my father, and an avid follower of the project from day one, preached a moving sermon while barely containing his paternal pride. The formal acknowledgements, rituals, and ceremony were followed by guided tours of the boat. It was a grand occasion.

As soon as the crowd left, the decks were cleared for a brief boat ride on the Sound to entertain guests and some of the older folks, some of whom might never have a similar opportunity. With Daugs monitoring the engine, Ken on the flying bridge, and a dozen volunteer deckhands manning the mooring lines, we were soon underway. This was my chance to check her out from stem to stern. In the engine room I found Daugs getting sweaty and glad to have company. He'd run across a leak in a fuel line. We talked solutions and decided we needed to shut down the engine for a while. No big deal, and my respect for Reverend Daugs increased impressively over the following thirty minutes. He repaired the leak by coolly cutting a short length of deck hose for temporary use to complete the short cruise back to the harbor. We docked with a high five.

Ken Olson at helm of the *Christian*
Ken Olson Family Archive

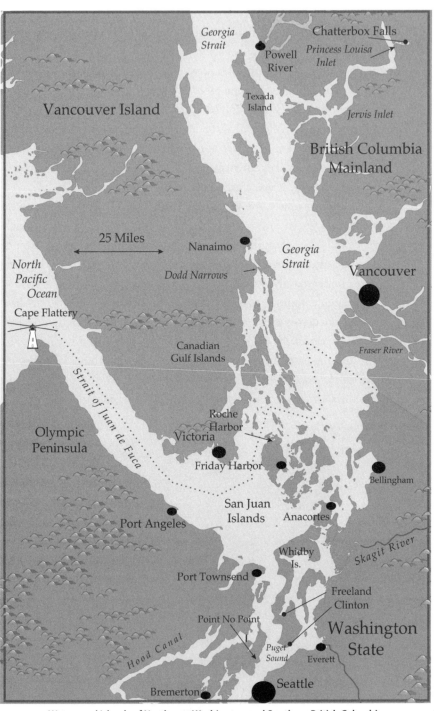

Waters and Islands of Northwest Washington and Southern British Columbia

FULFILLING THE DREAM

Promotion of the *Christian*'s mission was already underway a few months before her maiden voyage. This was to be a three-week cruise to Southeast Alaska to maximize people's interest and draw media attention to the unique new program. Equally important was scheduling and filling trips to keep the boat busy on its return home. One early flyer announced:

All Pacific Northwest Lutheran Churches

A SPECIAL GIFT
THE *"CHRISTIAN"* SEA & ISLAND MINISTRY
BECAUSE —
THE "CHRISTIAN" CATCHES YOUTH
while providing:
witness, worship & service to uncounted boating people;
a retreat facility for congregational groups

A NEW WAY —
Camp Tender, Puget Sound to Alaska, Minister Skipper, Year Around

AN INVITATION TO PARTICIPATE
OPTION I — A complete program of Christian inspiration and learning in the
context of the sea and islands of the Pacific Northwest.
OPTION II — Boat and skipper furnished upon approval of the Christian
program developed by your congregation.
Bring your own food.

Operational Day Cost: $6 each person
(food not included)
Summer Youth Day Cost: $7 each person
(food included)

*The Christian operates with 20–24 aboard multiple days; as an island camp
tender for 36–40 youth; maximum capacity day use to 50 persons.
Donations to help build this ministry are welcome.*
A "TRI-C BIBLE CAMPS" PROGRAM
* * *

For the maiden voyage, the complement of boat's officers, resource counselors, and teenagers added up to a crew of thirty, and the press continued to follow the compelling story of this unique ministry. The *Seattle Post Intelligencer* featured an eye-catching tell-all article by Don Page titled "Lutherans Go to Sea"—edited, excerpted, and quoted here:

THE DREAMBOAT is the M. V. Christian. Skipper Ken Olson is a sky pilot. Likewise, Ken Daugs, the Chief Engineer and First Mate. Quartermaster Marlene Johnson is a teenage water ski queen, and another teenager, Janene Solie, will teach seamanship. A full "crew" of two dozen teenagers will cruise up the coast, learning about Indian culture, Christian principles, camp lore, and togetherness. That's the way the Lutherans go to sea. And we dare you to think of a happier, better way.

DON'T GET THE IDEA the Christian is a luxury yacht. She's a workboat for the camping ministry. High school students of the camping ministry will work their way, standing watches at the wheel and in the galley—painting, chipping, getting their hands dirty in the engine room. Their additional "fare" will run $7 a day. "That covers everything," Rev. Daugs assures us. "Any kid can make that. We didn't want this program just to be for young people who could afford cruising."

THE FIRST CRUISE will take the Christian north to Petersburg, Alaska. The crew won't spend all their time aboard. They'll lay their sleeping bags ashore sometimes at parks and islands. They'll learn marine biology and astronomy. They'll catch seafood and prepare it fresh from the sea.

YOUNG MEN AND WOMEN of the Christian will visit with First Nation and Alaska Native tribes en route—study their art, architecture, and culture. They'll have two experts to help them. Mr. and Mrs. Tom Johnson are the special Indian "resource people" on this voyage. Both are just out of college—Johnson with a degree in architecture, his wife with a degree in special services to Indians.

ALASKA WON'T BE the only goal on the Christian's course. Pastor Daugs reminds us, *"Young people will be crewing, and at the same time, strengthening the faith they've learned in their homes and congregations."*

And proving too, Pastor, that the Baptists aren't the only ones with big things to gain by getting their feet wet.

The maiden voyage with crew aboard began by sailing south from Everett to Seattle for some final outfitting. A few days later they cast off for the Far North. All that was foreseen in *"Lutherans Go to Sea"* came to pass as if manifest destiny was on their side. The motley crew bonded beyond expectations. They called the sky pilot skipper and engineer, Ole and Daugs.

Says Daugs, *"You could sense the transformational difference it made in the faith of everyone aboard. For the kids, life on the boat became a metaphor for Christian life as an experience where there was risk, but they were safe as in God's hands."*

Retired Coast Guard Commander Paul Langner fondly recalls the maiden voyage from the unique perspective of the teenager he once was, who moved on to spend much of his career at sea:

My mother, a barber in Everett and Lutheran woman, has the gift of gab and a strong sense of adventure. She befriended Pastor Ken Daugs and his family. In conversation at the barbershop, she learned of the plans for the Christian and the vision Pastor Daugs had for the boat's calling. With a bit of a push, but no arm-twisting, I was signed up to partake in the maiden voyage. Up until this time my on-the-water experience was limited to small craft on Puget Sound and rowboats on rivers. I had never been afloat for more than a few hours, let alone days.

Following a pomp and circumstance commissioning ceremony at Everett Yacht Club, we "passengers" embarked on the Christian with visions of Alaska. Strangely, we turned south upon casting off and headed for Seattle for some repairs or outfitting. So our first days were spent on the Lake Union Ship Canal waterfront exploring the centers of the commercial fishing and yachting industry. The hearty Norwegian fishmongers used the same language their Swedish logging kin spoke. While I knew most of the vocabulary, I did pick up a few new idioms that would serve me well in a future life at sea.

Cleared to go, we headed back down the Ship Canal to Puget Sound. We had to lock-out through the Chittendam Locks in Ballard to get there.

Skipper Ken Olson and engineer Daugs were busy working out bugs in the throttle linkage and steering. As we entered the locks, they yelled down to a bunch of us on deck to make lively and toss a mooring line to the lock tenders. After a bunch of confusion, we landlubbers figured it out and Christian was made fast to the lock walls. As the kid who figured it out first, I made off the mooring line with a couple of half hitches around the horns of the cleat on the vessel's starboard side. I had no idea the lines would have to be tended as the water level in the locks dropped. So I headed to the bow to assist the girls attempting to get the other mooring line over to another lock tender. As the water dropped, the line I had made fast became taut. When Skipper Ken noticed the tightening line, he quickly came down on deck from the flying bridge to check the problem. When he attempted to slack the line, he found only half hitches, not lays of figure eights. I learned then, though he wore a turn-around collar on Sunday, he too knew the universal adjectives of loggers and fishermen. It was a lesson indelibly burned into this pea brain.

Finally free of land, Christian headed to the San Juan Islands for a bit of gunkholing in shakedown. Anchored in the north cove of Jones Island, passengers and crew made way by small boat to the state park docks. From there we explored the island and tasted the beauty and adventure forecast for the remainder of the cruise.

On the southern end of Jones Island is a large outcropping of granite polished by glaciers in ages past. The rocks overlook San Juan and Speiden Channels. I was awed by the spectacular view, the tremendous beauty of the rock formations, twisted madronas, and deep waters. Pastor Daugs led a sunset worship service amongst those rocks. This place, this time, there was no doubt in my mind of God's handiwork and his love for us.

The next morning we weighed anchor and resumed passage north. I am not sure if my compadres learned from the cruise that a vessel becomes like a living organism when lines are taken in and the deck rises to meet one's feet. I recall one girl in the crew who wanted to know why we didn't stop every night and continue the next day. Couldn't we just stop and start again?

Underway, we cruisers were encouraged to stand watch, take a trick at the wheel, and perform other work. Skipper Ken was quick to pass along his knowledge. I took in a world that cannot be described in words or photos. By magnetic headings, we were going far more west than north, how could that be? The charts didn't lie, but years of hearing "the North" and "North to Alaska" were hard to reconcile when the compass pointed more west by north, than north by west. But so it was, and the spatial concept of great circle sailing, albeit I would not master the understanding of spherical trigonometry for another few years, took root. I became fascinated with navigation as Ken laid out track lines and penciled in compass courses, I learned of the two compass roses overlaid on charts, the relationship between the true course and magnetic course, and the symbolism represented there for Christian faith—both guiding our way, but only one true, unchanging direction.

Standing watch or steering the boat, I discovered the comforting experience of the midwatches at night. Night watches are calm, quiet, deliberate, and peaceful, embracing routine and self-reliance. During daylight, humans insist on conversation. On night watch two people can go an hour without saying a word, yet communicate on the deepest level. When conversations occur, they range from expression of philosophical concepts and strange ideas to dreams and future plans to braggadocio of past exploits. What is said on night watch isn't judged or questioned, but accepted and ruminated upon. There may be some tall stories, but no liars.

Running the Inside Passage back then privileged me to see a raw and untamed world of rocks jutting out of water, scabbed hillsides where glaciers 50,000 years ago peeled off the topsoil, sand spits deposited from glacial till, and forests so thick and dark light did not penetrate more than a few feet from the edge. The wildlife, terrestrial and marine, was better than any National Geographic. Killer whales, seals, sea lions, porpoises, bears, and deer appeared just an arm's reach off the gunwales. The birds were incredible—fast-flying colorful little puffins darting ahead of our bow wake, big bald eagles ensconced in snags along the shoreline, "kawing" ravens, hovering gulls, gliding brown pelicans, and the first albatross I had ever seen—all had me transfixed. At night the churning phosphorous in the stern wake of the Christian glowed for more than a mile astern. As the bow sliced the gentle swells, the organisms bloomed, and the light show was fantastic. When a small school of Dahl porpoises showed up on our bow wake to frolic in the pressure wave, their antics set off similar "fireworks." My first experience of the unique blue, brittle, crisp taste of "bergy-bits" off floating icebergs, taken on board direct from the sea after calving off the face of Le Conte Glacier near Petersburg, Alaska, remains unforgettable.

As I type these notes, I still recall Skipper Ken pointing out Polaris and teaching me to tell time by the relative position of Dubhe and Merak. (bragging, I can still get within five minutes of actual time if I can see the full constellation and Polaris). What I know now is the seeds planted on that cruise were the beginning of what would lead to a career in the U.S. Coast Guard. I started out an enlisted man and worked my way up the hawsepipe to command cutters of various sizes. I sailed the Atlantic, Indian, Pacific, Arctic oceans, the Caribbean, Bering, and Mediterranean seas, and I wish to sail them all again. My fascination with navigation, seamanship, and ship handling continue to follow me today. A summer cruise on the Christian opened up an entire world for me.

Daugs' son, Duane, a teen at the time adds:

Ken made it a point to stop and anchor up at uninhabited sites with special attractions like abandoned ruins, hot springs, waterfalls, and ocean beaches for swimming. In Ketchikan we visited the Lutheran church where Ken's dad had been the pastor and the family had lived when Ken was a teenager.

I was on the high school swim team so it was natural for me to show off diving off the Christian to swim down and under the boat coming up on the other side. In those days bowel movements were pumped direct into the ocean from the heads. Swimming in it—not fun! So one time when I did my stunt I came up in the middle of it. The joke was on me as Ken and a couple of conspirators had slathered a coat hanger with peanut butter decorated with toilet paper. You don't forget those things.

Three weeks and 1,500 nautical miles later, the *Christian* was joyfully welcomed home. Everybody on board, except Skipper Ken, First Mate Solie, and Quartermaster Johnson, went their separate ways to bask in their adventure and return to life ashore.

Surely Ken was flying high, but he knew fulfillment requires consummation and the trip to Alaska was only the beginning of the venture. There was no time to relax. He was overdue getting back to his pastoral responsibilities. At the same time he had to juggle working with Tri-C and squaring away a new skipper(s) to take over running the *Christian*. A first move was to port the boat at Anacortes on the north end of Whidbey Island. This would be a convenient home port for Ken as it was closer to the San Juan and Gulf Islands cruising grounds, less expense than Seattle or Everett for moorage, and required no ferry ride to get there.

A primary stumbling block for the future of the ministry at sea was finding a licensed and qualified captain, secure in his Christian faith, who was able to coordinate with adult program leadership and work with youth as working crew. He would also have to be willing to live with seven-day workweeks all summer and a pittance as a paycheck.

Over the next ten months, into the early spring of 1972, three captains were found to skipper the *Christian* for a few weeks to a few months at a time, with Ken doing checkouts and going along on initial retreat cruises while Tri-C's Minister of Camping coordinated other aspects of the program. All were square pegs trying to fit a round hole. The boat worked fine traveling some 13,000 miles since launch. Contributions flowed into the Tri-C office to help cover expenses and loan payments. Retreat cruises filled to capacity. However, crewing the boat, passenger administration, and oversight of the financials— those tasks didn't always go so well.

Adding to the frustrations during the first few months of this period was a falling out between Olson, Daugs, and Tri-C supporters of the *Christian* and Bernard Kahn, Tri-C's executive director. The rub was mostly over coordination of the program. It culminated in Kahn's resignation in December 1971 and Tri-C joining a new Lutheran Outdoor Ministries Association (LOMA). This was a merger of the Puget Sound area Lutheran denominations' camping programs. Fortunately, LOMA was able to find and hire the very able Rev. Willfred (Will) Bigott as executive director and Minister of Camping in early 1972.

By spring the *Christian*'s mission was an acclaimed ministry. The *Christian* needed a minister/skipper who could wear any and all of the hats to make the program go. The light dawned on the LOMA board of directors and staff: the only qualified candidate they knew of was Ken Olson. The LOMA powers and Ken did the math. They came up with a package to call Reverend Olson to be director of the boat ministry of the Lutheran Church for the Pacific Northwest. What all that impressive title meant was he'd be directing the activities of and skippering the *Christian*.

A much-loved pastor for over nine years, he conducted his last services at the South Whidbey Island parish on June 11, 1972. The *Whidbey Record* had the story:

> Pastor Olson stated, "It's exciting to follow through on something you started as an extension of our churches' outdoor ministry program because it allows a more flexible, less rigid type of retreat than offered in the traditional summer Bible camp, creating closer fellowship combined with a real learning experience." He reflected on the Christian's first year of operation as a floating ministry, noting "it's been a great success and an

excellent program. To date, all types of groups have used the Christian, including college students and St. Hubert's Catholic parish in Langley." Olson adds, "I'm looking forward to my new job, but sad in a lot of ways to be leaving Whidbey. My family and I will miss South Whidbey and the many friends we have made here."

Ken's family—wife, Helen, and children Joanne, Danny, and Michael—moved to a small rented rambler in Everett.

Joanne says, "Dad was so busy with the boat, we rarely saw him. We kids had a good time while Mom worked as secretary in an insurance firm. She once saved change for two years so we could all go to Disneyland."

Ken was obsessed with a determination that the vessel was going to fulfill the dream on his watch come hell or high water. The challenge of becoming full-time minister/skipper of the *Christian* may have appeared exciting in the beginning, but the stress of at least feeling responsible for every aspect contributing and necessary to the success of the program would take its toll. Participation in planning, promotion, scheduling, financing, and personnel matters along with operating and maintaining the vessel were all in the job description.

There was too much work and too little income for one person managing a new program still in development. Ken drew a salary way too low for a father of a growing family because the Summer Youth Day ticket price had been kept at seven dollars per person per day, promising any teenager could earn the cost of going on the boat. Ken, on autopilot, overlooked his family in pursuit of his goal. He had something still to prove and failure was not an option. How much too low? The "per person per day" price was raised to fifteen dollars soon after a new director of boat ministry on the *Christian* succeeded Ken in 1974.

Ken Daugs and my brother Tim have told me, "The boat literally ran seven days a week most weeks for the next two years. The summers were mostly dedicated to week-long youth trips interspersed with a few three- or four-day cruise retreats. There was one three-week trip to Alaska. Customarily the *Christian* would come in to its Anacortes berth to unload on Saturday mornings. Following clean up, refueling, and loading of supplies, the group for the following week would board on Sunday afternoon. Departure would be early enough to clear the harbor for arrival at their first overnight anchorage that evening. Every trip was filled to capacity with a waiting list of people wanting to share the experience."

Rev. Bigott, who worked closely with Ken, extols the impact cruises on the *Christian* had on the crews:

The young people got a personal experience in caring for one another, helping one another, forgiving, and growing in the word. Stops at various islands gave them opportunities to share their faith with the people living or vacationing there. Ken was so very good with them. His approach to faith and gentle humor changed lives.

Dr. David Daugs, a younger son of Ken Daugs who went on *Christian* camp cruises as soon as he was old enough, says, "Ken influenced my decision to pursue ministry. At the time, I was intimidated by feelings of shyness and inadequacy for the calling. Talking with Ken gave me the courage and assurance to overcome my doubts."

As suggested earlier, Ken gave the kids the liberty to be themselves. He trusted them not to overreach beyond acceptable risk just as he trusted himself. Diving off the highest accessible dock, cliff, or board challenge we could find, and thought we could handle, was a thrill Ken and I never passed up in our youth. Both of us were still doing it in middle age. So it was natural for Ken to seek out sites for himself and like-minded kids and counselors to share the satisfaction. An early find were the cliffs at Prevost Harbor on Stuart Island in the San Juans. This offered work-ups up to fifty feet. Another discovery for Ken was the fun of diving off the boat, launching himself from the crow's nest. This challenged others to do it. One of them was David Daugs. His father is still boasting about how David holds the record as the only one who ever dove off the boat from the cross spar above the crow's nest.

With a new group of mostly hyperactive teenagers coming aboard weekly over the summers, some crew mischief was inevitable. It was the captain's job to deal with it. Ken certainly added a creative page in this anecdote, told now by his son Dan:

> *This kid brought a stash of pot with him for his week on the boat. One evening the kid and a couple of his buddies snuck off into the woods during campfire time to share a few tokes. Some snitch told my dad. Though pretty much a nonsmoker, he took a cigar with him to their hideaway. When he got there he lit up to hear their stories. Then he calmly shared some thoughts of his own and left the kids to think it over. That was it.*

Retired Bishop Lowell Knutson, whose children took trips on the *Christian* with Ken, says, "As skipper, Ken was more like a grandfather to the kids. Constraints were minimal. For example, the rule on the boat was only three people could be on the mast and in the crow's nest at one time. But the record was twenty-five!"

David R. Olson

One young person wrote of her experience and it was printed in the Oregon Outdoor Ministries Association newsletter in October 1972:

Upon The Water
By Kari Kvarsten
Sophomore, St. Marks, Salem

This summer, I had one of the most exciting and inspirational experiences of my life. It took place against the background of miles and miles of blue water dotted with islands. For one week I lived and worked with twenty-three other people, ages fourteen to eighteen, aboard the fifty-six-foot ship M/V Christian as we cruised the San Juan Islands of Puget Sound.

We "island hopped" through the Sound, visiting islands that were large and small, some uninhabited, but most having small harbors. The island I remember most vividly was Sucia Island, owned by the state of Washington. I remember climbing a hill covered with cedar trees and, reaching the top, looked down to see the crew waving from the shore of a blue bay that sparkled in the sun. I found a path that wound through green forest to the other side of the island. That night we had Holy Communion as the sun was setting. Afterwards, we sang and joked and talked into the morning hours.

The Christian took us in and out of Canadian waters. Many of the bays in which we dropped anchor were perfect for canoeing and sailing. There was a sail board aboard the Christian. One day four kids took it out. When they came back to the ship, on approach, a small gust of wind caught the sail. They shot past the Christian yelling for someone to catch the rope. Finally, on the third try, they made it in.

The most wonderful thing about the trip was what it meant to the people who participated. We left for home with a newness of life and stronger convictions in Christ. The talk sessions we had on the last couple of nights on board helped a lot. These sessions brought us together more than anything else. I was impressed to hear kids question things I had been afraid to question—and I was strengthened by the answers we found.

Recently I received a letter from a Portland girl whom I met on the cruise. I guess we feel the same way. She wrote, "My life was changed. Before the trip, I was discouraged with my life and the world, but now I feel restored and heartened in both my life and faith."

Another hallmark of boating with Ken was his fondness for cruising through the night. He was drawn early to the romance of running from sunset to sunrise. The turn-on was clouds and stars overhead, phosphorescent sea in the wake, northern lights, and twinkling lights of other boats and ashore—all contributed to the magic of the moments as expressed by Ken poetically:

Star Study on the *Christian*
Running, running by night,
fair tide, Orion on the quarter
dandling, soaring, adolescent,
feelings of love with girls,
soft, round, and warm,
tan beneath their Levis,
creating, creating everything,
looking for the swan.

Simply by being a boat named the *Christian*, coming in to anchor or dock in popular harbors with a boatload of kids on board, created an unforeseen and unpredictable opportunity for quiet Christian outreach. Curiosity would lead people with access to visit the boat to find out what was going on. They were always invited to come aboard where Ken, counselors, and youth were delighted to quietly explain the boat's mission, share their faith, and answer questions. Duane Daugs mentioned how, while cruising the Gulf and San Juan Islands years later, he would often run into other boaters who would remember the *Christian* and its unique mission.

Following the end of the summer youth program, the vessel was moved from Anacortes to a home port in Everett. This was more accessible to mostly Puget Sound churches interested in group charters. Docking here also allowed Ken to be home every night while in port. He could also more conveniently spend harbor days working on the boat, or away making promotional presentations of the program and attending synod and other meetings.

Charters for trips of one to three days came in a steady stream from a spectrum of individual church groups. These ranged from youth Luther Leagues through to women's fellowships, men's brotherhoods, and all church planning retreats. Since the boat interior was heated and cozy for all-weather cruising, winter charters were regular affairs. The holiday season was filled with a series of popular twilight evening cruises on the festively decorated boat with services and carols to celebrate the birth of Jesus. Will Bigott exclaims, "People were amazed the church would have a ministry like this."

The *Christian* was a success story. Approximately 2,200 people had been recorded cruising on the boat during 1973. Income was more than meeting expectations. There was confidence that prices charged for passages could be increased to write a better paycheck for Ken's successor. By the end of 1973, if a qualified successor could be found, Ken could feel good returning to parish ministry, promising more time to be with his family

Soon, a dream candidate serendipitously applied to serve the unique and changing congregation aboard the *Christian*. He was Captain Don Taylor, a licensed master of oceangoing vessels, Lutheran pastor with experience as a college campus minister, and a graduate of the University of Washington, School of Fisheries. When Ken got a call to be the minister at Our Saviour's Lutheran Church in Burien, Washington, on the South Puget Sound coast, he promptly accepted and moved with his family to Burien in April 1974. It was a wise move at the right time. Ken felt good about leaving the ministry in the competent hands of Captain Taylor.

ESCAPE TO SITKA

AUGUST 13, 1986

I have inclinations to leave off with life in society,
To find a completely pure way of existence. I know,
I am a little different in ways not like most people.
Now I want to indulge that, to leave and be alone.

—Excerpt from the journal of Ken Olson

The middle-class congregation at Our Saviour's seemed an excellent fit. The church wasn't far from Puget Sound and was peppered with young families interested in having an activist pastor whose strength was nurturing strong creative programs for restless children and youth. There was a close-knit group of men in their forties, fifties, and sixties who worked mostly in the craftsman trades and were hooked on sport fishing and boating. Bonding with their new pastor came naturally. They became Ken's steadfast supporters and friends for life.

Skiing was also a very popular pastime and there were ski areas an hour away in the Cascades, beckoning with accessible slopes and inexpensive facilities. Our Saviour's had the ideal pastor, still a star skier, to sparkplug a teaching program for its youth to get caught up in the bliss, beauty, and thrills of the sport. The congregation bought a retired school bus. Every winter Sunday after church, they filled the bus with kids and volunteer ski instructors to head for Snoqualmie Pass for the afternoon. Then, each summer, Ken skippered the *Christian* for a week to give Captain Taylor a break. The cruise was featured as a retreat week in which the early sign-up was often mostly members of his church to assure bunks on the boat.

After the *Christian*'s summer season ended, he would get the boat for another week to skipper a "men only" salmon fishing trip to renowned Rivers Inlet, British Columbia. Men from Ken Daugs' congregation often came along, as well as Daugs himself as trip retreat leader. Dad also made at least one trip serving as retreat leader, and I was another fortunate invitee. Also on most trips was a homeless fellow from the Lutheran Compass Mission in downtown Seattle. Ken would make arrangements with the mission chaplain for selection of the right guy. Staff would set him up with a duffel bag of outdoor clothing. Somebody going on the trip would pick him up at the mission on the way to the boat, where he became just another guy on the trip.

The fishermen in Ken's congregation had it organized for everybody on board to fish every day in an assortment of small outboard-powered boats. Daily limits were often caught by noon. They had freezers and ice chests aboard to preserve the catch. On the trip I made, Daugs provided lighthearted spiritual nurture with a nightly session reteaching the commandments like I'd never heard them taught in Sunday school. The impressive catch was divided equally among all aboard, including a share and more for the Compass Mission, on return to home port. Trip expenses were shared equally by the rest of the participants for a world-class fishing experience at a bargain price.

Everything appeared to go well for Ken and his family, too. The kids were thriving, and he and Helen were living active lives. Ken also found time to pursue his love of poetry. In 1976 this led to some new work he assembled into a booklet titled "Just a Few Poems For My Friends From the Summer I Knew I Was a Poet." This collection included the first version of his mental leap to visualizing the mysterious sacrificial life of the salmon as metaphor for the Christ-like life. He saw it, too, in a poem titled *Winging*, penetrating a Haida[27] myth that peered into the mysteries of bird migration. A copy is in the Pacific Lutheran University Library.

Anniversaries and birthdays were reason enough for Olson family reunions almost every summer. All were centered at the homes of Mom and Dad in the mountains, Ken and Helen in Burien, and Tim and Lorelie with their two golden retrievers in the city. All were joyous occasions except for the year following the loss of our Jef.

Then the unthinkable in a minister's life happened. Ken's marriage went off course during the summer of 1985. The impact wasn't pretty. Helen rented an apartment and moved out. Ken was devastated. He soon resigned from his parish with agreement to stay on as interim pastor pending appointment of a

---

27   The Haida are an Alaska Native tribe whose home is in Southeast Alaska.

successor. This allowed him and his son Mike to continue living at the parsonage for a few more months.

Feelings of real or imagined guilt, loss, loneliness, hopelessness, sadness, regret, futility, pain, self-doubt, disgust, frustration, and, ultimately, yearnings to start a new life swept over Ken in breaking waves. He had to move on. Fortunately, the group of men who had come to love their pastor, rallied and coalesced to help their friend through to a new life. Ken had managed to save some money in a personal individual retirement account. A craving bubbled up, swinging his mental compass to north, drawing him to return to his roots in Alaska. I surmise he experienced urges not unlike a migratory bird. He discerned his future in the life of the salmon as drawn in his poetry. Perhaps speculation reflected in free verse he had written a decade before crossed his mind:

> winging
> human reaching
> is a haida
> myth seeking
> migratory bird
> craving, a
> compass-sensing
> strangeness in
> praise and
> obedience, a
> for no-reason
> choosing

He saw his salvation and recovery in migration and transformation. Ever the writer, he took up keeping a journal to collect his thoughts and leave a record:

August 13—I have these strong inclinations to leave off with life in society, to go back, to find a completely pure way of existence. No doubt there is pain and death in nature, but it is of such a different kind. I know I should bring myself with me and all the years of accretions. I know I am a little strange and different in ways that are not like most people. Now it seems I want to indulge all of that. There is worst of all this deep and dreadful side of me only God can deal with. I have these times of working through when there is only darkness. Of course, there is the incredible shyness of my personality. Perhaps that is all there is to it. I just want to leave and be alone.

August 15—The intent of the trip of the Advena is to find out if it is really so. There seemed to be something about the boat, when I first looked at it, made me think I might have it. The auction, the hot sunshine, and the tallyho of it all with the shabby boats. The Advena had her bilges full of water—freshwater from having her hatches left open. Even the engine was in a pool of water. A broker told me she might go for between "five and ten thousand." After I had a good look, I set my mind on $5,000. Somehow, on the day of the auction, I couldn't let her slip away that easy so I bid to $7,000. I was very uneasy about it at that point—suspicious of a ringer. Saturday was the auction. She was to be taken for $7,400, one bid higher than mine. Sunday I sailed off on the Froya with my nephew Karl to Whidbey Island for a talk with the boat builders.[28] On my return home Monday night, Mike said the auction had called. Said the boat was mine as I had the next highest bid.

The *Advena* was a thirty-seven-foot ferro-cement hulled, Perkins Diesel-powered, auxiliary ketch[29] with six sails, including a main, mizzen, drifter,[30] genoa, and working and storm jibs. Ken forever after fondly called her his "floating driveway."

When fall arrived, he left the parsonage for a basement bedroom at the home of Lew Lewellen. He moved the *Advena* to moorage space at friend Roy Peterson's Ballard Oil Company dock conveniently located near marine repair shops. His vagabond life was divided between church work in Burien and boat work in Ballard for the remainder of the year. On a business trip to Seattle during this period, I found time to inspect the boat, including an hour working with Tim ripping wooden walls out of the cabin to clear for renovation and a better accommodation arrangement. I was delighted to find she was ketch-rigged to provide all the sailing options of that design.

He soldiered on at Our Saviour's to conduct his last church service in early 1987. Then he moved again to quarters provided by Tom Chase, his daughter Joanne's boy friend and future husband[31]. The digs were in Ballard, the Little Norway of Seattle, bounded by the Seattle Ship Canal on the south and Puget Sound on the west. Close to family and friends, he hung out there until restoration of the *Advena* was far enough advanced for him to move aboard the

---

28   Frank, Matt, and Archie Nichols.

29   A ketch is a two-masted vessel with a higher main mast forward and a lower mizzen mast aft, with the mizzen stepped forward of the steering station. It's a versatile rig with none better for dealing with storm conditions.

30   A drifter is a large triangular sail hanked on the forestay like a jib, sheeted aft, and of very light material to catch any wind.

31   Later, Ken had the honor of marrying Tom and Joanne in Seattle on July 1, 1989.

boat. Quiet evenings provided time to update his journal.

S/V *Advena* about to sail away from anchorage under Main, Mizzen and Drifter sails
Photo by Dave Olson

March 13—Yesterday was an important day. We took the Advena out for the first time to try her engine underway and to sail her. The wind was a little more than we wanted at a steady 20 knots. The rain came down in torrents at times. But she really sailed, and the engine performed well though not much power for the weight of the boat. Coming back into the lock entrance, three porpoises played about the bow despite other boats in the vicinity.

June 11—I must find time to recount all that has happened from the beginning of this quest or search I have set out upon. But just today, this beautiful morning, there are these thoughts. We leave the world to go into nature to participate and find rest and peace. But we must bring our sorrowing relation to God for our not following, for our not being, and then we must encounter a cross in nature and under the power of that cross find a place of rest and peace for sinners. Where God appears in nature there is a place of rest and peace for sinners. That is the sacramental principle.

June 12–17 (excerpts)—Dad and Mom have been on the boat. Mom, with her bad heart, managed to climb down into the cabin. She had that thoughtful wondering look—almost young again. Dad brought up the matter that we cling to life and cherish the earth when we get old while longing for our heavenly home. I asked him to explain the enigma—he couldn't. I said that is the problem I'd like to solve. I thought about being in love in nature, the feminine character of nature. The Holy Grail is a reality in the sense one might discover the sacrament in a feminine mode in nature. Is that pagan? But I have lost it. Perhaps I shall one day know it once more.

Over ten months, Ken and his friends, men who had worked and cruised with him on the *Christian,* accomplished a complete renovation of the *Advena.* Master carpenter George Sather, assisted mostly by Ken, rebuilt the cabin and installed a beautifully finished hardwood guardrail. A classic wooden dinghy was cradled on deck with a new outboard motor stowed below to get ashore from anchorages or for lifeboat duty. Added electronics included a VHF radio, radar, loran, and depth sounder, plus an Autohelm for steering relief while sailing short or single-handed. The galley was completely equipped with an oil-burning cast-iron stove and icebox. The main cabin had settees on either side with a nice galley table and featured a boom box with tape deck for onboard music. Bunks were two forward and one quarter birth.

The *Advena* had been transformed into a comfortable, solid, offshore cruiser equally serviceable as a cozy live-aboard for two or three people. Questions remained about the engine, but Ken decided to forego further sea trials. He was ready to go to sea.

On the morning of June 18, with eighty-two-year-old George Sather and teenage nephew Karl Olson as crew, Ken and the *Advena* finally cleared U.S. customs and took off for passage through British Columbia waters on the way to Sitka, Alaska. June 26 found them stuck two hundred and fifty miles north of Seattle, in Alert Bay,[32] with the engine going on binges of overheating and a burned-out starting motor. Adding insult to injury, Ken soon found out the starting motor on his old Westerbeck diesel was no longer in production. A search was initiated for a serviceable used unit. Hung up waiting, Karl and George went home to Seattle. Left alone Ken cast about making friends with people on boats in the marina, at local church services, and just walking around visiting the Indian potlatch museum and other local attractions. There were extended hikes to observe and resolve questions of identification relating to plants, edible berries, and birdlife as well as passing the time unloading dreams, disappointments, and thoughts on ministry in his journal.

---

32   Alert Bay is a small island village across the channel from near the north end of Vancouver Island.

June 29–July 15 (excerpts)—Yesterday was spent out with Dave on his Tuan with his five charter guests. Dave has a hydrophone for listening to whale talk. We spotted a fine family of orcas. It was beautiful and moving to hear them talking to one another as they moved along. This evening I went to Towers' cabin on the beach. Just as evening fell a show began. Killer whales came through close in to the kelp line, big and little ones. The bigs would stand up to spy out as the little ones jumped clear out. They all performed perfectly. The Towers sent me back to the boat with a vegetarian cookbook and enhanced understanding we mortals are in a death battle with human nature that is not nature's nature. I've been thinking of the pain and change within nature we call death, how it might be experienced by the animals, and how it is by us. How it reflects on the God we have and the nature of our existence. I'm still thinking that an outdoor mission program would be (1) to pastor nature; (2) to minister to nature and the people there. I'm also thinking of writing a program for one week called "Devotion For Those Who Go Outdoors." The simple truth might be that Christians should perceive nature differently than non-Christians. A place to retreat from the sort of untruth of the world, that nature is a place to be determined by man.

Ken at the tiller with George Sather in cockpit of *Advena* sailing from Ketchikan to Sitka
Photo by Dave Olson

* * *

With George back, Ken finally left Alert Bay on July 21. The engine, including its replacement starting motor, continued to be a problem, making day-to-day progress north challenging. But they did get some reasonable weather with fair winds, which gave them some good days under sail. On July 29, they limped into Ketchikan.

Since the plan was to spend about two weeks in Ketchikan, George soon took off on a flight to Seattle for another well-earned visit home. Ken needed a rest, too, and time to try and solve the continuing problems of overheating the engine. This was Ken's first visit to his boyhood hometown since he had made two-day stopovers there with the *Christian* back in the early 1970s. On those visits, though, he had been preoccupied with arranging and coordinating the activities of passengers intent on seeing and experiencing as much as possible of the town's attractions, including visits to the church where their skipper had lived and worshiped as a teenager. This time he had twelve days to reconnect with friends from those happy days.

He had a grand time in the evenings being hosted by the Vigs, Stenfords, Perrys, and MacMillans—all friends going back to school days and all families now. They welcomed him back as one of their own. Reflecting on all this in his journal, he noted, "Change is going on in me spiritually as to who I am and what I'm about. I am doing more living than I have in years." Interjecting the happy evenings were less-than-successful days working on the engine. These frustrations led him to conclude, "Possibly the engine is shot."

On August 10, I arrived in Ketchikan to provide another hand sailing the *Advena* to Sitka. I can't recall the communications leading to my involvement beyond welcoming the invitation to participate in visiting familiar waters one more time. I also looked forward to sailing a ketch-rigged vessel. What I do remember is a private conversation with Ken soon after I got to the boat. He expressed doubt he could overcome the engine problems to successfully complete the trip. The days among old friends had restored his spirit, but Sitka is where he had fast friends from the more recent *Christian* years on Whidbey Island. They were looking for him.

This sparked my interest in how the boat behaved under sail and a look at the inventory of sails and gear to handle weather. I liked what I heard and saw, especially the drifter for making headway in the light airs often prevailing in those waters during the summer. All of this was important to me because, for the past fifteen years, I had been sailing San Francisco Bay and nearby offshore waters, including racing experience crewing on vessels up to forty-three feet. We discussed the dependence on sails in olden times to navigate those waters. I told Ken, "I came up here to go to Sitka. Might take us a while to get there, but I'll be surprised if we don't make it."

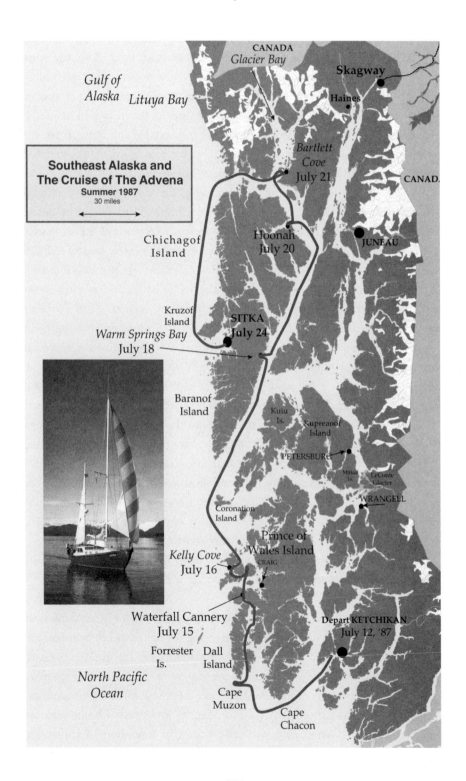

Southeast Alaska and
The Cruise of The Advena
Summer 1987
30 miles

Gulf of
Alaska   Lituya Bay

CANADA
Glacier Bay

Skagway

Haines

Bartlett
Cove
July 21

CANAD.

Chichagof
Island

Hoonah
July 20

JUNEAU

Kruzof
Island

SITKA
July 24

Warm Springs Bay
July 18

Baranof
Island

Kuiu
Is.

Kupreanof
Island

PETERSBURG

Mitkof
Is.

LeConte
Glacier

WRANGELL

Coronation
Island

Prince of
Wales Island

CRAIG

Kelly Cove
July 16

Waterfall Cannery
July 15

Forrester
Is.

Dall
Island

Depart KETCHIKAN
July 12, '87

North Pacific
Ocean

Cape
Muzon

Cape
Chacon

The next day was mostly spent buying groceries and other supplies and gear. Supplies included at least a dozen aerosol cans of ether fluid. A shot or squirt into each engine cylinder provides a kick to fire up a hard-to-start diesel engine—and hopefully get her running. This turned out to be a prudent purchase. I had no idea at the time how during the trip Ken would be unsuccessful on the first try, or even the second, getting the beast to go. Free time was spent making the rounds of the town for Ken to say thanks to friends for the hospitality he and George had enjoyed during their sojourn.

Up early the next morning for departure, George and I were standing casually talking on the dock next to the boat, hoping Ken would be quickly successful at starting the engine. We were interrupted by a mind-numbing crash coming at us out of the air overhead. Gazing skyward, we were transfixed by the sight of a float plane and helicopter in midair collision over the harbor channel, not far out from where we were standing. The helicopter came down in a shower of falling debris, including the bodies of the pilot and passenger. This was immediately gaffed and secured to a nearby seiner. Accompanied by a growing group of other boats and the sirens of police cars and ambulances, the seiner towed it all in a few minutes to the outside of the same dock we were tied to just thirty feet away. Police and medics were there in force. We witnessed it all. Ken noted in his journal, "Sobering! You could feel the dread and questions of death."

As soon as the hubbub cleared and Ken got the engine to start, we let loose the lines and motored the short distance out into the same waters just witness to tragedy. We found enough wind to raise sail, shut down the engine before it overheated and died, and set a course to sail southwest and away from Ketchikan to round Pennock Island. We were off on a balmy day of pleasant sailing outbound for Sitka.

August 12—Crossing Clarence Strait under sail heading west for Cape Chacon. The evening is beyond my description. Shades of rose and white. Even a hazy rainbow astern over Annette Island for a while.

With this entry, Ken hit the sack to get some sleep and leave me alone at the tiller enshrined in the light of the moon rising on the southern horizon. Less than an hour later I saw a large vessel approaching on an easterly course for port-to-port passing, unexpected for those waters. As it came abreast there was a call on the radio in the cabin: "Sailing vessel on course for Cape Chacon, this is the Coast Guard Cutter *Citrus,* please identify and provide home port and destination, over." Wondering what the heck this was about, I called Ken because the radio was over his bunk and he was the captain. Ken was already wide awake and responded, "This is the *Advena,* out of Seattle, departed Ketchikan this morning, and bound for Sitka. What is the purpose of your call?"

"*Citrus* back. Oh, we have some sailors lining the rail taking in the beautiful view of your vessel ghosting along in the moonlight. We just want to say hello and wish you fair winds and following seas on your cruise to Sitka. *Citrus* off and clear."

I don't know whether Ken or George ever went back to sleep. I spent the remaining hours of that watch basking in the beauty of the night and the thoughtful gesture of the sailors on the *Citrus.* The next day turned out to be quite different, though.

August 14, 1610 hours—A day of adventure! Began sailing past Cape Chacon[33] *in night headed for Cape Muzon. Began to be foggy and blowing. We intended to sail outside Dall Island (in the Gulf of Alaska) with moderate weather predicted. Then, in fact, encountered winds Dave thought eventually were gusting to 35–40 knots. We headed out in the fog perhaps toward Timber Island, but weather became worse and worse. Boat took on water through after hatch. At one point, found myself head down reaching into the bilge to clear the bilge pump intake screen. Boat was thoroughly doused. Not really ready for that kind of weather in high seas. George and I were both a little seasick. But Dave was terrific! He tended the sails and knew exactly what to do. Sailed back in fog toward Cape Muzon. With Dave insisting we had to bear up against wind as much as possible, hit her on the nose. Made it at last into Kaigani Harbor where I removed the thermostat because of heating problems.*

The next two-plus days were spent slowly sailing our way north up Kaigani Strait to the entrance to Tlevak Narrows. This narrows, translated from the Haida to be commonly called Skookum Chuck, thwarted easy passage to our next destination, Waterfall, where Ken and I had many fond memories of happy summers. This had to be run at slack water as ebbs and floods often ran at six knots with cross currents making for some mildly exciting times at the helm. We felt called to do it under power as it was too risky to try under sail.

On the early morning slack of August 16, Ken fired up the engine. We went in with the temperature gauge reading 210 degrees. Soon it increased to 230 degrees. Ken felt forced to ignore it as we had to clear a red buoy on the north side of the channel or be swept back through the narrows. The engine quit from

---

33 Cape Chacon is the well-known exposed southern tip of Prince of Wales Island. Dangerous nearby reefs make it a point of relief for navigators after rounding in foul weather.

overheating just as we were almost clear for escape south into Meares Passage. All three of us fell to quickly raising the drifter, main, and mizzen to hopefully catch enough wind to carry us out of the current. Then Ken went back to the engine to add water, replacing what had boiled out, and set up to crank the engine with twenty-four volts, if necessary. I went to work looking for zephyrs strong enough to put some air in our sails. We slowly sailed on for the short distance to Waterfall.

George and me on the dock at Waterfall Resort
Resort employee snapped the photo.
Photo collection of Dave Olson

We knew going in that the cannery complex had been sold years before to a private company that had converted it into a large, posh, five-star fishing resort. We were greeted by confirming signs on the docks and floats, PRIVATE PROPERTY—No Trespassing. Since we had a connection to the past, we moved to tie up to an outside float. An employee showed up to wave us off. Hanging off the float we explained our mission. He said, "Let me go talk to my boss." The boss returned with him. We repeated our story. He replied, "Your timing is perfect as all our guests are out fishing. How would you like a tour and then join us for lunch?"

The next two hours were a step back in time going through the beautifully preserved old buildings now tastefully converted to outfit, service, and house perhaps a hundred sport fishermen, along with processing and preserving their catches of salmon, halibut, and trout. After lunch, with perfect winds, we raised sails at the dock and cast off to the high fives of a half-dozen resort folks who had come down to see us off.

The rest of the day was classic sailing all the way to Noyes Island and Kelly Cove. We found enough wind left to sail in at midnight and drop anchor a hundred feet off the fish buying scow. What a way to end a day!

The next morning Ken and I jumped in our dinghy with cameras and loads of memories to row over to the buying scow to introduce ourselves. We found a young lady with a degree in marine biology running the operation. Late in the season fishing slowed and there were only five or six trollers left selling to the station. After a look at the docks, we rowed ashore to walk the beach and take photos of the engraved memorial stone honoring "Tonto Bill" Ingram who had fished every summer for decades out of Kelly Cove—long enough to become informally known and loved by all as the mayor of Kelly Cove. He had become Ken's other role model along with his skipper, Sevrin Hildre, during the summers he had decked on the *Rap III*. Tonto Bill had been the moving force in Seattle behind Ken's decision to buy his own boat back in the spring of 1951.

**Kelly Cove Fish Buying Station in 1987—a shadow of the operation
of Knaplund & Son in the 1930s and 1940s**
Photo by Dave Olson

He wrote in his journal, "Walking the beach, remembering, made me choke up." Me, too, as memories took me back to 1947 and my life-changing summer working for the founding owners of fish buying operations at the cove, John Knaplund and his son Carsten, as deckhand on their fish packer, the *Beloit*

II. I thought of my innocence, unaware back then that it was to be their last season. They had to give it all up because of the tragedy unfolding in the deteriorating health of Carsten. How fortunate I had been to have John as a mentoring skipper, and too dumb to say so while he was still alive.

I picture now, on that tiny square of hallowed ground next to Tonto Bill's commemorative stone, a granite block memorial inscribed:

JOHN KNAPLUND
Latter-day Viking of Kelly Cove
1881–1951
* * *

Returning to the *Advena,* we raised anchor and sailed away. Clearing the north end of Noyes Island, we beat our way northwest in the offshore waters making long tacks against southwest winds and a five- or six-foot southwest ground swell. These tacks were projected to give us a wide berth rounding Coronation Island, off the south end of Kuiu Island, for the turn north out of the Gulf of Alaska into Chatham Strait. This went on through most of the night. Ken's journal gave an account of that night and early morning:

> *August 17—We sailed all night having a hard time getting above Coronation [Island]. After getting four miles above, we made an attempt to round which turned out to be a mistake. The wind died with breaking seas on rocks less than a mile away. A frantic race followed to get the anchor gear ready and/or start the engine…*

At that juncture, with the main and mizzen mast booms secured, and the sails hanging limp and slatting with the action of the sea, George and I could only stand helplessly on deck, listening to the booming of the ever-closer breakers and calmly discussing tactics. We had no survival suits. Even if we had had one, a rubber life raft would probably have offered no escape, trying to row or paddle out against the incoming ground swell would have been difficult. We had a small outboard for the dinghy, but launching it would have been impossible. Our best chance for survival was to try anchoring, and, if that didn't hold, ride out engulfment in the surf to be cast up on the forbidding coast. There was reason for hope; the *Advena's* super-strong ferro-cement hull would survive the beating sufficiently to come to rest with a good possibility of getting ashore.

George's impassive demeanor was impressive. This gave me time to plan ahead. I recall thinking about preparation of easy release line tie-ins to the mizzen mast as the best bet for back-up security to just hanging on to the mast for dear life going through the surf. Ken continues, "Then at the last minute, I finally started the engine with breakers minutes away. Used 24 volts.[34] Really affected me. We could have lost everything, including lives."

It was a close call blessed by divine intervention or, at least, lady luck. The engine ran long enough to get us out of harm's way. Soon light winds came along for us to enjoy easy sailing up Chatham Strait to relax the next day at Baranof Warm Springs at the head of Warm Springs Bay. Located on the east side of Baranof Island directly across the island from Sitka, this five-star hot springs and postcard waterfall amidst stunning scenery has been a must-stop layover to "take the waters" for centuries. We began the day with a bath in the springs. Then Ken and I climbed up to a little lake to bring back seven nice cutthroat trout and enough blueberries for a cobbler. We feasted before ending the day in the springs. We needed this, especially Ken who was candidly noting in his journal, "I am getting tired and cranky."

Early the next morning, taking advantage of the outflow current from the river at the head of the bay, we sailed away under light winds back into Chatham Strait and north, into Icy Strait. Ken managed to get the engine started to get us to the outside dock for a brief stop in Hoonah late that afternoon for supplies and an early supper at the only restaurant. With a workable breeze, we were able to sail away from Hoonah bound for Bartlett Cove in Glacier Bay.

That night remains the single most exhilarating and memorable sailing experience of my life at sea. Ken and George took the first watch, staying awake long enough to sail through the first pod of spouting and bellowing humpback whales. Then I was on my own until the breaking of dawn on the horizon. Northern lights lit up the sky with a brilliant display after midnight. More than once, as we silently ghosted along under sail, at times through bands of thick sea fog, whales came up so close to the boat to blow, I could feel and smell the vapor from the spouts wafting over the cockpit and stern of the boat. I could see them. I suspect a few saw me. A couple of the slow-moving giants came close enough to make me feel like I might jump from the boat to land on their backs. I was surprised by the first one, but thereafter I relaxed to enjoy the show. I wished I knew more about their talk and songs.

We enjoyed an educational morning at the headquarters of Glacier Bay National Park, including an outdoor tour. After lunch at the lodge we cast off under sail in light rain and favorable northeast winds. Coming out of Cross Sound, passing the lighthouse at Cape Spencer into the Gulf of Alaska, Ken

---

34 This was double the designated voltage for that motor, risking burn out. Ken did it in an act of cool desperation and courage under fire.

and I were able to get patched through on the VHF radio by the Cape Spencer lighthouse keepers for heartwarming conversations with Mom and Dad. What a pleasure it was for them to hear from us! The weather had cleared. We were southbound for Sitka on a reach with favorable northwest winds to carry us through the night. You could see the isolated volcanic cone of Mount Edgecumbe, named by Captain Cook in 1778, visible on the southern horizon. It was the landmark early Russian mariners depended on to determine position while navigating their way to Sitka. I remember the sense of satisfaction permeating my bones. I thought we were already there.

By midafternoon of the next day we were off the west coast of Kruzof Island nearing Cape Edgecumbe for rounding east into Sitka Sound. If the winds held we could be in Sitka for a late dinner. We were also passing through a fleet of salmon trollers about to lift their gear to head for town, sell their catches, and tie up for the night.

Ken decided to get on the radio to see if his friend Gary Egerton, fishing the troller *Talatche*, happened to be out there.

George Sather, Gary Egerton and me in front of Gary's troller,
the M/V *Talatche* at dock in Sitka
Ken snapped the photo.
Photo by Dave Olson

Sure enough, he was and not far away. Soon he was over to welcome us to

Sitka. Ken told him about our no-good engine. Gary quickly offered to tow us into town. Ken and George were hot to accept. Not me. I got a bug in my bonnet to say thanks, but no thanks. My pride got in the way. We were so close. The thought of ignominiously finishing this singular cruise, so much of it under sail, so many adventures, on the end of a tow line? This was more than I could swallow. My pleas prevailed. Gary took off and we continued on our way. We did fine rounding Edgecumbe and into the Sound on a heading for town.

Wouldn't you know—the wind died! So there we were, going nowhere, ten miles from tying up, with slatting sails, wallowing in a two-foot ground swell. This was our lot for an evening when we could have been sitting in a comfortable restaurant, lingering over good wine, a tasty dinner, desert, and coffee served by a welcoming waitress.

My clueless selfish desire—to brag forever about how "we sailed from Ketchikan to Sitka"—had totally blinded me to the accumulated emotional and psychological burden Ken had been carrying over the past year. A broken marriage, resignation from his parish, buying and restoring the *Advena* to seek a new life, the long troubling cruise north with an all-but-useless engine, and the two close calls during just the past week added up to a heavy load. It hadn't dawned on me he would be a stranger in Sitka with only his two friends to hopefully ease the way to replacing the engine on his boat with limited funds. He had had enough! For the first and only time in our lives, but with good reason on his part, he lost it and we exchanged some heated words. Finally, some zephyrs of wind came our way to sail close enough in for Ken to go straight for a double-dose of starting fluid and twenty-four volts, start the engine for the last time, and power in to tie up at guest moorage. It was Monday, August 24, four-thirty in the morning. We were twelve days out from Ketchikan. We were all glad to be there, including me.

A day later, feeling happy perceiving Ken was happy, too, and with two salmon in my luggage compliments of Gary, I was on my way back home to the San Francisco Bay Area. Ken was looking forward to a casual get-together the next weekend with Gary, Gary's wife Martha, and a few of their happy-go-lucky friends.

RENEWAL

Love is nature's way of giving a reason to be living,
The golden crown that makes man a king,
Lost on a high and windy hill …
Love is a many splendored thing.

—Adapted from the lyrics of
"Love is a Many Splendored Thing"

KEN AND NANCY

Ken's connections to Gary and Martha Egerton actually reached back to Washington. Martha's maiden name was Nichols; her dad was Frank Nichols, who had been the Whidbey Island boat builder of the *Christian* years prior. During building, Ken got to know all of the Nichols kids who liked to play down at their dad's boatyard. After she and Gary were married, the attraction of a beautiful town near good fishing led them to settle in Sitka. By the time Ken arrived, they had many friends in the community. Their home was a float house at Birdsnest Cove off Jamestown Bay, a few miles outside of Sitka.

Ken joined the Egertons for dinner as soon as George and I were gone. Soon Ken got a slip for the *Advena* near Gary's boat, so it was natural for Ken to hang out with Gary down at the dock and at Gary's home while he got acquainted with his new surroundings. The Egertons hosted an impromptu party on Saturday, August 29. Ken was invited. Annie and Mike, fellow fisher people, showed up with their fiddles to contribute, with Gary on the guitar, to an evening of fun and music. Another guest was a lively close friend of Martha and Gary who divided her time between teaching school and fishing salmon as half-owner of a troller aptly named the *Spawn*. Her first commercial salmon fishing venture had been hand trolling out of Neah Bay in the Straits of Juan de Fuca near Cape Flattery. She was divorced and in her early forties with three grown daughters already pursuing successful careers. Her name was Nancy Brown McGrady. Recognition of a shared love of the sea, an instant bonding by water, gave Ken and Nancy cause to converse as the party lingered on, eventually turning it into an overnighter. Nancy recalls:

The next morning Gary was ready to take the party guests back to town when he remembered it was Martha's birthday. In the amazement and laughter of the moment, Ken, standing at the edge of the boat dock, was too tempting a target for Martha to resist, so she pushed him off the dock. He realized he was falling so he dove in, managing to lose his glasses. Ken, Gary, and I took off for town where I bought presents and a birthday cake for Martha, Gary bought air for his scuba dive tank, and Ken bought a cream pie. Soon after our return, Ken pushed the pie in Martha's face. This was followed by Gary diving for Ken's glasses and also a good bunch of abalone. Naturally, we all stayed to spend a second night at the cove to celebrate Martha's birthday and eat the abalone. Ken and I, in our sleeping bags, found a lot to talk about before we went to sleep. We spent the next day feasting on abalone and other good stuff. On the drive back to town, since Ken was a recently arrived solo sailor in Sitka and such a good friend of the Egertons, I casually invited him over for dinner later in the week.

Concerning Martha and the pie, Ken bragged in his follow-up journal entry, "I put it in her face perfectly." He also laconically noted, "Got somewhat acquainted with Nancy. Nice lady."

The next week began with a surprise for Ken from an unexpected direction because no one outside of family knew he was in Sitka or could be reached by phone through the Egertons. There is also no evidence of prior contact by Ken with the Alaska Synod office in Anchorage to indicate an interest in resuming parish ministry up there. Nevertheless, Reverend Donald Parsons, the synod's bishop, found Ken to tell him he was looking for a minister to become pastor of the small Island of Faith Lutheran Church in Wrangell, not far from Sitka. The week ended on another high note when he successfully tracked down a like-new rebuilt replacement engine in Indiana and secured financing to pay for it. Ken placed the order.

During midweek he reconnected with Joe Lewis, one of his best friends from high school days in Ketchikan. Raised in a downtown apartment by a wonderful hardworking single mother, Ruby, who managed a local restaurant, Joe still managed to get hooked on commercial fishing. Now here he was with wife Judy, settled in Sitka, and owner/skipper of the purse seiner M/V *Misty Moon*. He quickly invited Ken over to meet Judy and stay for dinner. The evening ended with Joe and Judy inviting Ken to hang out with them over Labor Day Monday.

By Friday, Nancy's dinner invitation had expanded to begin the weekend with Ken joining her for a drive to nearby Harbor Mountain for a hike to the higher elevations. Nancy says:

> *I remember when we really hit it off and realized we had a lot in common about values. We had climbed up Harbor Mountain, overlooking beautiful Sitka, and were sitting on a log. Ken asked me about teaching special education kids in school and how I graded them. My reply was, "I want them all to succeed in their own ways. Those kids earn A grades for their efforts." As we have both always rooted for the underdogs of life, something between us clicked that day.*

Labor Day at Joe's had ended with an invitation for Ken to join Joe, Judy, and their crew on the *Misty Moon* for a few days of openings[35] for salmon seining in Salisbury Sound north of Sitka. Regarding this respite from dealing with his boat problems and pangs of budding love, Ken noted in his journal on return to Sitka: "Judy is a perfect wife for Joe. Amazing—she not only cooks and looks after the crew, but she stacks corks[36] on deck during sets of the seine. She also has a little aquarium fish business in Sitka."

Reflecting a week later on the Labor Day weekend, Ken wrote:

> *September 13—Time has run together for nearly two weeks. It began by getting to know Nancy a lot better. The last week was spent being in love. I think I'm experienced enough to understand that. It all began with a drive up Harbor Mountain and hike into the high country, the heather, juniper, and marvelous views of ocean, mountains, and town below. Afterward, we had a salmon barbeque with huge king salmon steaks. I felt a real drawing to be near a woman again. There was so much open and inviting. The next three days were filled with all the longing and meaning of falling in love. I knew I was letting myself do it. We spent Labor Day at Joe's watching TV.*

---

35 "Openings" are designations, under regulations administered by the state of Alaska, of locations and times that commercial fishing is allowed. They are communicated to the fishermen and enforcement officials oversee compliance. All commercial fisheries in Alaska are controlled by seasons, openings, or boat catch quotas.

36 In purse seining, "corks" are small blocks of cork with a center hole in each. Hundreds of these corks are strung on the top line of the seine as floats. Stacking corks as the seine is hauled in is part of finishing a set.

How fast was Ken's life moving? Tuesday morning, back aboard the *Advena*, he wrote:

September 15—The world is incredibly beautiful and my mind is filled with thoughts. The chilly weather system has passed to the south. There has been a little north wind and breaking clouds. I am going to Wrangell today. Things are becoming clear. So much is etched in my mind from the last two weeks. I have been in love for the last time in my life. Is it the greatest? But one cannot compare the beauty of mountain top experiences. She is the most generous woman in the world. I would gladly live with her and marry her for the rest of my life. But that is impossible. For one thing, I have nothing. But more than that, there is the matter of the salmon (as in their struggle/my struggle) and my church/my wife (as in my ordination vows). Is it that I must be the outsider always? That I must choose the pain of struggle? She has become a sacred person to me, my love for her a sacred object. But I must not speak to her of that. Now perhaps I must come to terms in some existential way with Wrangell. Will it work? How I want to be honest!

We can only surmise the torture of Ken's apparently insoluble dilemma, confronted as he was by the need to reconcile "my church/my wife," a driving force in his mind and heart, with his impossible love for Nancy. Back in the early days of his decision to enter the ministry, before going to the seminary, he had loved a lovely young woman who loved him equally but felt she was simply not cut out to be a preacher's wife. She told him as much and this rejection had led to a severance of the relationship. Nancy's life choices had been the antithesis of those predicting happiness as a minister's spouse as well. What were the chances of a happy ending this time? The first move toward resolution was a brief trip to Wrangell to meet the Island of Faith congregation. A week later, returning to his journal, Ken wrote:

September 23—I've been to Wrangell. In Wrangell I sensed a kind of rough and ready town with a mix of all kinds of churches and preachers. My people were a true cross section, I think. Perhaps perfect for me. I got away for a few hours. Got a haircut from Clara, a Tlingit Indian barber. Found she was a young grandma who likes to cross-country ski. I went into a tavern. Not a pleasant experience. What is it about going into taverns alone? I stayed with Bob and Mary Drues. Ate moose steak. Now I've been back awhile. Went hiking with Nancy on Harbor Mountain Sunday. Martha and her son, little Levi, were with us. Found myself feeling extremely good and healthy again. Find my relationship to Nancy growing in strength. I'm over the first rush. It was great. Now we are talking a lot. So much feels right and good. Where she lives, how she thinks and feels, her talk about school, her kids—all together mean much to me. She is sensitive, very mature, and in control. There is wisdom in her from the years. How good she can make me feel. Also Martha, what a wonder of a woman! She is a true daughter of Frank and Peggy. I am being drawn by writing and Wrangell. I've had some talks with John Halaam, the painter from Shishmaref and Wrangell. He showed me his paintings. Perhaps I'm being drawn into some last romantic experience of truth, and some closeness to truth. Am I fey?[37] I think so.

Of this second hike, Nancy recollects, "When it started to snow, Ken gave me a kiss and said, 'You always kiss those with you at the first snow.'"

Carried by the flow, Ken was caught in a buoyant and fast-moving transformation of his life.

September 25—So many strange things going on in and with me. More life has happened to me in a few weeks than many a year. I tried marijuana a few days ago. Nothing exciting, but does seem to sharpen one's senses for a time. I've become very attached to Sitka, but feeling Wrangell is the place for me. Yesterday I learned I can go to Wrangell for sure. Nancy says she loves me. But we are both so wise and tried in life. Nancy brought up us joining the Peace Corps. It made me think very much about the future. I know I am drawn as if to some fate. To what extent Nancy is a part, I don't know. She already is in me, perhaps, no I am sure, more than any woman I have known. It is mysterious. Anyway, I feel warm and whole inside when I think about our love. How can it be happening?"

September 26—I think I will go south with Joe on the Misty Moon and drive my car up to Prince Rupert and thence by ferry to Wrangell. My deep-seated religiosity, and that I seem to have no inclination to settle down, maybe not to marry ever again, leaves me with an impossible relationship to Nancy. Is there hope? Nancy has a career here. For sometime we may have to spend big blocks of time apart. How will that work? I just can't come running here, find a job, and move in with Nancy. It would destroy us. I must follow my own destiny and so must she. My world has become so terribly romantic. I am so happy, but there is pain in that too. The problem

---

37 Fated or doomed.

is neither one of us are going to violate who we are for the sake of our being together because that would only destroy our love.

In early October Ken and Joe took off from Sitka on the *Misty Moon* bound for Seattle. They ran into a gale, giving them a harbor day in Ketchikan. According to Nancy, Ken used it to climb Deer Mountain. Later he told Nancy that near the summit he had carved on a tree KO+NM, her initials at the time. Of the remainder of the cruise south, Ken noted in his journal, "Joe and I took turns steering, five hours on and off, at night. Joe pretty much navigates with radar—no current tables, no real charts, and no logbook."

Following Ken's arrival in Seattle, Nancy flew down from Sitka for a busy weekend with him. Nancy says, "We stayed in a hotel. Much of the time was spent meeting each other's kids. All were so supportive and seemed delighted that we had found each other."

Ken portrays in his journal enjoying a wonderful meeting with Nancy's children at a family party. Of a later gathering of his family, he noted, "They seem to like Nancy very much." Relieved and uplifted by these feelings, Ken and Nancy enjoyed a euphoric parting at the airport.

Ken returned to Alaska via car and ferry with a stop in Wrangell to drop off his car. While in Wrangell, he met with a delegation from the congregation anxious to become better acquainted with their new minister. All went well. Then he boarded the ferry for return to Sitka.

Back on the *Advena,* he found the replacement engine delivered, but Ben Hubbard, the mechanic who would install it, would be away until November. This opened up time to ruminate and write.

October 29—My conversation with Michael Meier, the school board chairman (and pastor of the Lutheran Church), was extremely helpful. How shall I understand myself now? I have someone who loves me and someone who hates me. Are they both right? I've become engaged in the life in Sitka. Am I still on some quest? I think so. My life and feelings about myself have changed. Nancy has become precious to me. I was more alone than I knew. How patient and kind she is. I think she has needed someone like me more than she has admitted to herself. And I feel all unworthy because my vocational future is so uncertain. How little I have to bring to her with my still unsettled marriage break-up pending. And my Christian feelings and thoughts? What is happening to them? Yesterday, Nancy and I had quite a discussion about faith's meaning in relation to love. Faith, belief, hope, and trust establish the realities that love deals with. How interesting and full my life has been with her. It's as if some great cure is taking place within me. The outcome is not sure or clear yet. I believe it can all work out if I have the courage to accept it. Meanwhile, I am working on the engine.

November 9—I've been in Wrangell for nearly a week. It has been okay, but has me uneasy too. How unsuited I seem to be, to be a preacher. I had the service yesterday. So many strong feelings are coming through. I've been reading The Diary of a Parish Priest again. Now it strikes me, if all goes as planned, I will be bringing the boat to Wrangell at the beginning of the Advent Season. I'm conscious of my great turbulence to be faced in the next few months. How dearly I cherish my new love and feeling cared about by a woman. In Wrangell I seemed to hold up pretty well with all the new relationships. What a delight it was to be with the Rylls. Mother and daughter have an extraordinary relationship; beautiful to behold. Sharon teaches little kids in Sunday school. Al is deeply involved in his boat. He's very analytical keeping track of barometer and temperature day by day. They are so hopeful I will be a good pastor to them. It is humbling.

November 13—I'm learning how much courage it takes to live and love and take it into one's self. I feel good about my relationship to Nancy. But people may misunderstand. I have no control of that. Have I a right to happiness? Must I die to be Christian? Yes, but in what way? Am I squirming and avoiding the issue? There is the feeling that I can be more productive through what Nancy gives me—a strong sense of worth and confidence as a man. I feel so close to Nancy and not wanting to hurt her in any way. How little and vulnerable she seems to me at times, and so brave. I can't comprehend her courage as a person. It is astounding and so forthright. I learn from her. I have to go to Wrangell tomorrow for Sunday services. I hope I feel more at ease in church and have something meaningful to say. Am I living a lie with them? I hope not. They must come to understand me as I am, but not in such a way as to hurt them.

December 1—Ben and I finished installing the engine the day before Thanksgiving. Joanne and Tom were here for the weekend. Wonderful to have Joanne here. How good Nancy is! Joanne and she seem to get along great. Put up Christmas decorations. Saw them off feeling sad with Nancy.

A day later Al Ryll, a pillar of the Island of Faith congregation, arrived to help Ken take the *Advena* to Wrangell so the church would once again have a resident pastor. Also, Ken would continue to live on the *Advena* while he got settled in his new surroundings. Of Al's time in Sitka, Nancy writes:

I remember Al coming to my little cottage with Ken to meet me. From there we went to dinner together. He was so nice to me, but I knew it was a bit of a stretch for him to understand all that was going on between Ken and me. He and Ken had an interesting theological discussion as Al was very literal in his biblical interpretations and, you know, Ken was much more open to possibilities.

Years later, after Ken died, Nancy says, "Al told me Ken was the best friend he ever had. Coming from a very private, reserved person, I was very touched when he told me that."

Commenting on the same dinner, a few hours out from Sitka on the *Advena* with Al, on their way to Wrangell, Ken noted in his journal: "Nancy and Al had a good chance to get acquainted. Al seems to like Nancy, too. Now Al and I are coming into Salisbury Sound underway to Wrangell. Everything is going fine." It was for Ken and the *Advena*, but not for Al.

December 14—So much has happened. While underway in Peril Strait with Al, a helicopter passed over contacting us on the radio. The pilot told us Al's son had been killed in a biking accident in Hawaii. He was there to pick up Al for his return home to Wrangell. The next day, in a snowstorm, I motored the Advena back to Sitka and caught the next plane to Wrangell to be with Al and his family. I stayed in Wrangell through the weekend. On Tuesday, Eric Kading, who loves to sail, flew back to Sitka with me. We took off and ran one day and night till four-thirty in the morning to snowy Petersburg. Three days to Wrangell. Now I'm all settled in at Shoemaker Harbor marina with electricity, water, and phone. Cat goes wild sometimes wanting to play. What is troublesome is I now know I want to be with Nancy. And I will be here and that seems impossible for her.

As lovers will find a way, so did Ken and Nancy by cobbling together arrangements to celebrate much of the Christmas holiday together with their families in Seattle. Nancy remembers meeting Ken's mom and dad, and Ken meeting hers, and they both remember how understanding they all were, seeming delighted they had found each other. Nancy recalls her Methodist dad saying privately in jest, "Well, you might have found someone besides a Lutheran."

Nancy returned to teaching and her home in Sitka. Ken, now the minister of Island of Faith Lutheran Church in Wrangell, returned there to resume his pastoral duties while continuing to live on the *Advena* at Shoemaker Harbor. This is a breakwater-protected public marina four miles south of Wrangell that is totally lacking in any business establishments in the vicinity. It was built to provide inexpensive but secure boat moorage to accommodate the one hundred-plus vessels home ported in Wrangell, for which there was no room in the small harbor centered on the town waterfront. Perhaps one-third of the boats are liveaboards, mostly because their owners are either transients or can't afford a house in town. It is a quiet place ideal for solitary pursuits like writing.

Living alone, surrounded by salmon waters, gave Ken time to revisit his long-standing fascination with the mystical migrations and martyrdom of salmon. Pondering the necessary suffering of the salmon in their life cycle, he wrote, "Gives me a better understanding of the key role of transcendence in human life, and that all human knowledge and morality is based upon its presence." This led to writing a twenty-seven-page mystical, theological, and philosophical discourse he titled *Salmon Are Christian*. To my knowledge, Ken was the first Christian thinker to make the theological leap and see the sacrificial drama in the lives of salmon as the Christ-like activity of believers in ultimate resurrection. He saw the salmon's oblation to secure procreation as a metaphor for the martyrdom of Christ. Following are excerpts from the preface, two poems, and a few provocative verses ruminating on life, death, and dying in a third poem:

Preface

Call me ADVENA Ken as is the oft followed custom in small boat harbors. I bought her at auction in 1986 for $7,000. Information about the owner was protected. After the purchase, my brother[38] and I raised the main to find near the top a prominent Latin cross with a stylized dolphin around it. With the romantic goal of sailing the boat north to St. Augustine Island39 where I would scale its volcano, I left Lutheran ministry. In my heart was a private, dangerous, not unfamiliar, purging kind of intent. However, owing to a favorable providence, some wandering brought me no further than Shoemaker Harbor, Wrangell, Alaska. Though not gifted at writing, in lieu of climbing that mountain, this is what I have written …

Salmon Are Christian

In a glance
of transfiguration
into humanness
spawner-salmon

---

38   Tim, who helped Ken with restoration of the boat.
39   Near Anchorage, Alaska

shoaled, break
into sere air—
fear is in the sea,
queer signals
and currents
that prevent, then
ever more and more
allure as a mask of
divine desire appears
ever more and more
in the creator image
ever more and more
ominous and wonderful
drawing upward into
the river and the
ever more and more
roar of the cataract to be
ascended.

Those Priestly Ones

Then Christian … the salmon creatures
waited upon the seeming blasphemy
and painful arts of being human,
while within that longing profoundly
holy was yet expressed
in eager reaching,
wanting still those dark thoughts
to fall away like flapping ravens;
and so, in endless purpose
to give life for life
by pressing earth's cold-water sands
with bodies spent and useless,
believed in such acts of the impossible
as birth from on high and resurrection.

When the Branch Becomes Tender

Actually as well as mortal, we're natal.
How we got here and how we leave is

So cleverly covered, who would suspect?
Something might be up.
Death's in the domain of nature.
To die is most physical, we all will.
But to die in the prime of life?
That's unacceptable.
There's an unearthly element.
Each one departs with a shudder.
There's a sublime aspect to everything.
Science can't study it.
Spirit's a transcending of transcendence.

Ken never considered the work a finished manuscript. He worked on additions and revisions off and on for the rest of his life. He included excerpts from the original and additions in other writings contributed occasionally to church-related house periodicals. If he had lived to retirement, I think he would have completed and probably published the work. While still living on the *Advena,* he did have the foresight to make copies of the draft and distributed them to family, relatives, friends, and fellow clergy. I treasure mine.

Nancy says Ken wrote her a letter daily during these months of separation, which accounts for the three-month lapse of entries in his journal during this period. Fortunately, she saved those letters and later, looking for something else, she wrote:

> *I found this tied-up bundle of letters Ken wrote me during the winter of 1987–88. Couldn't put them down till I reread them all. He was the romantic poet. Reading them again moves me. One proposed our marriage... the ending of another one of them reads:*
>
> *Oh Nancy, sweet Nancy, do you dare to touch me with your soul?*
> *Oh Nancy, sweet Nancy, one day our lives will part;*
> *Then will there be some treasure in your heart?*
>
> *Well, the treasure proved to be there strong and remains ... I was surely blessed to have those experiences and my life has been changed and made all right and complete. One of the touching things is Ken typed this poem on his little old portable typewriter that left dark spots in the spaces because the keys were gummed up.*

* * *

**Ken and Nancy enjoying a respite from responsibilities
at a remote cabin on the Stikine River**
On the British Columbia mainland, the Stikine River is traveled by small boats out from Wrangell. Ken
and Nancy reached the cabin on such a craft.
Photo collection of Nancy Olson

Ken eventually resumed journal entries.

*March 4—I awoke to the sun coming in the wheelhouse window. Frost
on the floats and mist over the mountains, but a strong sense of a new
season. What a winter it has been. The cold snow and the way the seawater
held the snow till it looked like you could walk on it; the long walks in the
woods to behold the towering ice at the frozen waterfall. And the talks with
liveaboard boater friends Tim and Laura on Laura Lynn, and Bob and
Holly on the Hattie, sharing their problems with me. Sometimes I've felt
my life to be a little like walking on the water. If I don't keep my eye fixed
on Jesus, I'll sink in the alarms of life, I've thought. Life is as simple as that.*

*March 5—Went to a local pastor's gathering. They talked about how
strong the Baha'i Faith following was becoming in the world and Wrangell.
I was thinking about survival of species and bird life. Hell, they're for
undoing that.*

Pondering Ken's March 5 entry, I think back to Ken's previous entries
envisioning an outdoor mission program to pastor and minister to nature; that
is, the natural world was not made just for man to ravage for his own selfish
ends. I speculate Ken had moved beyond the largely accepted church

obliviousness to the destruction taking place in the physical world around us. He had come to a mystical appreciation of the place of God's world created for all life to share equally abundantly. This moved him to dismay with the priorities of his colleagues.

I know he walked his talk in his personal life. The only weapon on the *Advena* was an old twenty-two-caliber revolver owned fifty-fifty by Ken and me while we were teenagers in Alaska. He never bought another gun nor ever hunted for game following his return to the Great Land. Ministering to nature implied stewardship for all of God's creation. The mandate for preservation and conservation was implicit in this ministry. This was a decade before the founding of Earth Ministry in Seattle and a number of similar organizations across the nation, which put Ken ahead of his time.

March 14—Things are on track. I had a good time in Sitka and accomplished something. Thinking—the world is perfect if love is the thing. The pain and uncertainty perfect it. God is the ultimate force on earth. Jesus is the new Adam. The King is Lord!

March 29—The barometer is up and I saw the first huckleberry blossoms today. I have some marvelous thoughts about participating nature. I'm working hard at getting ready for Nancy to visit me.

April 5—Nancy has been here since Thursday. It was a beautiful weekend. We went sailing on Saturday out to Elephant's Nose and back to Wrangell. Sunday services went fine with Nancy here.

April 8—Storm warnings up for winds to sixty knots. I've thought some again of writing this life into some kind of a story. I might call it "My Boat, My Home—The Advena Story."

* * *

THE *CHRISTIAN*

During Ken's time on the *Advena*, the *Christian* was continuing its mission of floating faith ministry. Through the late '70s, Captain Reverend Donald Taylor had continued the popular program and punishing cruise schedule initiated by Ken without respite for himself as successor, wearing the many hats incumbent in the job. By fall 1978, Taylor was ready for return to the much less hectic life of a parish minister.

Unable to find a qualified minister/skipper, Rolland Burrows, a licensed captain and devout layman, was hired in the spring of 1979 to take over as captain. While waiting for him, for the April through May weekend retreat cruises, Taylor had his nineteen-year-old son Martin, an aspiring seminarian who was already licensed and very familiar with the boat, skipper the trips with others on board who were qualified to contribute spiritual leadership. Burrows continued this practice coordinating with the Lutheran Outdoor Ministries Association (LOMA) Minister of Camping while remaining in touch with Rev. Taylor. Thus, young Martin Taylor skippered the boat full-time for the summer of 1982.

Don Taylor came back as primary minister/skipper in 1983. By that time the need for an upgrade and call for a bigger boat had surfaced. This culminated in a proposal to lengthen the boat to increase the size of the main salon and space below deck for dividing guest sleeping quarters into small two-person staterooms. All of this was designed to better accommodate adult couple retreat cruises. A fund-raiser campaign brochure invited people to "Invest in this ministry, be a partner with us. Adventure with us in expanding this ministry to older adults!" The solicitation was successful enough for boat owner and program sponsor LOMA to support going ahead with the project. The bigger boat was creatively accomplished by cutting the existing boat in half and lengthening it by adding nine feet amidships. Nichols Bros. Boat Builders completed the work in time for cruises to resume in the spring of 1984. The upgrades resulted in expanded accommodations and a faster boat.

By 1987 serious friction had developed between Captain Taylor and LOMA management. Martin skippered the boat through the summer of 1987. Rumors circulated LOMA was dipping into revenues from the *Christian*'s operation. Subsequent events tend to confirm this was probably true as LOMA later filed for bankruptcy. All this festered into a falling out. At the end of the 1987 summer cruise season, Don Taylor walked away, leaving the vessel marooned at its marina moorage in Anacortes. LOMA management made little or no effort— or, if they did, it was unsuccessful—to find a replacement for Taylor. This left the *Christian* abandoned to rust with unpaid moorage bills and other expenses piling up on the ledger. Meanwhile, a dispute simmered over the vessel's future. This was the woeful state of the *Christian* during the fall of 1987.

* * *

RECLAIMED

Through the bleak winter of 1987–88 the *Christian* lay deserted at the dock in a backwater Anacortes marina appearing abandoned to barnacle growth below the waterline and the ravages of salt air above. Unfortunately, what to do about the *Christian* was only one of the financial and operational headaches afflicting LOMA. The board of directors decided to sell the boat in February 1988, but they were reluctant to sell her for private charter work. This would be a betrayal of the vessel as a venture of faith. Tax issues were also foreseen going down this road. Somebody at LOMA looking for other possibilities, knowing Ken's history with the *Christian*, got Ken's phone number on the *Advena* in Shoemaker Harbor, Alaska.

As fortuitous timing would have it, visiting Ken on the *Advena* was none other than the Reverend Donald Parsons, bishop of the Alaska Synod of the Evangelical Lutheran Church in Alaska. He was down from Anchorage to get better acquainted with him and his congregation. Reverend Parsons recollects:

> *There we were, sitting in the cabin, when the phone rang and this man from the Puget Sound Lutheran Camping Ministry called to talk and ask if we'd like to have the Christian in Alaska for ministry in Southeast Alaska. They wanted to develop a closer relationship with a church-related mission enterprise. Ken and I brainstormed how the Christian might fit into our synod mandate to share our faith. The possibilities were exciting!*

Ken visualized a creative new mission for the *Christian*. Perusing a map of Southeast Alaska, he identified seventeen isolated waterfront communities reachable only by boat or plane and lacking any religious, social, or basic medical services. What if a circuit was established for the *Christian* to make regular visits to these villages offering the vessel as their church for religious and related services? Would there be a welcoming reception? Could financial backing be found to try out the mission and then maintain it, if successful? Support of the larger church body of the Alaska Synod would be a prerequisite to securing this foundation and establishing this unique congregation. Would they share the vision of Ken and their bishop? Would this premise include acceptance of the real financial risk the collective synod congregations they represented would be taking on purchase of the *Christian* and coverage of the mission start-up costs?

Toward that end, the farsighted Bishop Parsons took a leap of faith and went to work forming an M/V *Christian* task force with representation in several congregations around the state to provide leadership for favorable synod action if the opportunity to buy the boat materialized.

One major problem for the anticipated minister/skipper of the *Christian* would be finding an onboard assistant to help run the boat and onboard programs while managing a busy galley and commissary. Early on the bishop must have asked Ken where he hoped to recruit the right person for this important job. My guess is from the beginning Ken foresaw the answer. How about Nancy with her social concerns, teaching background, and boating experience—a perfect fit for first mate on the *Christian?* Would she welcome the challenge? He broached the subject at the first opportunity and followed up with more serious discussion during Nancy's Wrangell visit to see Ken in early April. Adventurous, romantic, go-for-it Nancy hardly hesitated before responding with a resounding yes. Finally, if all the other players signed on, could a mutually beneficial agreement be reached with the small financially struggling Island of Faith congregation to divide Ken's time between their church and his proposed floating circuit? There was good reason to think so.

Throughout this period Ken was intermittently in conversations with the close-knit group of men, mostly from Ken's former parish, Our Saviour's Lutheran Church in Burien, Washington, who had made annual retreat and fishing cruises on the *Christian* led by Ken during the 1970s and early 1980s. They were saddened over the possibility the *Christian* might end up in commercial service and hoped to find a way to keep it from happening. They formed an informal ad hoc "Save the *Christian*" group. Their initial action, knowing little of Ken's new ties to Nancy, his Wrangell parish, and Alaska, had been a call to try and talk him into returning to Seattle to skipper the *Christian* in her original mission and program. They now knew that wouldn't happen.

With the arrival of spring, the LOMA management and board of directors reached a decision to sell the vessel to a best-offer buyer. The board scheduled an open meeting in mid-April to settle disposition of the vessel. By that time, Ken's friends had spread the word to increase their number to represent over a dozen families united in their determination to save the *Christian* for continuing ministry. When word of the meeting reached the friends, they banded together to attend and persuade board reconsideration of how the boat might be saved to resume service in its dedicated mission. They showed up together and rose one by one to make their case. Impassioned pleas fell on deaf ears. The board, sympathetic but feeling caught between a financial rock and a hard spot, was resolved to sell.

Fortunately, among those attending was William (Bill) Ruthford, a creative

Redmond, Washington lawyer in private practice. He had also been involved in family-related commercial fishing ventures as a cannery worker and around fishing boats since he was a boy. His only connection and knowledge of the *Christian* had been gleaned from his daughter Emily's account of a summer youth camp on the boat during her teens. Bill was there, knowing nothing of the situation beyond what his church's pastor, Rev. Paul Running, had told him. Paul had a personal interest in the circumstances of the *Christian* and its future. Knowing Bill as a lawyer with an interest in boats, he thought it might be worthwhile for someone like Bill to be there and observe the proceedings. Bill agreed to go and he did. He heard the fervor to find a way to continue the vessel in ministry. Their petitions gave him an idea. He asked the board for a recess so all those of like mind might adjourn to a side room to discuss the situation. Mr. Ruthford already had a solution to suggest, but the board didn't know that. He got his recess.

Ruthford proposed immediate agreement by the group to form a nonprofit entity to raise the cash to buy the *Christian* within a reasonable time frame. The investors' checks would be accumulated in an escrow account until the necessary sum was on deposit. In the event of failure, funds would be returned to the respective investors. Mr. Ruthford would do the legal work pro bono. An ad hoc volunteer committee was organized to move ahead immediately. They returned to the board meeting where Ruthford set forth their proposal. Board discussion followed of basic provisions for acceptance, which was determined to be $115,000 cash within twenty days to pay off all existing liens, including assumption of a loan secured by the vessel. The board was certain the group could never meet the deadline. Ruthford, representing the proposed buyer, agreed to those terms.

Before leaving, the committee met briefly to reach agreement on holding a formal organizational meeting within a day or two in the choir room at Our Saviour's Lutheran Church in Burien.

"Lutheran Marine Ministry was born there, but when the minister who had succeeded Ken at Our Saviour's heard about it," Ellis (Lew) Lewellen says, "he kicked us out so we held all the rest of our meetings in the Star Light Lounge of the K-C Restaurant."

Bill Ruthford adds, "The early bar customers at the lounge were really puzzled to see this group showing up for coffee, late in the morning, almost daily, to hold a meeting beginning with a short prayer."

With the necessary paperwork filed, and a bank account established by banker/treasurer Dennis Daugs, Ken Daugs's brother, the group set about enlisting additional support for their cause. Their petition was for investments in the project to buy the boat. According to Lew, "Check amounts ranged from $1,000 to $20,000." In a partial list of the seventeen investors, all apparently with the approval of wives recalls Lew, were John Black, Jerry Heinie, George Sather, Dick Lewis, Rufous Alberts, and Bill Ruthford. In early May, the day before the deal's expiration, "I had the sweet pleasure of going to the LOMA office and laying a certified check for the required $115,000 on the director's desk," says Ruthford. "The man was speechless in disbelief!"

The investors in Lutheran Marine Ministry bought the boat unseen as to condition. LOMA could only provide them with the name of a man in Anacortes who had worked on the boat for Taylor before he walked away; he had boarding keys and knew where the boat was berthed. George Sather and Lew, both possessing detailed knowledge of the boat from stem to stern, volunteered to promptly go up to Anacortes to find out what they had bought. They found the contact, who turned out to be a good guy. He showed them the boat and helped them make arrangements for immediate movement to a marine way for long overdue clean up and servicing. Then he started the engine and, with George and Lew for deckhands, ran the boat over to a boat yard to end the day in dry dock.

Following the report of the boat's condition to a meeting of Lutheran Marine Ministry and conversations with Ken and Reverend Parsons in Alaska, a conclusion was quickly reached to ready the boat as soon as possible for cruise to Sitka to seek purchase and take-over by the Alaska Synod. In early May, volunteers worked for two weeks to get the boat ready.

Meanwhile, Bill Ruthford was busy cleaning up purchase paper work while others were planning for the cruise north and lining up the roster of people interested in joining the crew on such short notice. Interest in making the trip quickly shaped up to include many spouses of the men of Lutheran Marine Ministry. After all, it was their boat, too. All of the out-of-pocket day-to-day personal and collective additional expenses continued to be borne by the owners of Lutheran Marine Ministry with no firm assurance of what the disposition of the *Christian* might be following their arrival in Alaska. It was a venture of faith.

While all this was going on in Anacortes, Bishop Parsons was busy alerting the synod task force of the purchase of the *Christian* by Lutheran Marine Ministry and plans for sailing her to Alaska to present her to them and the other delegates at the Synod Assembly in early June in Sitka.

Following notice of the purchase, Ken sought leave time from his congregation to skipper the boat for the cruise to Wrangell and then on to Sitka for the Synod Assembly. Fortunately, they supported him even as they knew the relationship with their new pastor was already headed for an uncertain future. There was also work with Bishop Parsons on the proposal for the synod purchase and sponsorship of the ministry.

**Group of investors in purchase of M/V *Christian*
who crewed cruise to Sitka from Anacortes**
Captain Ken Olson is on the right.
Ken Olson Family Archive

It would be delicious fun to know what was going on in Ken's mind through those hectic months of March, April, and into May, mulling over what was going on in the offices of LOMA and the Alaska Synod, both many hundreds of miles away. Unfortunately his journal entries during the period were mostly about the weather and Nancy, and offered nary a clue. The only references are three vague sentences:

April 5—There was lots of talk last night about the Christian again. Everybody is thinking about a program of sacramental insight up here in Alaska.

April 16—I've had news the Christian is likely too expensive with the taxes against it to be worth buying, maybe $125,000, who can say.

May 9—I'm going south to pick up the Christian next Sunday.

Contrasting Ken's expressions of the depths of his feelings for Nancy with his laconic, disengaged reportage of reclamation of the *Christian* speaks volumes of change in Ken's life. He could live without reconnection working out because a future with Nancy and a congregation in Wrangell promised a period of peace in his life. But how long would he have settled for such a life before becoming restless with a compulsion to do something new and different? No matter, there was no respite this time. The Lutheran Marine Ministry partnership literally delivered the *Christian* into his hands with a mandate to pursue another vision of new ministry.

* * *

REUNION

When Ken arrived in Seattle on May 15, he went directly on to Anacortes. There was a joyous reunion as he found all his old Lutheran Marine Ministry friends operating on fast tracks to assure cruise time for delivery of the *Christian* in Sitka by June 1. They had to be ready for presentation of the boat and visualized ministry for purchase and sponsorship by the delegates to the Alaska Synod convening June 3. There had been four projects to accomplish in about seven weeks, which felt like very limited time:

1. Twenty days to raise bridge funds to buy the boat;
2. Two weeks to restore the vessel to Bristol condition ready for sea;
3. One week to finalize plans, organize the crew, and provision the boat for the eight hundred-mile cruise from Seattle to Sitka; and
4. One week to complete the voyage.

This left little room for holdups due to weather, mechanical problems, or unexpected hang-ups.

Fortunately, Ken already knew the routine to successfully oversee the final two projects. Equally important, so did his friends as they busily went about firming up the complement of those who would share the trip, purchasing supplies and completing the many other preparations for the voyage. They were ready for sea with a few days to spare.

The cruise to Sitka with stops in Ketchikan and Wrangell took about ten days. The atmosphere was like a family reunion except the people were sharing crew responsibilities along with endless yarns of the past. With an abundance of experienced crew aboard, Ken had time to work on preparations for presentation of the boat and proposed program to the conference. They enjoyed a cool cruise.

* * *

FLOATING MINISTRY

The *Christian* was welcomed to Sitka by a group already on hand for the Synod Assembly. They were eager to see what their bishop, Don Parsons, was excited about as a unique venture of faith for their synod. From this reception until the delegates went home, there was never a dull moment on the boat. Tours of the vessel were in constant demand with no shortage of guides. Ken was even persuaded to put on the captain's uniform he abhorred.

The delegates liked what they saw and heard. Following discussion in session, they voted for the organization of Lutheran Island Ministry and election of a board of directors made up of mostly synod members. An outsider named to the board was lawyer Bill Ruthford to represent Lutheran Marine Ministry, owner of the *Christian*. The group's primary responsibilities would be to find a source or sources of funds to purchase the *Christian* and cover the projected cost of covering ongoing operational expenses thereafter. It was an act of faith to believe they could accomplish this.

The funds didn't exist at the synod and there was no way the member congregations could find the money within their memberships. Meanwhile, the Lutheran Marine Ministry investors were continuing to meet monthly payments on the loan secured for the boat. They were anxious to get out from under the ongoing obligations incumbent as owners of the vessel and disband. Thus, the board's first job was to cobble together and activate a plan to raise sufficient "bridge" money to cover the total expenses of operating the *Christian* while making visits to the outlying villages expected to be the major focus of the ministry. Ken and Nancy needed to introduce themselves and the *Christian* to the people and determine the interest and support they could expect for the ministry among those people. The success of those visits would be critical in determining the fate of the ministry. The new board met briefly before the close of the conference and decided to get together for a working meeting in conjunction with a synod council meeting in Anchorage set for September 30.

One of those attending the 1988 Synod Assembly was David L. Miller, senior features editor of *The Lutheran*, the monthly magazine of the Evangelical Lutheran Church. The July 13, 1988, issue included this *Inside Cover* brief by Mr. Miller:

> No, Alaska Synod Bishop Donald Parsons and the group in prayer on
> our cover is not praying the boat doesn't sink or for safety before casting off
> on a pleasure cruise. Their prayers are focused on the ministry the synod
> will soon launch when the good ship Christian cruises among the hundreds

of islands scattered throughout southeast Alaska. The vessel had journeyed from Anacortes, Washington, to Sitka so delegates to the synod's conference could try it out and consider if it had a place in the synod's ministry.

It does. Voting members overwhelmingly approved the $125,000 purchase and now are looking into financing it. Several outreach possibilities are being considered for the boat. Many island communities, usually with populations of twenty up to two hundred, have no church and limited worship opportunities. The Rev. Ken Olson will skipper the vessel and provide worship and pastoral services. The boat will bring vacation Bible school to the children. Also, a doctor and a nurse have expressed interest in operating a medical mission from the boat. This approach to ministry seems appropriate where everything the people do is related to the water. This fact was not lost on delegates who traveled to Sitka the only two ways it can be reached—by ferry, which comes twice a week, or by plane.

Miller didn't mention the part Nancy had already embraced to play as Ken's first mate on the boat, which was critical to the success of the ministry. Perhaps he wasn't aware of how important her role would be, or he just wanted to avoid explaining their relationship as it still existed during the conference.

Ken and Nancy had been committed to marry for months. What they desired was an opportunity to be with friends to celebrate their marriage where their love had begun and blossomed. So Ken and Nancy remained on the *Christian* in Sitka for a rest and worked on follow-up of the Synod Assembly vote for establishment of the ministry. This respite included time for Ken and Nancy to be married at Martha and Gary Egerton's float house in Birdsnest Cove surrounded by loved ones. Reverend Michael Meier, good friend and pastor of the Lutheran church in Sitka, tied the knot on June 20, 1988. The happy couple went from there to an overnight honeymoon at nearby Goddard Hot Springs. Nancy says, "This formality was followed by busy months of honeymooning work on the *Christian* where Ken and I lived aboard until we bought a small waterfront home in Wrangell."

The marvel of their marriage is it paired lovers uniquely equipped to be partners in accepting the challenge of successfully developing the Lutheran Island Ministry. Who else might have done it? It was truly "a marriage made in heaven," evolved from a fortuitous encounter at a casual party, to fulfill an unusual mission. Makes you want to believe "God works in wonderful ways," doesn't it?

Ken in skiff with *Christian* anchored behind him
Ken is on his way to shore to meet with residents.

Photo by Nancy Olson

THE "GOD BOAT" MISSION

Every floating vessel is built for a purpose subject to classification.
"Classes" range from canoes to cruise ships and aircraft carriers.
Thus the Christian *came to be dubbed the "God Boat."*
In a class by herself!

The first year of marriage for Ken and Nancy was wrapped around live-aboard life on the *Christian.* Home was the boat at Shoemaker Harbor four miles south of Wrangell.

Nancy at work in the galley of the *Christian*
Nancy is holding a bowl of bread dough.
Photo by Ken Olson

While Nancy was teaching and Ken continued to pastor his parish in Wrangell, Ken was also involved in resolution of boat ownership/sponsorship issues, preparation of the future floating parish program, exploratory voyages on the *Christian*, and completion of other groundwork and organization of the ministry. Additionally, he was a key person in the critically important collective search for grants, contributions, and angels to fund the enterprise. I think Ken doggedly worked at this always aware of how often success and failure are separated by small turns of fate. He had faith *something* would turn up.

Soon after the *Christian* tied up at Shoemaker Harbor, an opportune visitor was Reverend Stephen Kristenson, Director of Ministry and Flight Operations with the Lutheran Association of Missionaries and Pilots (LAMP) Canada based in Edmonton. Since 1970 LAMP pastor/pilots had been pursuing a ministry not unlike that envisioned for Ken and the *Christian* except they were traveling by small plane from one remote village to another on their mission circuits. The popular ministry had grown and eventually reached a size warranting division into LAMP USA in Brookfield, Wisconsin, and LAMP CANADA in Edmonton, Alberta. One of the areas LAMP leadership had identified as promising possibility for ministry was expansion into Southeast Alaska. The decision was to check out Wrangell or Sitka as a potential LAMP base. Steve got the assignment. Recalling his visit to Wrangell, Steve writes:

Imagine my surprise on arrival in Wrangell to find Ken and the *Christian* there. Surprised, because my connection to Ken and the *Christian* went back to 1970 when I was a seminary intern at Trinity Lutheran Church in Tacoma, Washington. In that capacity I accompanied our youth group on cruise outings aboard the *Christian* with Ken as skipper. I got to know Ken through those great trips, some very memorable. My guess is our first cruise on the *Christian* was in 1971. Our most memorable trip with Ken was from Anacortes to Victoria. Underway outbound my wife, Jane, made an orange Jell-O salad and put it in the fridge. On entering the Strait of Juan de Fuca we ran head on into a strong west wind that created some impressive waves with spray reaching the crow's nest. The Jell-O coated the inside of the fridge. I suspect the stains were there for years. So here were Ken, and the *Christian*, in Wrangell.

* * *

Can you imagine Ken's surprise when Steve showed up in small-print-on-a-map Wrangell? And then find Steve working for LAMP in a ministry similar to that visualized for Ken and the *Christian*? It was natural for them to talk about how they might work together and, more importantly, how the *Christian*'s proposed ministry might fit into the LAMP mission and how LAMP might be the angel for financial deliverance of the *Christian* to continue in its dedicated calling. I wouldn't be surprised if Ken ended the day with a nip of Scotch and a prayer of thanksgiving.

As a result of their conversations, Steve became a member of the board of directors of Lutheran Island Ministry just in time to participate in the board's first major meeting in late September in Anchorage. Steve says, "I suggested to Les Stahlke, LAMP executive director, that LAMP look into bringing the *Christian* under LAMP's umbrella as funding for the boat and its ministry was very difficult to obtain from the very small base of the Alaska Synod. Les was very enthusiastic about the idea." That meeting also led to activation of plans for the synod to cast its net among congregations in Alaska and the Pacific Northwest seeking contributions to cover operating costs of the Lutheran Island Ministry. The board met again in late October, and then in Wrangell and Sitka in January and April 1989 respectively. Enough funds dribbled in to keep the ministry afloat from month to month—but barely. Ken and Nancy pushed ahead with faith they would accumulate evidence of ministry success to warrant more permanent resolution of the financial issues before the money ran out.

By June of 1989, well-received church services aboard the *Christian* had been held at communities located on the west coast of Prince of Wales Island, like Edna Bay and Craig, with communion, if desired. Other ports of call had included Myers Chuck, Port Protection, Point Baker, Klawock, Tokeen, Hydaburg, and Thorne Bay, establishing welcoming locations for continuing visits. The *Wrangell Sentinel* reported these visits in an article on August 17 titled "Floating Ministry: Lutheran Pastor, Wife Take Services to Communities":

Ken said, "We got a grand reception. People just naturally come aboard and want to talk." Nancy averred, "In Hydaburg, for example, the children from the Haida tribe flocked to the vessel. They were zooming around everywhere. They told us everything about their town." Ken added, "There are really four different cultures in Southeast Alaska. There are people in logging, people in fishing, settlers, and the Native community. All of them look at life differently with varying beliefs and goals for the region's future." Nancy, summing up, said, "It's been a real eye opener and privilege to be out there."

Ken and Nancy were ready to host ten important key supporters of the program on a representative circuit of the ministry in early July. Among them were Bill Ruthford, accompanied by his wife Marcie and daughter Emily. This was Bill's opportunity to see the fruits of his work two years previously saving the *Christian* for service as a vehicle in continuing ministry. Another passenger was the same David L. Miller, senior features editor of *The Lutheran*. He returned to his office in Chicago to write "An Alaskan Odyssey: Pages from the Log of a Missionary Journey" as the cover story for the August 30, 1989, issue. Here are excerpts:

> *The M.V.* Christian *plies the heavy currents northwest of its home port, Wrangell. Today the sea is flat, and the spruce and hemlock clad hills are wreathed in cloud. Only a few bald eagles swoop across the water's face in search of salmon on their journey home to spawn and die. The aroma of supper filters from the galley to the wheelhouse where the Rev. Kenneth N. Olson, skipper of the boat, steers to the evening's destination. Three of his 10 passengers study the map as he points out the route. They are not just along for the scenery that overwhelms the poet's eye. They have come to see the birth of a new ministry.*
>
> *Olson points out with uncharacteristic directness, "This is a boat with a mission. Its mission is displayed on the face of the bridge—the outline of a fish (an ancient Christian symbol) is superimposed with a cross." For more detail, a plaque hanging in the main cabin fills in the blanks with language that bristles with adventure. "Lutheran Island Ministry is a ministry operating the M.V.* Christian *as a vessel for Christian outreach and service. Its purpose will be to carry the gospel to communities and isolated places on the water."*
>
> *Olson speaks more simply: "I see the people, and I want them to know the gospel. We want to be part of their lives." He trails off in sentences that have no end as he often does when he struggles to analyze his reasons for doing a ministry for which he is not being paid. This is not the* Christian's *maiden mission voyage. That occurred in May. But many in these islands will learn of the boat and its mission on this voyage. Will they welcome the boat or see it as an intruder from a world they want little part of? Some have come here to find tranquility in a place where the earth is not entombed in an asphalt grave, a place ruled less by the clock than by the timeless patterns of nature.*
>
> *Olson is far more concerned with the curse of almost every young ministry—money. A few individuals and congregations give what they can to keep it going. The boat will be able to operate 12 months a year in this climate moderated by the sea. But then again it might not. There is no money to pay the mortgage. There is not even enough to buy fuel for the voyage after this one. But there is ministry to be done.*

Labouchere Bay: *The camp on this quiet cove is little more than a bunk house for single men and a strip of mobile homes sitting about 70 feet above sea level. But there is a school relieving parents of responsibility for educating their children. Cindy, in her 30s, and two young boys are waiting on the dock. As the boys explore the boat, she focuses on Bible school for the village's children. "The kids are excited," she says. "I can get 20 together— there are only about 30 in camp. It would also be great to have a schedule so we can plan on when you are coming in and have regular services." As she and Olson discuss Bible school they partially fulfill a concept of the ministry to the collective villages as a parish. There is a desire to operate on a congregational model where the 4,000 people of these villages help plan the worship and education events and carry out the ministry when the boat is not tied up at their dock. This is not yet one big multipoint parish. But there appear to be several "Cindys" poised to make it a reality.*

Note: A month after this trip, Ken and Nancy returned to Labouchere Bay to host twenty-eight children filling the Christian for Vacation Bible School. Teenage girls took turns attending to the needs of two four-year olds while the Olsons and other adult helpers taught classes and supervised other youth activities.

Edna Bay: *As on most of the islands, people in this village built their own homes from lumber cut from the nearby forest. They produce their own electricity, and get water from springs. Unresourceful people don't last long here. But they do want help with their Christian fellowship that meets most Sundays. After conferring with Judy Slattery, who met the boat with a lonely smile, and Sherry Miethe, a leader of the fellowship, worship is set for 11 a.m. tomorrow.*

But worshipers who walk or come by small boat are not late. Twenty-two people come and crowd the Christian's main cabin. Miethe, who this week had to kill a bear that had been creating havoc around her house, cradles her guitar and begins. "I am Sherry," she says, "and this is Aaron (a 16-year-old playing the boat's tiny pump organ), but the name we should remember is Jesus." Miethe leads a half dozen songs before Olson reads the parable of the Good Samaritan and shares a few meandering comments about the story. He invites worshipers to share their thoughts and experiences, which they do for 20 minutes. Olson finishes with a prayer.

As the meal is made ready, children explore the boat, and adults swap stories of their common life—fishing, boats, gardens, even of delivering babies that won't wait for a plane trip to a hospital. It's like church dinners everywhere, including the ever-present element of tragedy.

Craig Yates is new in the bay. He just arrived from Klawock to start a new life. His 19-year-old son drowned there in a boating accident five weeks ago. At worship he thanked people for "taking care of me. If it wasn't for that I wouldn't have gotten through."

* * *

The day after the accident the *Christian* was in Klawock and "had won the town's heart" by serving for a few days as the quarters and base for the search and rescue operation and as the staging point for searchers who came there to rest, compare notes and eat. "Ken Olson worked for my dad thirty years ago," Yates says. "He knows boats, and he knows people. I hope this ministry works out. We need the fellowship, need to help one another. The boat can be important to us."

Leaving Edna Bay is difficult. Today the faith of those cut off from a broader Christian community was stirred up by a blue boat giving them extra reason to come together.

Throughout the summer and into the fall, communications between LAMP and Lutheran Island Ministry (LIM) continued in a slow-dance courtship. The LAMP boards of directors got together for a joint meeting in Fairbanks in early November. Accord was reached to proceed with meetings between LAMP, LIM, and Lutheran Marine Ministry (LMM) to reach agreement on LAMP's purchase of the *Christian* and assumption of responsibility for operation of the vessel including crew compensation. Rev. Stahlke found a donor in Calgary able and willing to fund the existing marine mortgage on the *Christian*. On behalf of the synod, LIM agreed to continue providing pastor/pilot leadership of the ministry. Documentation completing the deal was signed March 9, 1990, at a board meeting of LAMP USA.

Seven rewarding years followed for Ken and Nancy aboard the *Christian*. Nancy writes:

Such amazing memories I hold dear of that time for Ken and me traveling by waterways to live amongst the people of Southeast Alaska. Some, especially my old fishing buddies, referred to the Christian as the "God Boat" as its circuit ministry came to be a participant in the lives of them and their families. Edna Bay, Tolkeen, Craig, Klawock, Port Protection, Wooden Wheel Cove, Point Baker, and the large logging camp at Labouchere Bay, all located on the shores of inlets, bays, and harbors along the multi-hundred-mile west coast of Prince of Wales Island, were all ports of call on most port-to-port trips.

Every summer during July our job description changed. Hoards of youth and children and a few adults came aboard for Vacation Bible Week cruises. It was a pretty loose operation mixing some sit-still sermonizing with fun short adventure cruises on the Christian. It was their opportunity to learn about the boat underway. A favorite stop on many of those trips was at Eagle Island in Sea Otter Sound. It had a white sand tropical island beach just inland from the open ocean with swells breaking from miles out. The beauty was breathtaking. The beachcombing for shells, clams, and crabs was fascinating along with giving the kids a chance to mingle and learn some social skills along the way.

We were there to offer support in many very life-changing situations over the years. We would drop all and travel far to be with communities in times of crisis. This would often lead to a hasty revision of commitments as once we were out on the west coast of Prince of Wales Island, it only made sense to stay over for a Sunday and then make other hastily arranged stops on our eventual way back to our home port in Wrangell.

One time we went to Edna Bay to be with the families and neighbors following a drowning tragedy just before Palm Sunday. This led to us boating over to Craig for Ken to provide Palm Sunday services. Then it was back to Edna Bay for Easter Sunday where about sixty came aboard for services. On the trip back to Edna Bay, having and needing a day off, we anchored in a little bay north of Tonowek Narrows. Ashore, we hiked up to the ruins of Chief Tonowek's village on a grassy hillock overlooking the Narrows. There was evidence of where the Native peoples had their gardens. You could feel the presence of people working there so many years ago, gathering fish and gardening in the summertime. It was all very beautiful!

* * *

Although much the same, each year on the boat was different with diversionary mini-ventures to keep the juices flowing. One was delivering a herd of goats for a LIM congregational project in Edna Bay. Occasional grounding of commercial air service would lead the *Christian* to deliver the Wrangell High School basketball team in time for a game in some city like Ketchikan or Petersburg. Every winter trip of any distance could entail layovers due to adverse weather and sea conditions.

Every summer Ken and Nancy hosted visitors traveling with them for various purposes and durations. Each summer also featured hosting at least one church group for a one-week retreat cruise. During more than one summer the national Lutheran Council of Bishops showed up for a retreat cruise, usually with a different theme, through unfamiliar waters, and visiting new places. Bishop Parsons recalls:

> *One that really stands out for me is the time we conducted a weeklong continuing education retreat on the* Christian *for twenty-five bishops and wives representing synods nationwide. The cruise began and ended in Ketchikan. It was titled "Caring For Creation from the Perspective of the Tongass National Forest." We engaged people from the National Park Service, Alaska Fish and Game, the U.S. Forest Service, the Southeast Alaska branch of the Sierra Club, and, representing local commercial interests, Ketchikan Pulp and Paper whose CEO was a member of First Lutheran Church there. Can you think of a more diverse group? They came aboard on separate scheduled visits to speak to us about the issues. We got Roger Vegdahl, the LAMP pilot flying out of Wrangell, to coordinate with us. He picked up each person, or persons, and delivered them to the boat with his Cessna 185 on floats to wherever we were anchored. We had seven days of sunshine. Ken and Nancy were superb hosts, both skippering the vessel and taking part in conversations.*

Can you imagine the impact this creative week had on those twenty-five bishops and their spouses, gathered from every corner of the nation? Living afloat on the *Christian* in anchorages offering opportunities to go ashore in the heart of the creator's forest? Or the impressions those visitors to the boat took back to their colleagues of their exchanges of views with the bishops?

The *Christian's* Lutheran Island Ministry was always to isolated island communities with one notable exception. Meyers Chuck is on the mainland at the northwest tip of the Cleveland Peninsula, forty miles northwest of Ketchikan and sixty miles southwest of Wrangell. The beautiful island-studded harbor looks out on Clarence Strait, a major waterway for north or southbound Inside Passage traffic from kayaks to cruise ships. A small river draining a nearby inland lake provides an abundant water supply. The place came to be called Meyers "Chuck" because a short walk up from the outer-harbor shore brings you to what appears to be a small lake. But it isn't. It's actually a sort of inner-harbor saltwater basin with a channel connecting it to the outer harbor. You can run small watercraft in and out at high tide. These small bodies of water are called "chucks." They offer total security in any weather.

It was a magnet attracting white settlers, mostly commercial fishermen and miners, who began making permanent homes there in the late 1800s to be serviced by a store, poolroom, and fish saltery. By the early 1990s, when Ken, Nancy, and the *Christian* first started regular visits to Meyers Chuck, the population had shrunk to about twenty residents—a few more in the summer—and evolved into a fascinating mix of families with children, lone wolf characters, retired couples, and creative professional artists. Only a few lived along the original village waterfront. Most had homes located along the shore of the nearby back channel, the back chuck, or on an island in the harbor reached by a short hike or boat ride. Everyone had an outboard-powered skiff for getting around. Commercial fishing was the major source of income for those who needed one. A few others worked part-time building vacation homes for summer visitors to buy or rent. The post office was on an island in the harbor. It was tended by the cheerful Cassie Peavey, a lifelong resident and part-time postmistress, whose husband was a fisherman. Initially led by Cassie, the artist group had a quaint small cabin co-op shop for selling local works and crafts. Members took turns minding the store when visitors showed up or by appointment. Eventually Nancy joined them as a contributing artist exhibiting for sale her native cedar weaving baskets and related art. Ken and Nancy loved the people and the "Chuck," and the people loved them in return.

The itineraries of the *Christian's* visits to the various communities occasionally began, and ended, with pick-ups and drop-offs of passengers, often groups, at cities in the cruising area serviced by commercial airports. Ken and Nancy would passage back home to Wrangell with only the two of them on board. When appropriate, and with adequate lead time, they would take advantage of these trips to invite family to show up and share the passage, including a few extra days for sport fishing and/or stopping at scenic or historic sites. Nancy's daughter Kerri and her fiancé, Dan Pack, were along on one of them in early 1996. They made a layover pastoral visit in Meyers Chuck. The young adventurous couple fell in love with the place.

Ken married Kerri and Dan in Portland in late October. In early November the couple moved to Meyers Chuck to make their home and set up a sea kayaking service. Scheduling the itinerary of the *Christian* for a last-of-the-year cruise of the circuit, Ken included a stop in Meyers Chuck for Thanksgiving with the newlyweds. From there, Ken and Nancy took off for the west side of Prince of Wales Island to make a round of ministerial visits to the communities located along that coast. They returned to Wrangell in mid-December.

Every Christmas brought a welcome letter from the port-to-port pair bringing us up to date on their year. Here are excerpts from their 1996 letter—Nancy first:

Another incredibly busy year! We remodeled our hovel in Wrangell. It now has sixteen feet of two-story living space out over the water with an added living area, bedroom, weaving room, and bathroom—insulated, but unfinished. Daughter Kerri is now married to Dan and they are living near us in the tiny village of Meyers Chuck. They're starting a bed and breakfast sea kayaking adventure business there and loving it. Ken has given me a present of an acre of land in Meyers Chuck. The property includes a shore-bound float house plus Greasy Gus's old falling-down cabin, and a working band saw mill in the woods. I have to get busy cutting lumber to finish our Wrangell house. We took the Christian to Seattle for bottom repairs last spring. We had endless trips on the boat visiting the people in the nooks and coves of SE AK, plus bishops trip and adult/youth training trips. We have a great life! We still have Ken's lonesome cement sailboat. At least two more years on the big boat and then…who knows?

Peace, love and laughter, Nancy

Hi! This is Ken. I learned starting this way from a community building workshop. As things went this year, ditto what Nancy, well said. Which leads me to mention (though you may get this after Christmas), Jesus was born in the barn. Just remember that.

Ken

P.S. from Ken: "Though she creaks, she holds!"

P.S. from Nancy: "If you haven't anything to do, don't do it here."

SKATING TO NIRVANA

Nirvana: A blowing out of the flame of life; the state of perfect blessedness achieved by the extinction of individual existence and by the absorption of the soul into the supreme spirit.

—Webster's Dictionary

Clear-sky cold weather systems blowing in from interior Canada are expected a few times every winter in Southeast Alaska. On arrival they stabilize to promise clear below-freezing conditions, usually prevailing for one to three weeks. There is often adequate time to ice over already cold freshwater ponds and lakes. Ice over four inches thick is deemed safe for skating.

Captain Reverend Ken Olson liked to celebrate the birth of Jesus sharing Christmas and traditional holiday festivities aboard the *Christian* at one of the communities participating in the ministry. Meyers Chuck was the destination in 1996. Let's let Nancy recall the story leading up to the climax:

About that amazing Christmas of '96 in Meyers Chuck, well, that was the year. It was so cold we had heard even the back chuck at Meyers Chuck, a mix of fresh and salt water, was so frozen you could walk on it. So, before leaving, Ken told me to stick in those special skates he had received years before as a gift from son Michael. He had told me before, "Someday there will be freezing weather with no snow and I will be able to use those skates." Contributing to the anticipation was knowledge of a small lake a short hike from the "back chuck" promising winter sport. We knew some residents also liked skating and would be eager to share the festive enjoyment.

We docked in Meyers Chuck in the afternoon of the twenty-third. Ken finished decorating the Christian *with a lighted Christmas tree attached to the mast, lighting strung around on the railings, and lots of green added in the cabin. The next morning, Dan and Kerri, Ken and I walked way up the hill behind Hunleys and cut down the most beautiful little pine tree. We dragged it down and over to Kerri and Dan's house. In the afternoon, Ken and I visited the people in the Chuck to wish them a happy holiday. Then we went over to Dan and Kerri's for a traditional Christmas Eve decorating the tree and singing carols. Ken read the Christmas gospel story. Also, a story poem passed down in the family about a little boy who played with his toy soldiers until an angel came one night and took the boy away, leaving the tin soldiers on the shelf lonesome and wanting the little boy back. Our Meyers Chuck friend Benny was with us, and it all seemed perfect.*

After breakfast Christmas morning it was time to go skating. We went up to a small lake behind Bob Hunley's house. There were nine or ten of us including the Hunleys, Herb and Shirley Lee, our family, and Ken Buffa.

Buffa was a quiet, friendly, footloose and penniless bachelor who had shown up in Meyers Chuck many summers before, decided he liked the place, and went no further looking for a place to live. He found a small parcel of ground back in the forest behind the village where he built a shack from cast-off lumber, scrap materials, and equipment. We befriended him, welcoming his sharing in the ministry of the Christian.

It was a beautiful sunny day. The ice was so thick. We had such fun. We started out skating around the little lake. We were all pretty bad at skating except for Ken and Ken, who were both surprisingly graceful. We called them Brian Boitano (Ken Buffa) and Hans Brinker (Ken Olson). The Kens discussed their love of skating and how they skated in their younger days. They talked about how nice it would be to skate on the big lake up the hill. They tried to get some other people to go, but no one was interested. Somebody had a hockey puck so some of the more active skaters scrounged and found a few shaped tree branches to serve as sticks. A rip-roaring hockey game followed, banging and chasing the puck all over the pond.

Then we all gathered back on the Christian. *Ken conducted a service of readings and music. This was followed by an amazing traditional dinner of prime rib, Yorkshire pudding, and Jackie's famous cheesecake. Ken Buffa even joined us and we all seemed so happy.*

Before Buffa left the boat, the two Kens decided to take advantage of the continuing freeze and fair weather, head up to the frozen lake the next afternoon, and skate to the upper end of it. Thank heaven Dan did not go on that skate—a newlywed and all.

* * *

The next day dawned clear and cold. After a late breakfast the two friends made fast work of the one-mile boot trail hike over frozen muskeg to the shore of the lake. On arrival they walked out on the lake to check the ice and be assured it was more than thick enough for safe skating.

Skaters at Meyers Chuck pond on Christmas Day 1996
Ken and Nancy are on the far right. Ken Buffa is sitting against the tree in the center.
Photo collection of Nancy Olson

I know they did this because Ken and I had participated in similar checks all the way back to our early teens in Minneapolis when we lived a block from a lake that froze in the winter for skating and ice boating. We made the same checks before skating on small lakes near Ketchikan during our high school years. Additionally, we participated one evening as part of a chain of four or five high school student skaters, lying prone on the ice stretched out from shore, in the rescue of a fellow skater who had been the first to blithely skate out into the darkness on Upper Ward Lake near Ketchikan and fell through the unexpected thin ice. Reinforcing my certainty of Ken's precautionary check is that the thickness at that lower end of the lake when measured the following day was six inches—two extra inches of ice over the minimum for skater safety.

After their check, they put on their skates, cached their hiking boots at the foot of a tree, and took off. Breathing the crisp mountain air, gliding along on a cradle of virgin crystal black ice, totally free, in a bubble of solitude—it must have been a heavenly experience. I remember from our youth the elation I felt skating with Ken and friends in similar surroundings during Ketchikan winters.

Ken skating on Meyers Chuck pond on Christmas Day 1996
Ken played hockey on his high school team.
Photo by Nancy Olson

What might Ken, the poet, have been thinking as he contemplated the passing scene? Maybe he recalled this verse he had written in an earlier life:

Passage

These morning breezes!—Blessing drowsy senses,
Shaggy unkempt firs and cedars waving
Incensed wakening branches while fiery rim
Of sun splays fireworks blinding tints on heights
To reach before I die. A bell rings!—How many times?
Could I count them if I tried? Should I live
To be a million, shall I know the hues
And faces on my white woven cloth shall leave

Their traces? Shall I lay again at rest. Sleeping wonders
New performing, dreaming, watching faraway places,
Stars and planets with their infinite spaces—just so
And this way? And when I from them awake, shall I
Draw again from dancing colors dawning splendor
This poet's pilgrimage of passing nature?

—Ken Olson, 1976

* * *

The lake is about three miles long and shaped like a pair of eyeglasses. The upper and lower elongated ovals are connected by a natural channel that probably shallows and narrows to about one hundred yards in width. The channel then deepens again going into the upper oval creating a separation of the waters between the lower and upper lake. Apparently neither of the two Kens was aware of this circumstance nor the possibility that there might be much deeper water with warm springs at the bottom for warmer water feeding the upper lake. They casually skated the one and one-quarter miles to the narrows and then onto the longer upper lake. A half-mile in, skating abreast thirty to fifty feet apart, some distance out from and favoring the eastern shore, the unthinkable happened. The ice broke under both of them.

December days are short in Alaska. Bob Hunley, one of the Kens's best friends, a permanent year-round resident with his family in Meyers Chuck, became concerned as dusk approached and the Kens had not returned. He had thought of accompanying the Kens on their skate of the lake, so he was interested in the story they would tell on their return. Meanwhile, since they were only supposed to be gone a few hours, Dan and Kerri went over to the *Christian* to share their concern with Nancy. Thus, Bob found Nancy, Dan, and Kerri on the boat when he arrived to voice his fears, and discuss what might have happened. They placed a call to the Alaska State Troopers to report that Ken Olson and Ken Buffa were overdue returning from their skating trip.

Bob was determined to go up to the lake to find out what might have happened. Dan wanted to go along and he did. They took along a pike pole, cell phone, flashlights, VHF radio, rope, first aid kit, and other rescue equipment. On arrival at the lake, they put the canoe, kept up there year around for summer boating, on the ice. After loading their gear, Bob and Dan, each with one foot in the canoe and the other on the ice pushing, one in the bow and the other in the stern, proceeded to move up lake with the canoe for flotation, if needed, and following by flashlight the skate markings that had left a trail on the ice.

Bob, fearing thinning ice, had checked the thickness when they started out and rechecked a few times along the way. Dan remembers:

We followed the tracks as they twisted and twirled doing figure eights and loops. The nearly full moon shone off the ice. It was a bit eerie imagining these guys skating around just hours before we got there. Bob would call down to Nancy occasionally to tell her our progress. At this point, I was convinced we would run into them sitting on the ice or the shoreline. I guess I must have realized the possibility of finding holes, but it seemed pretty farfetched to me. I think Bob knew better. As we got farther along the ice got thinner and thinner. Bob kept measuring it. We started to get a little concerned for our safety, but figured we would be all right with the canoe. Past the narrows Bob shone the light on what looked like a hole in the ice. I still couldn't believe it, but as we got closer, it was definitely a hole. Then we saw another hole. We decided we shouldn't get too close since the ice was already broken up. One distinct memory I have is Bob calling Nancy on the radio. He said very matter-of-factly, "He's gone, Nancy." Silence on the other end. I wanted to tell him we didn't know for sure, but I figured Bob knew what he was talking about.

Bob says:

We eased the canoe up closer to the holes. They were about thirty feet apart. I estimated the hole left by Ken Olson to be about fifteen feet in diameter, his gloves left on the ice facing the beach and marking his battle. Ken Buffa left a small hole indicating he evidently went down quickly. We found no sign of life indicating one of the Kens might have gotten out and made it to shore. After calling Nancy, I also called the State Patrol to relate our findings. There was nothing more we could do except return to Meyers Chuck.

The larger hole my brother left showed signs of a valiant struggle, of him breaking ice and trying to get out on to firmer ground before succumbing to hypothermia and drowning. How did my brother die? I don't know. I visualize he fought to live until he died moving on, and through, to nirvana, to be with God, without fear or regret.

Nancy called at about three o'clock in the morning to tell me what had happened. Her self-control under the circumstances was remarkable. She asked if I would break the news for her to Ken's children and my brothers. Betty suggested waiting until morning. We lay wide-awake talking to cope with our sorrow. About six o'clock we made the short drive over to Ken's daughter Joanne's home to tell their family what had happened. The four of us, Joanne and her husband Tom, and Betty and I, clung to each other sharing our grief.

Fortunately, Nancy was surrounded by her daughter Kerri, son-in-law Dan, and the close-knit community who already knew her like family. One was Benny. Nancy says, "As soon as he heard on the radio that Ken had passed through the ice, Benny got in his boat to make the six-mile run to the "Chuck" to be by my side the whole time and tell me what a good friend Ken had been to him."

Nancy had many decisions to make and she promptly made them all. What to do with Ken's remains? Cremation. Which organizations to alert as soon as possible? Island of Faith Congregation in Wrangell, Alaska Synod of the Lutheran Church, and the Lutheran Association of Missionary Pilots. Finally, she made arrangements for her and the *Christian* to return home to Wrangell. The way she did all this in the midst of heartbreak remains indelible in my memory.

The *Ketchikan Daily News* reported the tragedy in its December 28 edition:

Men drown on skating trip near Meyers Chuck

KETCHIKAN (AP)—Two men died in Meyers Chuck on Thursday when they fell through the ice on an unnamed lake while skating. Alaska State Trooper Lt. Warren Tanner said Kenneth Olson, 65, and Garret "Ken" Buffa, 56, apparently died Thursday afternoon. Olson lives in Wrangell and Buffa is a Meyers Chuck resident. Olson and his wife, Nancy, were celebrating Christmas there with family members, according to Ketchikan resident, Kate Berntson, a family friend.

Divers from the Ketchikan Rescue Squad arrived Friday morning, found a second hole, and retrieved the bodies, Tanner said.

Olson is a pastor with the Evangelical Lutheran Church. He is also skipper of the Christian, a boat used in Southeast Alaska for church work.

Alcohol is not suspected in the drowning, nor is foul play, said Tanner.

"These people apparently started skating on thick ice and then skated over to thin ice," Tanner said.

* * *

Over the years I have listened to one or two people second-guess the Kens' prudence skating on that lake. Bob Hunley went back up to the lake the morning after to witness the rescue squad divers's recovery of the bodies. He says, "There were a half dozen guys standing around on the edge of the hole. The ice was six inches thick over shallow water between the hole and the shore, but abruptly thinned to three inches where the Kens had broken through." I think the Kens were free skating with their attention drawn to their surroundings.

I can visualize the time it took to go from safe to dangerous as a matter of a few seconds. What happened was just bad luck. If I had been there, I would have gone down with them.

Bob Hunley's theory is the cause of the thinning ice was warm springs at the bottom of the upper lake. These created a thermocline in which the warm spring water, constantly rising, slowed the freezing rate at the surface, resulting in thin ice. Nobody knew about the existence of the springs. The Kens were probably the first people ever to venture on that lake in winter.

Reverend Stan Berntson, the pastor of First Lutheran Church in Ketchikan and a close friend of Ken and Nancy, had been among the first to hear of the tragedy. He had acted quickly to recruit Leonard Leach, a church member with a skipper's license, to take him on his boat, the F/V *Tawego,* to Meyers Chuck that same day. On arrival, after tying up the *Tawego,* Stan and Leonard moved to the *Christian.* Nancy, Kerri, and Dan were waiting for them. Soon, with Leonard as captain, and Stan, Nancy, Kerri, and Dan as crew, they took off on the *Christian* for Wrangell. Nancy writes:

It was windy, raising a sea, and still so very cold. By the time we pulled into the dock in Wrangell, the front of the *Christian* was all iced up. It looked like a scene from "Jaws." There were so many people there to meet us. I remember Deena, a girl who lived on a boat across the dock from the *Christian,* who hugged me when we landed, and said, "Ken baptized me."

News of the disaster quickly went out to the multitude of family, friends, colleagues, and church members Ken had served over thirty-five years of ministry. Lutheran pastors who had been among his closest friends rallied around Nancy and the family to share their sorrow and help with arrangements for memorial services.

The first service was an outpouring of love on New Year's Eve afternoon in Wrangell. It brought together the close-knit communities where the people had come to know Ken, and he had come to know them, over the past eight years. Members of Island of Faith and other churches and civic organizations, boat people in maritime pursuits, and ordinary people from all walks of life were there. The service was held at the Presbyterian church to hopefully be sure of room for all. The Order of Service cover pictured Ken with the *Christian* in the background and the words "loving husband and father, skipper, pastor, and friend—a good man." Al Ryll who had come to Sitka in 1987 to help Ken sail the *Advena* to Wrangell read the Gospel. Al also read a poem by Soren Kierkegaard, chosen from the book Nancy reports Ken had left open on the table in the captain's stateroom on the *Christian* before he left that fateful morning to skate the lake with Buffa. Sarah Hunley, from Meyers Chuck, proffered a memorial of Ken Buffa. Dan Pack, Nancy's son-in-law, read "The Ordinary Man" by Robert Service. This was one of Ken's favorite poems. Reverend Fritz Youra, the host pastor, offered the homily. The reception was hosted by Island of Faith and held at Father Jerry Hall.

A second service was held on January 3 at Central Lutheran Church in Anchorage. Carrying forward commonly held themes from the service in Wrangell was "A Tribute To Ken" contributed by Jim Drury, pastor at Sitka Lutheran Church. Here are excerpts:

Many of you knew Ken as pastor/pilot of the *Christian,* the LAMP boat plying the Prince of Wales Island waters bringing ministry and love to people in isolated communities. This was a team ministry, shared by Ken and Nancy, lovingly called "the first mate." Together, they lived the Good News of Christ's love wherever they went. To Ken, no person was marginal, all part of God's creation and worthy of respect and care. To people in need of respect and care, he gave freely.

Ken possessed a rare combination of openness and ease that made adults trust him instinctively and children love him immediately. Husband, friend, father, brother-in-Christ, mentor, pastor—Ken fit each of those roles uniquely and filled each with remarkable purpose: witnessing to Christ's love.

That we have lost this great soul is God's gain and our grief. Nancy, we love you. Ken, rest in peace.

* * *

Meanwhile, wheels were turning to organize a memorial service in the Puget Sound region where Ken had lived most of his life. Joanne was busy calling friends and colleagues of her father to share the news. An early contact was retired Bishop Lowell Knutson who had known Ken for decades as a friend and pastor. His children had made summer Bible camp cruises on the *Christian* with Ken. Lowell had been one of the passenger/crew on a weeklong national Council of Bishops' Retreat on the *Christian* in Alaska in the early '90s. Lowell soon showed up at Joanne's home for the finalizing of plans for the service. Lowell immediately volunteered, saying, "This is a service I want to do." A discussion ensued of where to hold it. Joanne had been thinking of Ken's former church, Our Saviour's in Burien. Lowell said, "Too small. How would it be if I could arrange to have it at Our Saviour's in Everett?" We were all familiar with the beauty and size of this sanctuary. We quickly agreed, and Lowell immediately confirmed availability for the following Monday, January 6, at one o'clock in the afternoon. An offer by the host congregation to sponsor the reception following the service was thankfully accepted. We discussed favored readings, hymns, themes, and other suggestions with Lowell. One concern related to the number of clergy who would want to be heard and keeping the length of the service within bounds. This was important because of anxiety for the large number of elderly seniors expected to attend—some traveling from some distance away. Lowell left to ask the synod office to notice the member churches of the service, line up the participants, and draw up the bulletin for printing.

The next steps for us involved getting obituary notices with confirmation of the memorial service to the newspapers. These papers followed up with separate stories. The January 1, 1997, *Seattle Times* Regional News featured a lengthy story by staff reporter Carol Beers, headlined "Fisherman and Pastor Kenneth Olson Found Happiness in Adventure." The account covered his entire unique life and work including numerous quotes from people who knew him.

The memorial service to celebrate the life of my brother remains indelibly imprinted in my mind. Arriving at the church, I was amazed to have to look for a parking place with two buses full of people at the door. The service was a summing up and moving reinforcement of the themes from the previous services. Participants had flown in from Alaska, Wisconsin, and North Carolina.

Bishop Donald Parsons built his homily around Ken as an extraordinary "ordinary man." He reflected on how the arrival of the *Christian* had brought a sense of safety and security to the outposts of Southeast Alaska. Dan Pack's remarks concerned Ken's friendship with Ken Buffa and how their relationship stood out as an ultimate example of Ken's ability to relate to everyone, regardless of age, religion, or status in society. Dr. Don Johnson, director of the Lutheran Association of Missionary Pilots, told us how Ken's wisdom had inspired his life and the LAMP ministry to remote villages across Northern Canada and Alaska. One of the Nichols brothers spoke of the influence Ken had on his life while growing up on Whidbey Island. A young man told us how Ken had helped him grow up. Numerous others rose to recall happy occasions and remind us of Ken's quirky sense of humor.

Our brother Jerry movingly represented our family. Bishop Knutson ended the service with a reading from Micah 6:8, "What does the Lord require of you, but to do justice, to love kindness and to walk humbly with your God!" You could sense the feeling running like a river. All four hundred or more of us knew Ken had lived that life.

The bulletin for the memorial service included a simple poem written by a sleepless hurting poet, after midnight, two days after the crushing calamity:

Ken Was the *Christian*

M/V Christian *is a mission boat,*
To seaside hamlets, all remote,
Word carrier for the heavenly host,
To island shores, the Alaska coast.
Missionary was Captain Ken,
He decided where and when,
The Christian's many ports of call,
To bring good news to one and all.
Mostly ministry—joy and hope,
To parents and children—ways to cope,
With peaks and deeps, to gain foresight,
To stay the road to heaven's light.
Though the thought may seem absurd,
Ken was the cargo of the living word,
Bringing comfort to those in sorrow,
Jesus' promise of eternal tomorrow.
Mission—a privilege of serving,
Living a dream—at times unnerving,
Touching lives of unique congregation,
Gave to his life a constant elation.
Ken was the Christian,
He it was who made its mission,
Captain of the savior ship,
Shoved off to make another trip.
Leaving gloves—in farewell nod,
He has gone—to be with God.
This our loss we must bear,
Seeking solace in Our Lord's Prayer.

December 28, 1996

David R. Olson

THE CONVERGENT LIFE AND

THEOLOGY OF KEN OLSON

Fame is Fleeting—Vanity is Delusional

Easy to Say—Hard to Believe

During the winter of 1988, as mentioned previously, Ken found time to set forth his provocative insights on Christian faith in *Salmon Are Christian*, a short booklet he completed and distributed to friends and relatives. Humbled and perplexed by the bearing of his thinking, I never responded in a way that did justice to the work. Attempting to tell his story now, I've felt the need to include some exposure to his novel theology but sensed that capturing the essence of it remained beyond me. I knew him in a relationship with no secrets, but didn't *really* know him. Recognizing this reality, I sought elsewhere for insight. And then, rummaging through some saved correspondence I thought I'd already explored—there it was. Somehow Nancy, without realizing it, had passed to me an old letter she had forgotten or misplaced. On discovery, I read the letter and felt blown away. Since the letter was unsigned, I contacted her to identify the writer.

The only person Nancy thought could be the letter's author was Lee Griffin, a LAMP pastors' counselor with an interest in theology, who often attended LAMP meetings on the *Christian*. He was the head psychiatrist at Medical Lake Hospital in Spokane, Washington. She remembered, "He and Ken always had very interesting talks each time we were together." She sent me his phone number.

Upon receiving my voicemail, Cynthia Griffin called back. "Wonderful to hear about this," she said. "Lee has some memory problems, but I'll ask him. Could you e-mail me a copy?" I did.

Cynthia called again. She said, "It's a beautiful letter. I'd be pleased if Lee wrote it, but it doesn't look like his work and I did all of his typing. He can't recall anything like that. Let me put him on the phone. Maybe you'll make a connection." Lee and I enjoyed a good conversation, but he could recall nothing linking him to the letter.

I reread the letter trying to think of anyone who I knew or had heard of who might be the writer. The only name that crossed my mind was my brother Tim, but the letter was personal to Nancy. If Tim, she would have mentioned the possibility. I e-mailed Nancy—the writer was not Dr. Griffin.

She replied, "David, maybe I'm losing my mind, but the only one it sounds remotely like what I remember is brother Tim."

I e-mailed Tim with "Marvelous Mystery Letter" in the subject line: "Hi, Tim. Did you write this amazing letter? If you did, I'll be on my way to cloud nine!"

"Hi, Nancy and Dave. Yep, that letter was from me. For some reason I thought about it at some point last year, but it had disappeared. Not in the computer and I only had a couple of pages stuck in a folder. I'm curious as to how it surfaced."

Dated March 28, 1997, three months after Ken died, this is what the letter said:

Dear Nancy,

I actually began this last January and I'm still not satisfied with it. Still, if I sit too long, I'll never get on with it.

To Think of the Life of a Man

In a time that breaks
In cutting pieces all around,
When men, voiceless
Against thing-ridden men,
Set themselves on fire, it seems
Too difficult and rare
To think of the life of a man
Grown whole in the world,
At peace and in place.
But having thought of it
I am beyond the time

I might have sold my hands
or sold my voice and mind
to the arguments of power
that go blind against
what they would destroy.

—Wendell Berry

* * *

It does seem "difficult and rare" to think of a man "grown whole in the world, at peace and in place." I'd like to think that Ken was such a man. Only Ken could know that, and I do not doubt that knowing that, he could not express it except in metaphor. To do other than that would be to catch himself in a Kierkegaardian double-mindedness and become precisely that which he was not: a thing-ridden man—a man of some importance. I suspect that during his life, Ken struggled with a dilemma: How is it possible to lay claim to what is "important" to living in the world while remaining unimportant in the world. We live in a time where "who a person is" often replaces "what a person does." He found his solution in his living and in his poetry.

The core of Ken's thought—and this is explicit in sermons, poetry, and essays—is that an individual is *nothing*. When Ken considers nature's unfolding through the evolutionary process, what does he find a person to be? "That Nature cares is one of our 'sweetest illusions.' After all Nature shows little concern for individuals or even species so long as others replace them and evolve to ensure an ongoing abundance of happens." It's a mere disposable blip in the inexorable trudging of time. What does Ken find when he considers a person from a Christian perspective? "As long as you feel yourself 'better,' then you cannot love your neighbor as yourself.

Jesus said, "Do not be given any name of distinction such as teacher, father, or master. The first shall be last and the last first."

I know what I would say: "Our Lord Jesus Christ was nothing, oh, remember this Christendom."

Ken's compassion, his courage, and his sense of humor are bedded deep in the two poles of *nothingness*, physical and religious.

It is one thing to suggest as was done at Ken's memorial service that Ken had friends that were "marginal." Not even "respectable." But it is quite another to suggest that Ken was one of them, a marginal, not even a respectable man. I think that most of us find this unacceptable, and want to find a way around it; in short, to make Ken respectable, even *better*, make him a hero. Like the

English in *Lord Jim*, we want Ken to be "one of us." We know how Jim didn't measure up and why the imperialistic British could not tolerate this. A review of Ken's life and thought reveals that not only didn't he measure up to the standards of our "thing-ridden culture," in an ironic way (and at considerable difficulty for him) his life was an insult to it! He neither aspired to own "things" nor did he aspire to position and recognition. Ironically, because of what he did, the way he did it, the way it turned out, however, we are not inclined to consider him a failure, but rather a success. That makes us who hang onto our "things" and our "positions" a bit uncomfortable.

I heard the statement, "People don't know who Ken was." What is to be done with that? What even is meant by it? Several possibilities exist here. One has to do with familiarity with what he has been up to for the past several years. For instance, distant relatives and friends will hear of his death, but know little or nothing about what he was doing with his life, maybe not even know where he was doing it and with whom. To tell that he married you, was a grandfather, navigated the waters of Southeast Alaska, that he wrote poetry, that he treated everyone as the Bishop said, "as one of God's beloved people" is one thing; but to stop there is difficult. For there is another sense of *know* and that has to do with *who* and *what* he was, his identity. That he was a poet? A philosopher? A theologian? A friend to the marginal? A deep thinker? A skipper? A pastor? Who would question it? It is even more difficult to stop there!

Yes, there is something else in this becoming known; it is to apply the quality of being BETTER to Ken. It is of greater value to be *known* than *unknown*. In that way, to make him more *known* than he was is to change who he was. So what do those of us who admired Ken do with him in order to make him "one of us"? We are tempted to provide him with a mantle, precisely the kind that he never wore and would have rejected had it been offered to him. Ken becomes not only the "ordinary man;" Ken becomes the "Extra-ordinary Man" who managed to pass himself off as the *ordinary man*. He becomes not merely a marginal man working with people in Southeastern Alaska island communities; he becomes that "Man of God" that can reach the marginal people in the place where they live. Who can tell? With the right editor, the right biographer, he might become a person of influence, of some notable importance. The quality word GOOD rests easily above Ken Olson and Ken Buffa on the front of the memorial service bulletin, but reverse the placement of the two names, wouldn't most of us still feel that Ken Olson belongs in the upper space? Knowing what I know, would I really think it was right if Ken Buffa had the higher place? And in that very instant, that very passing thought, that blip of a synapses in my brain, I have voided the center of Ken's thought and the way he struggled to live his life. What he was is lost. What is gained is that he becomes "one of us," recognized, someone, one of the *better* people, his name just a little higher on the marquee of who is and who isn't in this life.

To quote Ken at length:

"My own inward (hence spiritual) reason for keeping in mind what, though strangely obvious, I have found with some difficulty is that it affords an easy and quick way to recognize in myself what I have come to think about as a pervasive and personal human fault. It is like an ironic litmus test. When I feel better I know I am doing something wrong. Not only are the cumulative effects of this evil apparent as in sexism, ethnicism, racism, speciesism, and the like, but also in the slightest indication that I for any reason think of myself as better. As a clergyman how I feel when I do the Sunday service is a fair example. It could be the way I hold my face when I speak or my tone of voice. I am better than parishioners. When challenged I am aroused. I may not say everyone is like this, neither is it possible to judge another person. Not even ought I make a guess which might only reflect on myself. What I can say—when I think about it—is that this is what characterizes the world, some are like this, I am like that. Jesus asks me to renounce this world. He said evil comes out of the heart. I know that it is within me."

I find that in his writing, Ken made no claim to righteousness because he didn't feel better than anyone. On the contrary, while Ken felt kinship to the nobodies of this world, I think he struggled with his feeling of being better than the thing-ridden people, the people of position, the people of privilege, the "rich-fuckers." He wrote, "To acknowledge what is understood in this fashion as in myself is to at first painfully laugh, than to feel shameful and childish. How I want to be—ontically. emotively, and ironically—better!" Ken turns the way we would measure success upside down; he takes Jesus at his word. Ken isn't saying, "Oh, we shouldn't look down on the marginal, those barely surviving on the edges." He is no bleeding-heart liberal finding a way to make it possible for those living unrespectable lives to be rehabilitated and to live like us. He is saying that the traditional way we measure success is a delusion. We are all in the same boat on the same ocean with the same prospects. No wonder he kept smiling and saying, "Do you get it?" Who would guess? We are too caught up in what we have, too complacent justifying what we have, and too fearful that we might lose it. To acknowledge Ken's life without grasping what Ken meant by all his deliberations on what it is to be *better* demands that Ken be transformed into something that he struggled not to be.

Would it be best to leave Ken in death where he chose to be in life, hard at work in the backwaters? I not only think so; it is the only possibility. Something else can be done with our memories of Ken, but not with Ken. The poem Dan [Pack] read recognizes it; the poem Sam read recognizes it. All kinds of people have internalized the way Ken lived. There are, however, some suggestions that I would like to make about Ken's writing.

I am concerned that what he wrote and did will get lost. "Poetry is a series of explanations of life, fading off into horizons too swift for explanations." Carl Sandburg said that and Ken's poetry fits that definition very well. Ken's poetry juxtaposes the radically natural and the radically transcendent. The human being exists at the nexus of the two. Ken's language uses earth/sea/sky imagery extensively and leads the reader to transcendent meanings. Because I have earlier editions of a few of his poems, I know that he worked on them and changed them, attempting to make the words fit closer to both the concrete facts of the experience that stimulated the poem and to lead toward the meaning inherent in the facts.

On the cover of the collection of poems that David O. [Olson] sent out, Ken writes "Just a few poems for my friends from the summer I knew I was a poet." On the cover page of the writings from you, he wrote, "Though not gifted at writing..." Ken was more a poet than an essay writer. His prose often uses esoteric language, is loosely organized, and is often elliptical. His themes, however, are consistent and insistent. One of his major themes is what he calls the "true" tenth commandment, "Thou shalt not be better." Another is the sorrow of the rich young ruler who turns away from Jesus and another is participation, the active connection between the individual and the natural world; God becoming human. Someone else may find other themes. Most important writers have a few themes that they chew on and on and on. Well, Ken did that and I hope they don't get lost.

I would hope that something like you suggested on the phone about gathering material together could be done, including reminisces and anecdotes from this life. I would hope that his poems could be gathered together with later revisions separated from earlier drafts. His prose could be edited; or possibly, someone who has knowledge of Ken's sources, and also participated in intimate conversations with Ken, could take on the project of turning Ken's thoughts into a coherent whole. Ken often referred to Ernest Becker's *The Denial of Death*, which draws extensively from the writings of S. Kierkegaard and Otto Rank. Becker makes a point about Rank that he isn't read or known that much because his writings weren't as readable or complete as some of the other great psychoanalysts like Jung or Adler. Ken could use an Ernest Becker. It can be done and I think it would be a worthwhile project.

After Ken's service, I heard more than once the forever-asked question, "Why Ken?" I'm not sure when Ken wrote this poem or whether he'd worked further on it:

Explanation

Christianity's in faith simply the things are:
radically physical and radically transcendent.
They're not opposed.
That's spirit.
To die is most physical.
We all will.
But to die in the prime of life?
That's unacceptable.
We share this passage.
It has to be.
We want what's invisible.
When everything's taken, why there's nothing left!
It's a test.
We don't really know what comes next.
For humans a certain way is meant.
I see Christianity so purely existing judgment fails.
God is wholly here all forms always in the other.
Transcendent."

Maybe Ken's answer is in these lines. "We don't really know what comes next" and for Ken "a certain way is meant." For me, Ken has "grown whole in the world, at peace and in place."

In Ken's words:

"In dark-truth to suffer transcendence, to acknowledge a cross, feel drawn to Jesus, be changed inwardly—that is what it means to be a salmon … a Christian. With love."

Chapter 20

RIVER LIFE RETROSPECTIVE

THE ROAD TO OUR RIVER

Moving on for our family after losing Jef in 1982 wasn't easy, but we knew we had to and she would have wanted us to. An opportunity surfaced for me to quit my job at Regan Holding Corporation and organize a specialized wholesale life and annuity insurance brokerage in Northern California. It would be a participant in the same nationwide network I'd helped build over the past few years. Backed by Betty, and with the support of John and Lynda Regan because I'd be organizing a company of brokers to sell their plans and policies, we incorporated as Advanced Insurance Marketing, Inc.

We had $10,000 in savings to spend finding out if I could make it. I opened for business in our garage remodeled as office space. Betty paid the bills from her dental hygiene income during the ensuing months. The savings were soon spent on advertising AIM, the acronym bestowed on our business, and travel conducting workshops for insurance brokers convincing them to sell our plans. Enough signed up to start hiring office help. With the popularity of the products slowly taking off, my time became hectically divided between office responsibilities and travel commitments.

Two years into this run, one late afternoon still in my garage office, Betty burst in excited about something.

"I quit cleaning teeth for Tony today," she announced with no forewarning.

Since she got along great with her boss, Dr. Anthony Smith, DDS, I was befuddled.

"You what? What are you going to do?"

"I'm coming home to manage the office," she said.

Within weeks we moved to a small suite in a beautiful contemporary office park, and it was the best decision we could have made. Betty was a natural manager and "numbers cruncher" allowing me to concentrate on working with brokers marketing products. By 1989, AIM, Inc. was national with hundreds of affiliated brokers in city centers as far apart as Miami and Seattle. We qualified as invitees to numerous business conferences overseas as distant as Wellington, New Zealand, and Santiago, Chile. In 1992, our best year, over $60 million in premium flowed through our office to be processed by a staff of six employees under Betty's supervision. We were major minority stockholders in Regan Holding Corporation and I was serving on their board of directors.

This prosperity freed me to pursue other personal interests. One was Pilgrim Park Apartments, an eighty-three-unit Title 8 financed complex for low-income families developed by First Congregational Church of San Rafael. Soon after joining the congregation I had joined the Social Concerns Committee. Then someone approached me about becoming a member of the Pilgrim Park board of directors. Within a year or two I began service as treasurer. Seeing the need, I conceived, organized, funded, and oversaw a successful summer youth program for twenty-plus kids living in the development.

I was also delighted to crew for Ken on the *Advena* from Ketchikan to Sitka in 1987, as well as sail the *Advena* in Southeast Alaska waters during the summers of 1989 and 1990 in exchange for buying and installing a few vessel upgrades plus annual maintenance. Longtime sailing partner Gene Dyer joined me in the installations and preparations of the vessel for sea. With Betty and assorted friends, including Gene, sharing the adventure as crew for separate segments of the voyage, I cruised almost two thousand miles over three months at sea. *Aboard the Advena: Alaska Summer 1989* storied a part of that cruise and was coauthored by me and friend Louisa Arndt who crewed for two memorable weeks.

Life for Betty and me at work and play continued to be a joy until 1993, when we were caught up in a turbulent falling out between Regan Holding Corporation and one of its primary insurers. Then, in early 1994, at home in Lucas Valley, California, almost off the wall, Betty said, "Dave, how about selling our business and retiring to Washington?"

With our children, relatives, and roots up there, and feeling reasonably secure financially, I instantly answered, "Let's do it!"

In late June we combined my 65th birthday with a big "farewell to friends" bash. By late July we were settled in Redmond, Washington, looking for a house.

* * *

FINDING HEAVEN AT HOME

A year later we moved twenty miles east to North Bend. The area was more rural and had been recommended to us by relatives, Joanne and Tom Chase, who already lived there. We began volunteering at the local Helping Hands Food Bank in 1996, shortly before Ken's death. Among the volunteers was Bob Tabor. We became friends. Working together at the Food Bank ended once at the Tabor's home where Bob gave me a tour of the property located on the west bank of the south fork of the beautiful Snoqualmie River. In 1998, Bob and his wife decided to move to California. I invited Betty over to meet the Tabors and see the house. Six months later we moved in.

With headwaters at the summit of Snoqualmie Pass in the Cascade Mountains, the wild South Fork of the Snoqualmie River drops 2,500 feet in twenty miles of rapids, including two beautiful waterfalls, to flow past our home. The snow I ski on in January melts to stream past our home in July. The back door is sixty feet from the riverbank with ready access for birding, fly-fishing, meditating, and whitewater kayaking. Since moving in, we have been reveling in those pastimes as participants and observers. We feel surrounded by the grandeur of God's creation.

Since 2006, we have had a bench for contemplation, conversation, and reading at the top of the bank. In front of it is a kiosk with a see-through top. Beneath are celebratory reverential poems of nature, especially the river and mountains, for enjoyment from the bench. The bench and kiosk are made of ancient old-growth cedar provided by the Snoqualmie Tribe. Both were custom-built from plans by master carpenter and designer Terry Diraison, who had been on that fateful Bear Creek Spire trip. The site is a memorial celebrating the lives of Jenifer, Ken, and all who have died in the outdoors they loved. In front of our home is a plaque that reads, "Welcome to Paradise." On permanent display in the kiosk is my paean to the wild river Betty and I love:

Our River
Home on our river, here we play,
Allured by magic on display,
Sparkling torrent lightly kissed,
By the dawning morning mist.
Reveling in our river's year,
Winter, summer, spring and fall,
Changing seasons, we love them all.

David R. Olson

Winter fly-by soaring eagles,
Stormy weather, flocks of sea gulls.
Spring melt flows lure river rats,
For white water runs in kayaks.
Summer we marvel the cutthroat rise,
To leap and catch a careless fly.
Early Fall flows slow, sedate,
For us and friends to meditate.
Later flash floods, raging bold,
Presage return of bracing cold.
Prepare for winter to unfold.
On this river, decked in winter white,
Cast our ashes on a full-moon night,
On rushing waters for us to flee,
To eternal peace in a welcoming sea.

—August 3, 2010

Our River

* * *

If someone someday feels called to gather at the river a few friends and family to cobble together a casual memorial service to make something of my life and what I did with it, I would want those doing the eulogizing to play down stories about my activism and adventures. Instead, I hope they will have gleaned from this modest work a glimpse into the spirits of my parents, Ken, and Jef, and perceive how their lives influenced mine.

I grew up nurtured in the spirit of Jesus' activist life of faith and have reflected it in small ways throughout my adult life, but their deaths, each in its turn, awakened me to the lives each of them had lived. They changed me, bonding us by water, and sensing eternal peace awaits in a welcoming sea.

* * *

Index of Poems

Maps and Photos

Maps

Photos